1981

Controlling Stress and Tension:

A Holistic Approach

Daniel A. Girdano, Ph.D.
Ecotopia Institute
Winter Park, Colorado

George S. Everly, Jr., Ph.D.
University of Maryland

PRENTICE-HALL, INC. Englewood Cliffs, New Jersey 07632

Library of Congress Cataloging in Publication Data

GIRDANO, DANIEL A.
  Controlling stress and tension

  Bibliography: p.
  Includes index.
  1. Stress (Psychology) 2. Mind and body.
I. Everly, George S., (date)   joint author.
II. Title.
BF575.S75G57   158'.1   79–14381
ISBN 0–13–172114–3
ISBN 0–13–172106–2 pbk.

© 1979 by Prentice-Hall, Inc., Englewood Cliffs, N.J. 07632

Printed in the United States of America

10 9 8 7 6 5 4 3

Editorial/production supervision by Ruth Anderson
Interior design by Katharine Glynn
Cover design by Mark A. Binn
Manufacturing buyer: Harry Baisley

PRENTICE-HALL INTERNATIONAL, INC., *London*
PRENTICE-HALL OF AUSTRALIA PTY. LIMITED, *Sydney*
PRENTICE-HALL OF CANADA, LTD., *Toronto*
PRENTICE-HALL OF INDIA PRIVATE LIMITED, *New Delhi*
PRENTICE-HALL OF JAPAN, INC., *Tokyo*
PRENTICE-HALL OF SOUTHEAST ASIA PTE. LTD., *Singapore*
WHITEHALL BOOKS LIMITED, *Wellington, New Zealand*

To Dottie, Scout Lee, and Jonathan Livingston Seagull,
who individually and collectively have helped me learn to fly
and to
George S. Everly, Sr., and Kathleen W. Everly
for their love, understanding, and support.

Contents

Preface

For some time we have been hearing of the dawning of the Age of Aquarius, predicted to be a time of enlightenment when the individual will finally reach his or her full potential. One sign that such an age may in fact be coming is the increased realization of the human potential for self-direction. People are beginning to restore their sense of balance with the environment and have "rediscovered" self-responsibility as a major factor in health and illness. Thus, the age of passive medical care is coming to a close. The time has come for health professionals to truly educate members of our society in the art of self-health and in the role of self-responsibility for gaining and keeping a high level of wellness.

A major factor in the maintenance of health is the ability to live in harmony within society, while keeping to a minimum the detrimental effects of one pervasive by-product of modern society—excess stress and tension.

Technically, we all possess the ability to reduce stress arousal and thus prevent stress-related illness. This potential is far from being fully developed, because most of the stress control techniques currently being taught are lacking in two essential ingredients: depth and scope.

Depth refers to the depth of knowledge presented about the nature of the problem of stress and about the intricacies of the stress control technique. Often those who are presenting the technique underestimate the motivation and abilities of their students. Also, these teachers may forget that knowledge forms the cornerstone for compliance with the sometimes tedious effort and practice necessary for success; indeed, knowledge may serve as the "mother of invention"—if enough is known about the technique, the individual can improvise and fit it to a particular problem or situation. In many techniques, the mentors may intentionally withhold knowledge because they desire strict adherence to one dogmatic interpretation of the technique.

The second essential ingredient missing in most stress reduction techniques is scope. Most techniques are one-dimensional, trying to solve a complex problem with a simple solution. When these systems are successful, it is usually because individuals, while practicing the technique, slowly and unconsciously condition themselves to change other stressful aspects of their lives. More frequently, however, the stress engendered in the total lifestyle of an individual is too pervasive to be changed with any single technique. The progress is slow, frustration and boredom ensue, and the practice is abandoned.

Stress is a multidimensional phenomenon, and if its detrimental effects are to be reduced, the individual's entire style of living must change to some degree. There must be a reduction in the stressfulness of the environment and this must be accompanied by an attempt to change some stress-producing personality characteristics. A technique, or better yet, several techniques of relaxation must be mastered, and nutritional and exercise patterns must likewise be altered.

Success in the control of stress and tension demands a *holistic* approach. This method operates on many levels, encompasses both the internal and external milieu, and combines several techniques into a complete system. We started using such a system several years ago when it became obvious that the techniques currently available were failing to sufficiently prepare or motivate participants, thus resulting in extremely high failure rates.

The holistic system consists of three phases which parallel the three parts of this book. Part I discusses the problem and our potential for achieving a solution. It examines the relationship between mind and body, the nature of stress and the stress response, the psychosomatic theory of disease, and the mechanisms that link stress and illness, and presents the design for the holistic approach of intervention.

Part II deals with the broad concept of the stress-producing environment, dividing it into specific underlying causes, and gives you the opportunity to assess the stressful factors in your own life. Through self-assessment exercises, you construct a personal stress profile, which represents a unique and important aspect of this approach because success in controlling stress and tension is enhanced by knowledge of conditions, attitudes, and behaviors which contribute to the stress response.

Part III consists of techniques used to alleviate stress and tension. Some are specific to the causes of stress described in Part II, while others are general techniques for reducing stress reactions. Detailed instructions are provided along with discussion of the basic mechanism underlying each technique. The reader is encouraged to build his/her own stress management system which incorporates aspects of all of them. To that end, knowledge about the technique is as important as the technique itself. The hoped-for outcome is not the immediate adoption of any one technique, but the ability to create a total, personalized system of controlling stress and tension.

STOP!!

Preliminary Self-Assessment Exercise

Before reading Part I, complete this exercise to rate your reading style.

Between these covers you will find information about disease, about stress and stressors (the triggers of stress), and about techniques which many people have used to reduce stress in their lives. Two basic kinds of readers will choose this book.

Reader I, realizing he/she is under pressure and probably under stress, skips the Preface and speed-reads the first few chapters to get to the meaty part about the techniques for stress reduction. After all, learning how to get rid of stress is the reason for the book, isn't it? Being a good intellectual, Reader I picks out one of the techniques which appears to have merit, dissects it to try to find the trigger mechanism, and tries it out for a couple of days. When peace and enlightenment do not engulf his/her body, frustration sets in, and figuring the technique is just a rip-off, Reader I goes out to buy the next book on the shelf.

Reader II, realizing he/she is under pressure and probably under stress, reads the Preface to obtain insight into the authors' reasons for writing the book and then closely reads the first few chapters and comes to realize that stress is more than an isolated incident: it is the product of an entire lifestyle. This reader discovers stress reduction can be most efficiently accomplished by the holistic approach—which operates on several levels and ultimately leads to a less stressful lifestyle. After reading the introductory chapters, Reader II goes on to read subsequent chapters, practices and learns many different techniques, and more important, comes to understand the relationship between these techniques and a natural state of balance. This natural state of balance— call it knowing, intuition, insight, faith, philosophical growth, or enlightenment—sustains motivation past the awkward learning stage, past the expectation plateaus, until tranquility is not just an intellectualization, but a feeling. It starts to govern Reader II's life choices to the point that managing his or her life to reduce stress is not an active chore of endless compromise, but a natural selection of lifestyle dictated by a philosophy of natural balance, both within the organism and between the organism and the environment.

Now, what style reader are you?

I am Style I. _____
I am Style II. _____

part I

Body and Mind in Health and Disease

Introduction

This book is divided into three parts: Part III is about what you can do, specifically, to reduce stress in your life; Part II seeks to better describe the causes of your stress; and Part I provides the foundation that will promote a better understanding of the hows and whys of the stress response. If we were writing a cookbook, we might leave out Part I because the reader's attitude is likely to be, "When I am hungry, I want to eat, so just tell me how to cook the food." But not all needs are as direct as hunger. Many, like health, get confused in social and psychological processes of adapting to our environment. Part I is about the need to be healthy and how stress interferes with our ability to meet that need. It takes an in-depth look at what stress is, how we come under stress, why we are so susceptible to it, and how stress leads to illness. The primary vehicle and unifying thread in this process is the Psychosomatic Concept. This concept of illness explains how our environment and social interactions, our perception of our environment, and our personality and emotional states act to produce a physical stress response, as well as how stress arousal can eventually lead to illness. It reveals a map of the interrelationships between the mind, the body, and our social environment.

1

The Evolution
of Mind-Body Unity

The illustration on page 5 shows mankind's evolution from a state of natural balance of mind-body components, through a mind-dominated period, back to a mind-body unity. It shows the nature of the problem as well as its resolution.

These changes in man's approach to mind-body unity or disunity have profoundly affected our health. Physically, there are only minute differences between modern man and the caveman. We have the same central nervous and endocrine systems—that is the brain, nerves, and hormones—that allowed our ancestors to meet physical emergencies. What has changed is the extent to which the conscious mind has taken control of the body and the extent to which our total being has been transformed into *ego consciousness*, that is, into logical, rational thinking that protects and preserves the psychological self. In other words, there has been an emphasis of personality or ego and a de-emphasis of our physical aspects.

The ancient Greek and Far Eastern philosophies did not separate mind from body, did not even recognize differences between physical matter and spirit, or for that matter, any differences between the inanimate and the animate. Gradually there was a change from the mind-body unity philosophy (known as holism or monism) to a separation of mind and body (dualism). With the dualistic philosophy of Descartes in the seventeenth century, Western man further identified with his mind rather than with a complete mind-body organism. Man was considered an ego being carried around inside a machine-like body which was ruled and used by the mind. "Lower" animals were seen not as beings similar to man though functioning on a different plane, but rather as inferior life. Indeed, nature itself was treated as inferior as the natural environment became a resource or commodity to be used by man.

The philosophy of Descartes compartmentalized life into specialties— science, religion, philosophy, politics, medicine—with each segment of society being governed by specialists. Man was either philosopher or scientist or politician or doctor. No one man could be all, even though those activities related to each individual. It is no wonder that people grew passive in the areas outside of their individual expertise. Even the care of one's personal health was left to others.

As the balance between the mind and the body gradually shifted in favor of mind dominance, the products of the mind (technology) advanced, often unchecked. Modern man has now become so dependent upon machines, external expertise, and a gigantic bureaucracy to run our complex society that most of our activities seem to be various forms of endless technological education whereby we attempt to learn to use our resources most efficiently. Alvin Toffler in *Future Shock* describes the rapidity of the seemingly endless changes that overwhelm us to the point of producing a shock reaction to our systems.

The increased birth rate and the growth of urban areas have resulted in overpopulation, noise, air, and water pollution, job dislocation, and decrease in individual privacy and in self-reliance. As a result of improved methods of communication and transportation, we have been driven to accomplish more in less time. Trying to keep pace with our technological advancements has drastically affected our value systems: basic values which once took generations, even centuries, to change, are now in a constant state of flux. For example, family structure, religion, education, work, communication, and sexual identity are now constantly changing, some for the good of human growth, some not so good; but most important to the basic concept of this book is *change* itself, because it epitomizes psychological pressure.

Coping with change has become a preoccupation in our society. The coping styles in turn have become mind games. Thus we have developed a vicious cycle: increased thoughts lead to stress arousal, and the conceiving of ways to reduce stress just adds to the arousal. The harder we try to reduce stress, the more stress we subject ourselves to, so we try even

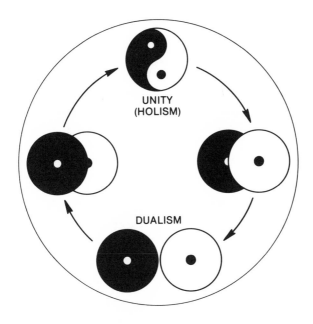

UNITY
(HOLISM)

DUALISM

harder. In our efforts to *think* our way out of this dilemma we have created a condition in which our most important channel to the basic natural truths (our bodies) has been demoted to a second-class status. We do not act as we feel; we act as we think we ought to feel, or as we would like to feel, or as others expect us to feel. But we cannot totally subdue the innate stress response that we share with the caveman. That vestige of our physical past is ever present to remind us that we cannot totally "civilize" this natural creation. It reminds us we cannot conquer nature; we are nature. The denial of this naturalness pits mind against body, a needless battle that has no winner.

> *Stress.* A term used mostly in physics to mean strain, pressure, or force on a system. When used in relation to the body cells, it describes the effects of the body reacting, that is, the buildup of pressure, the strain of muscles tensing. In the context of this book, stress is taken to mean a fairly predictable arousal of psycho-physiological (mind-body) systems which, if prolonged, can fatigue or damage the system to the point of malfunction and disease.

Perhaps we can learn a lesson from some of our less intellectual earth-mates—not necessarily a lesson in how to live, but perhaps in how to

5

show freedom of expression. For instance, let's consider my dog, who is a pure example of healthy freedom and naturalness of expression. As she runs across a field with boundless energy, she appears to spring off all fours at the same time; not chasing or being chased, she leaps and turns with muscles rippling as her entire body seems to explode with the sheer joy of moving, of freedom, of just being. One day I followed along, at first trying to imitate her movement, then finally just running, moving, jumping, my body directed by my body rather than by my mind. Every now and then my thoughts would flash an inhibition about how ridiculous my behavior must look to others, but the ecstasy of my body's flow would not allow the thoughts. At last, I dropped to the ground, exhausted but not tired, my mind active but not reactive. My thoughts were mine, not reactions to situations imposed by others. For a moment, I was envious of my dog, but why? Mankind is endowed with everything she has. We can feel, we can think, but—much more—we can know, and beyond knowledge we have the potential for true enlightenment. When did we lose the freedom of spirit to run, leap, or dance? How long has it been since we lived in harmony with nature instead of battling to conquer it?

One does not have to "go back to nature" to be more natural. All one must do is to stop gratifying the mind at the expense of the body. We have tuned our ear to the message of the mind; now we must do the same and listen to the message of the body. However, it is difficult to hear over the din of the engine; and even in quiet, it is impossible to hear over the constant chatter of the mind.

Distress and tranquility are opposites. When distressed, the mind is bombarded with stimulation of thoughts, plans, schemes, worries, constant reenactment of an event or mental preparation for it. Tranquility is quiet, it's peace, it's somewhat of a void which can be filled with a sense of feeling the self. You cannot act or create if you are reacting. You cannot "feel" your body when your body is feeling the pain of stress. Your spirit cannot be free as long as it is burdened with worry.

Distress. A concept popularized by Hans Selye to differentiate the stress which is inherent in all reactions, positive and negative, from the usually more chronic debilitative stress of negative events.

Thus, the answer does not lie in the search for new knowledge or new truths, because there are none. The fantastic proliferation of knowledge in recent centuries has not led to new enlightenment. Man has not become wiser, he is not significantly happier, and in many respects he is less healthy. But happiness is relative and can to a degree be conditioned; health, on the other hand, is more absolute and thus becomes a concrete focus of our attempts to regain our balance.

We will further explore the trend back to mind-body unity in Chapter 3. First, it is important to have some understanding of the nature of health and disease.

2

What Disease Is

It may appear somewhat ironic that a book about the maintenance of health should start out with a discussion of the opposite condition. Nevertheless, we will take disease as the starting point, for all too often one's interest in health begins when health deteriorates and pain and dysfunction begin to dictate a lifestyle of diminished capacity. Disease or the fear of diminished capacity has become the motivator for studying stress, now a well-documented precursor of illness.

This book is not about disease, nor is it about psychology, physiology, or medicine. It is a book about the philosophy behind the choice of a lifestyle which is likely to promote health and happiness through the reuniting of mind and body.

DISEASE

Virtually everyone knows disease. It is a condition of the body which presents symptoms peculiar to it, these symptoms and the ensuing condition setting the disease apart from other body states. Medicine has characteristically dealt with the symptoms of organic diseases, but there are three categories of disease processes which are germane to the study of stress:

1. Organic diseases
2. Conversion reactions
3. Psychosomatic diseases

While these disease processes are interwoven, there are some important distinctions among them. The following analysis of these should provide a firm basis for the understanding of the stress-disease relationship.

ORGANIC DISEASES

Organic diseases are diseases which adversely affect the structure and function of the human body. They are caused by invasion of the body by foreign elements such as microorganisms and pollutants or by some natural degenerative process. Organic diseases can be divided into two major categories: (1) infectious and (2) noninfectious.

> *Structure.* The cellular construction of the body.
>
> *Function.* The act of engaging in some behavior.

Infectious diseases are communicable—they have the ability to be transmitted from one host to another and are generally considered acute, short-term diseases. The infectious illnesses are typically caused by microorganisms such as viruses, bacteria, fungi, parasites, and rickettsia, which cause damage to the body by releasing poisons or toxins and/or by reproducing in overwhelming numbers and thus interfering with normal body function. Common infectious diseases are the common cold, influenza (flu), and pneumonia.

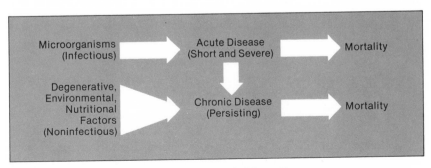

Figure 2.1 The Organic Disease Process

Noninfectious organic diseases are not considered communicable, though they can be just as harmful to the structure and function of the body. Common causes of such diseases are degenerative processes, heredity, birth defects, nutritional habits, noxious environmental factors, and other cellular and metabolic disturbances. Many forms of heart disease, arthritis, senility, and various malnutritional disorders are examples. They are what we would call chronic diseases. Figure 2.1 represents the organic disease process.

CONVERSION REACTIONS

Though not a major disease type, conversion reactions are important to our discussion of stress because they are sometimes confused with psychosomatic diseases and because they are stress-linked.

Conversion reactions have been traditionally considered a neurosis, that is, a mild emotional disturbance. In a conversion reaction the coping mechanisms do not properly adapt to a stressful situation. There is the loss of some function of the body without any underlying *structural* impairment to explain it. Conversion reactions, then, are functional physical disabilities that are used as coping mechanisms in the face of unbearable stress.

The most common functional impairments occur in the sensory and voluntary nervous systems. Typical conversion reactions of the sensory systems include deafness and blindness, and typical conversion reactions in the voluntary nervous system include paralysis of some limb or the inability to speak.

Due to the fact that no organ destruction underlies the physical symptoms, conversion reactions are considered neurotic mental disorders. The rare phenomenon of conversion reaction goes back to early Greek medicine. Hippocrates believed that this illness was caused by a woman's need to bear children, and thus used the term "hysteria" (Greek for "uterus") to describe it. Modern medicine recognized conversion hysteria as a maladaptive coping mechanism of both sexes in reaction to a stressful situation. The case of Ron demonstrates a classic conversion reaction:

Ron was 18 years old when he joined the Army simply to please his father, a retired Army captain. Ron had found Army life very difficult because of his devout pacifist philosophy, but even though opposed to the Army in general, he was able to function until he was placed in hand-to-hand combat training, at which point he refused to participate. Consequently, his superiors threatened to give him a dishonorable discharge. Ron knew this would emotionally destroy his father, and the situation placed him in a highly stressful position of conflict, torn between pleasing his father and living up to his moral obligations to himself. When the morning came for the next combat training session, he was unable to get out of his bunk. Both legs appeared to be paralyzed from the hips down to his toes. Extensive physical examinations over the course of several weeks proved the legitimacy of the functional paralysis, yet revealed no organic cause. Several months went by and Ron was finally given a medical discharge from the Army based upon his condition. After two months of bed rest at home, Ron was able to regain complete use of his legs. A brief analysis will show that Ron faced what he perceived to be an overwhelming conflict between the Army and his father on one side, and his own moral attitude on the other side. When the conflict became too great, his body responded with an unconscious maladaptive coping mechanism (conversion reaction paralysis). This response in the face of the stressful conflict solved his problem by giving him a "legitimate excuse" for not complying with the Army's combat training. As is typical, when the causes of stress were removed, the conversion reaction subsided.

Figure 2.2 shows the process of conversion reactions.

PSYCHOSOMATIC DISEASE

The term "psychosomatic" was first used in 1927 by Felix Deutsch to describe the mind-body interactions in illness, and the first major publications on this topic were written in 1935 by Helen Dunbar. The basis for the psychosomatic disease concept is that the mind plays an important role in many different diseases. All psychosomatic diseases affect the structure and function of the human body. There are two basic types of psychosomatic diseases: (1) the psychogenic, and (2) the somatogenic.

The *psychogenic psychosomatic* disorder refers to a physical disease caused by emotional stress. There is structural and functional organ damage, yet no microbial invasion or natural degenerative processes. This phenomenon has been traditionally considered as "physical disorders of presumably psychological (emotional) origin." Backaches, skin reactions, peptic ulcers, migraine headaches, and some respiratory disorders are a few common examples.

Bronchial asthma is a condition which often falls into this category. An all-too-frequent situation can be illustrated by the following case.

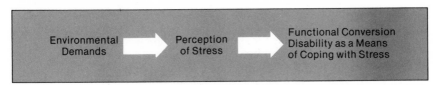

Figure 2.2 Conversion Reactions

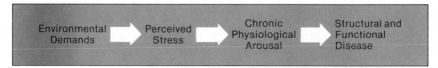

Figure 2.3 Psychogenic Psychosomatic Disease

Karen, who had no previous history of bronchial asthma, developed a rather severe case by the end of her freshman year. Her most severe attacks occurred just before major exam periods. A summer free of attacks ended with a major attack a week before the beginning of the fall term. It was obvious that while successful at school, she was not adequately coping with it. Her fears of failure and not living up to often-expressed expectations of excellence of her parents were translated into a psychogenic psychosomatic disorder.

Figure 2.3 is a representation of the psychogenic psychosomatic process.

The *somatogenic psychosomatic* disorder is less clear-cut conceptually. In this case, emotional disturbances such as anxiety, anger, fear, and frustration increase the body's susceptibility to organic diseases. The somatogenic phenomenon is an important concept that has far-reaching implications for health. Therefore, a more detailed analysis seems in order.

In 1965, Renee Dubos noted that even infectious organic diseases do not commonly occur simply from some pathogenic (disease-causing) microbes entering the body. In the following passage, he notes the role of what we are calling the somatogenic psychosomatic phenomenon:

> The sciences concerned with microbial diseases have developed almost exclusively from the study of acute or semi-acute infections caused by virulent micro-organisms acquired through exposure to an (external) source of infection. In contrast, the microbial diseases most common in our communities today arise from the activities of micro-organisms that are (always present) in the environment, persist in the body without causing obvious harm under normal circumstances, and exert pathological effects only when the infected person is under conditions of . . . stress. In such a type of microbial disease the event of infection is of less importance than the hidden manifestation of the smoldering infectious process and the (stressful) disturbances that convert latent infection into overt systems and pathology. [1]

Thus, stress may act as a catalyst for some already present organic disease to (1) allow the organic disease to establish a "foothold" in the body from which to spread destruction, or (2) accelerate the rate at which some

[1] Renee Dubos, *Man Adapting* (New Haven: Yale University Press, 1965), pp. 164–65.

disease may spread throughout the body. Thus, almost any organic disease may have a somatogenic psychosomatic component, depending, of course, on the psychological makeup of the individual.

The somatogenic phenomenon appears to act by lowering the body's resistance or immunity to disease. As was pointed out by Dubos, in somatogenic psychosomatic illness, being infected or having some organ system begin to degenerate *is not* the critical factor determining the course of the illness; rather, it is the body's ability to defend itself against these otherwise common infectious and degenerative processes of everyday life. We now know that distress impedes the body's ability to defend itself against all diseases.

A common example of this phenomenon interacting with an infectious disease is in the analysis of tuberculosis. Tuberculosis is a respiratory disorder caused by the tubercle bacillus, a bacillus not uncommon in crowded industrial cities—making the disease a potential hazard for vast numbers of individuals. Yet, why is it that more people do not contract fully developed cases of TB?

The most obvious answer lies in the body's defense mechanisms against such diseases. The body can usually fight off such invading microorganisms before much harm has been done. Indeed, in many urban dwellers a chest X-ray will actually reveal tiny tubercular scars upon the lungs, indicating points at which the tubercle bacillus was contracted but was effectively resisted by the body. Stress researcher George Solomon (1974) suggests that during a stress reaction the body's natural immune system may be hampered in its defensive role so that various microorganisms which would normally have been destroyed may prove too strong an opponent for the body's defenses. The result is some illness.

College students seem to be especially vulnerable to this situation. The financial pressures of college, added to the normal clothing, transportation, and socializing costs, lead many to seek employment. So after classes, studying, and socializing they often work instead of sleep.

John, a graduate student, worked five nights a week during his junior and senior years, averaged three hours of sleep a night, and ate when he could find the time. He was a man in motion, and although he kept a B+ average, he lost a substantial amount of weight, and his relationship with his girlfriend became an on-again, off-again affair. About midway through his senior year, John began having respiratory problems which were subsequently diagnosed as tuberculosis. John grew up in an urban area known for its concentration of heavy industry. Like many of us, he probably carried the tubercle bacillus for years, but the stress imposed by his recent lifestyle weakened his defenses and John landed in the hospital. His recovery was a lengthy one, with frequent relapses requiring hospitalization. It seems clear that John's lifestyle and attitude toward life affected his illness. He is now a graduate student, is engaged, and while the schoolwork is demanding, John is quick to balance it with rest and relaxation, and has effectively warded off his disease state.

The concept of somatogenic psychosomatic illness has far-reaching implications. It may explain the mysterious phenomenon of "spontaneous remission," the sudden and unexplained disappearance of a disease. Perhaps the only reason the person initially contracted the disease was that his or her immune system was only partially functional because of some adverse stress reaction. Yet when the stressor is removed, the person fully recovers because the body can fight the infection with its entire immunological arsenal. The somatogenic phenomenon may also explain the "spontaneous relapse." In this case, a patient, thought to have recovered, suddenly develops the full-blown illness again without significant reexposure to the disease. Here, perhaps the body has recovered from most, but not all, of the infection and, under stress, the infection is allowed to revitalize its growth in the body. Similarly, during conditions of severe stress, the slightest reexposure to the microorganism might have a profound effect.

> *Stressor.* An event or condition that may be purely physical, social, or psychological—including anticipation and imagination—and that triggers a stress reaction.

The somatogenic psychosomatic concept, though relatively new to Western medicine, represents one of our most substantial advances in the study of mind-body interactions, for it implicates stress in diseases from the common cold to cancer. We are only now beginning to understand the mind-body phenomenon as research efforts continue to demonstrate the strength of that relationship. Figure 2.4 represents the somatogenic psychosomatic phenomenon.

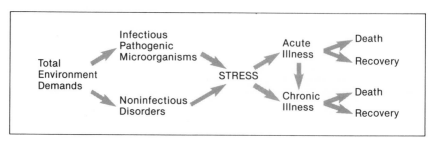

Figure 2.4 Somatogenic Psychosomatic Reactions

3

The Psychosomatic Theory and the Holistic Approach

Certainly, not all diseases are psychosomatic, but almost all diseases do have some mind-body involvement. Hinkle summarizes this point:

> It is evident that any disease process, and in fact any process within the living organism, might be influenced by the reaction of the individual to his social environment or to other people. [1]

The information received from the environment, the way it is perceived, evaluated, and given importance, and how these influence thought processes and muscle activity—these factors can all contribute to the development of disease. The pathway from the social environment to ill health is a complex one and involves the interrelationship of mind and body, as diagrammed in Figure 3.1. Even positive events can produce a measure of stress when they demand change and adaptation, but most stress begins with the negative, painful, and unpleasant events of our lives. An inseparable aspect of environmental stress is our varied and complex social interaction fraught with feelings, expectations, and often frustration.

[1] L. E. Hinkle, "The Concept of 'Stress' in the Biological and Social Sciences," *Science, Medicine, and Man*, 1:43, 1973.

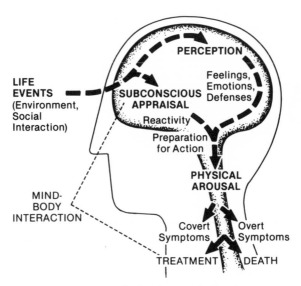

Figure 3.1 The Psychosomatic Concept

The information from the environment is processed by different pathways, two of which are represented on Figure 3.1. One pathway is thought of as being largely subconscious, and is thus named the *subconscious appraisal pathway*. This pathway contains physical and emotional reflexes that act to prepare the body for action. It is important to note that this system only prepares and that this preparation is independent of the final action. It is the second or voluntary pathway that determines whether this arousal is necessary and used or inappropriate and harmful. If the subconscious appraisal pathway is stimulated, coping action may eventually be required, and if it is, this system, through its innate physical and emotional reflexes, prepares the body for action.

The second pathway, that of perception, evaluation, and decision-making, is responsible for voluntary action. How you perceive an event largely depends on your concept of self, ego strengths, value system, and even heredity. The emotions that are aroused are tempered by your psychological defenses, which you gained from your past experience. These lead to physical arousal and you feel a need to act. Action itself is also complex; often the reaction to a stressor is no action at all, as you weigh the possible consequences (e.g., you may hold back a harsh comment to a superior).

As can be seen in Figure 3.1, both pathways can lead to physical arousal, so arousal is not totally dependent upon voluntary action. If the body prepares itself for action, defensive postures, worry and/or fear, and if the action is thwarted, the person is often left with chronic low-to-moderate tension. Prolonged physical arousal can go unnoticed, because the symptoms are not overt and do not produce pain or discomfort. However, if fatigue of an organ system ensues, or if the system malfunctions, noticeable symptoms appear.

At the core of the psychosomatic theory lies the concept of mind-body balance or unity discussed in Chapter 1. Spurred perhaps by threats of ecological disaster or by innate needs to feel self-control, human consciousness is gradually turning inward and people are beginning to understand the need to restore harmony to their lives. We have seen that balance between the environment and the human organism and balance within the human organism itself is not new thinking, but a resurgence of ancient philosophies which centered on unity and the interrelationships of all things. The ego consciousness—defense of self —of the individual becomes secondary to a collective consciousness of all things. This is the *holistic approach* to life.

Let us stop here and reflect on this most important concept—ego consciousness—for it is responsible for most of our stress-related health problems. Overcoming the ego consciousness is the only means to restore and maintain the best possible health. The dualistic philosophy—that is, the separation of mind and body—has led to the self-as-divine concept. We stress the state of mind over the state of the body. Psychological stability is more important to us than physiological stability. Thus, most of our activities are centered around pleasure, happiness, and ego gratification, often at the expense of mind-body wellness. In our devotion to psychological stability and adaptation, we are losing the ability to perceive imbalance and the will to rebalance. But a philosophy of balance dictates that one cannot satisfy the mind at the expense of the body; one cannot preserve the species by consuming other species or the environment.

Until recently in the United States, Eastern mysticism was just that— mystical wisdom of the old masters. The Westerner, who has come to believe only what is external and what can be proven by the scientific specialists, could not accept this philosophy. But the so-called "new" scientific facts are verifying much of the ancient teachings. The mind and body state of tranquility became a "reality" only after it could be measured with electrical instruments. The ability of the yogi consciously to influence heart rate, skin temperature, perspiration, and other autonomic functions was always fascinating, but it was given renewed attention when it was objectively measured, and more important, when it was accomplished by thousands of "average" humans. Out of this renewed interest have come investigations into alternative forms of treating illness. Newer types of treatment will return to a more holistic form of health care: the individual will have more responsibility for health maintenance, and will be viewed not merely as an aggregate of organ systems, but as an individual with a lifestyle of habits and activities affecting health.

Passivity about our health developed both from an over-reliance on

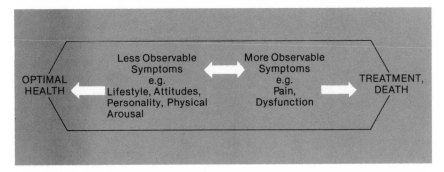

Figure 3.2   The Health–Illness Continuum

health care specialists and from a lack of knowledge about the disease process. The holistic approach views the body processes as not being completely involuntary. It holds that the individual should play an active role both in maintaining good health and in treating ill health. It dictates that the ill can no longer be seen as innocent victims of their bodies, completely absolved from any responsibility for the illness.

There is a general misconception that illness starts when the symptoms first appear. In most illnesses, however, the more observable symptoms are preceded by less recognizable and less disabling symptoms which go unnoticed to the unaware. In the case of psychosomatic illnesses, more observable symptoms are preceded by malfunctioning of an organ system, preceded in turn by fatigue of an organ system, due to prolonged physical and emotional arousal, usually in response to a social or environmental situation. This process is outlined in Figure 3.2.

We are conditioned to act on health matters only when we hurt or when organs no longer function properly. Our motivation to intervene at this stage is shown in Table 3.1 as Level One motivation. When we intervene at Level One, it is usually by seeking treatment through the health care system. However, the underlying physical arousal may have been persisting undetected for months, even years, before symptoms showed. If we were better attuned to our bodies and were trained in making the proper observations, we could intervene at an earlier stage, and thus prevent our bodies' even reaching Level One.

Table 3.1

MOTIVATION HIERARCHY

Level One	Treatment for ill health
Level Two	Prevention of ill health
Level Three	Enjoyment of healthy behavior

Emotional arousal, which usually precedes physical arousal, can also be classified as a less observable symptom, even though we usually know when we are being aroused. Although we are aware of emotional arousal, most people do not link it with physical illness and, even more significant, we tend to become tolerant of emotional arousal. Because our bodies and minds adapt, hyperarousal seems to be the normal state. How often have you, after finishing a prolonged project or when just starting a vacation, experienced an extreme sense of relaxation and "let down"? It is only then that you realize just how tense you were, though at the time, that was "normal" for you. Often there is an extreme difference between the relaxed state and what we perceive to be our "normal state."

Other less observable symptoms include certain attitudes and personality traits. Research has firmly established that certain personality types are more prone to illness than are others. In this book there are several tests for self-assessment of the personality traits and attitudes which are often linked to illness. The holistic approach to stress control also attaches much importance to lifestyle. Evidence shows that some lifestyles clearly promote the development of psychosomatic illness. Thus, where you live, how you live, how you work and play can also help determine your health or illness.

The ability to recognize the less observable symptoms comes with training. One essential in the training process is knowledge. In the case of many individuals, if they just know what activities to do and why these should be done, they will be motivated to move toward a healthier lifestyle. So knowledge is at the core of Level Two on the motivation hierarchy in Table 3.1: healthful behavior as an insurance against or prevention of ill health. Most people who take up jogging or running do it as an insurance against cardiovascular illness because they know the detrimental effects of a sedentary lifestyle. To a large extent, the knowledge and activities presented in this book are aimed, at least initially, at this level of motivation.

Very often, however, while changing some stressful aspect of your life or while practicing a relaxation technique, the motivation level changes to Level Three, as one begins to feel very comfortable with the activity—and vaguely uncomfortable without it. The activity becomes pleasurable, it produces a tranquil, satisfied feeling, and is then repeated not necessarily with prevention of illness in mind, but because it is rewarding in itself. As one becomes conditioned to the activity, he/she moves toward optimal health.

The most significant contribution of the psychosomatic health and illness theory is that it demonstrates how it is possible through knowledge and training to alter, intervene, or prevent the detrimental effects which our environment, our perception, and our imagination have on the arousal of the control systems of the body.

INTERVENTION POINTS

Accepting the premise that many diseases are psychosomatic, there are several points at which intervention in the stress–disease cycle are possible. Remember that stress operates in many dimensions and not always predictably. How stressfully we react to our environment is determined to a large extent by our attitudes, values, personality, and emotional development, as well as our ability to relax, our diet and physical activity patterns, the ability to modify our lifestyles, and other such factors. Understanding this concept of stress makes one realize the futility of trying to deal with a complex problem with one activity or technique. Since stress reactions occur in various ways and on various levels, stress management should be holistic, that is, be approached from numerous and varied perspectives, incorporating the mental, physical, spiritual, social, and environmental interactions.

Holism. The concept underlying an approach to controlling stress and tension that deals with the complete lifestyle of the individual, incorporating intervention at several levels—physical, psychological, and social—simultaneously.

Intervention in the psychosomatic disease process may be accomplished by: (1) techniques designed to minimize the frequency of stress, (2) techniques designed to allow one to become better prepared, psychologically and physiologically, to withstand excessive stress, and (3) techniques designed to utilize appropriately the by-products of excessive stress arousal (see Table 3.2).

TECHNIQUES TO MINIMIZE THE FREQUENCY OF THE STRESS RESPONSE

Social Engineering

Our environment is filled with stressors. The action or behavior of each individual or institution in the world becomes the input to other individuals. As we go about our daily activities, each individual with whom we interact, the people we live with, those in the next car, the ones we pass on the street or sit with in meeting halls, and to some extent those we see on television, present some manner of stimulation. Obviously the more people, the greater the opportunity for contact. The intimacy

Table 3.2

THE HOLISTIC APPROACH TO THE CONTROL OF STRESS

1. Techniques to Minimize the Frequency of the Stress Response
   Social Engineering
   Personality Engineering
2. Techniques to Minimize the Intensity of the Stress Response
   and Reduce Emotional Reactivity
   Meditation
   Biofeedback
   Neuromuscular Relaxation Training
   Autogenic Relaxation Training
3. Techniques to Utilize Stress and Promote Body Consciousness
   Body Awareness Activities
   Ego-Void Physical Exercise

of that contact is also of prime importance, for not only does the behavior of others become our stimulation; if we know them well enough, so do their thoughts, dreams, and unspoken expectations. All of life's pursuits create potential stressors—from noise and pollution to competition for a seat on the bus, a place on the highway, or a position with the company. Generally speaking, more people means more complexity in social as well as in institutional organization.

One of the easiest and most effective techniques of stress management is to identify stress-promoting activities and to develop a lifestyle which modifies or avoids these stressors. A change in lifestyle may be as simple as getting out of bed earlier or driving to work by a different route, or as complex as choosing a profession, a mate, or a life goal. *Social engineering,* shown at its intervention point in Figure 3.3, is the technique of willfully taking command and modifying one's life. In one sense, it is the most conscious point of intervention; but as stress management becomes a way of life, one begins unconsciously to modify one's position in relation to sources of stress by selecting a less stressful lifestyle.

Social engineering strategies may be simple or extremely complex (based upon the nature of the stressor). But one thing is definite—there are virtually unlimited strategies available to the imaginative mind. In this book you will find many guidelines you can follow to make social engineering a valuable asset in the holistic approach to reducing stress.

One social engineering strategy involves the *analysis of biological rhythms.* Our social world runs on time—meeting time, plane time, bedtime, wake-up time. Our natural world also runs on time—solar or light time, lunar time, seasonal time. Our bodies also have a series of time clocks, such as temperature time, metabolism energy time, and hormonal

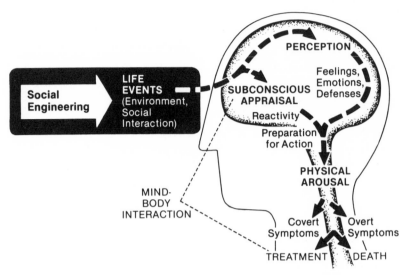

Figure 3.3 Social Engineering as an Intervention Technique

time. We have to balance work and recreation schedules with what is socially and economically efficient. This is often accomplished at the expense of being out-of-phase with our natural biological rhythms. The consequence of that may be increased susceptibility to illness, increased irritability, and emotional instability. If you know more about your natural biological rhythms, you can direct your activities to more closely coincide with these rhythms. You will be able to better understand, expect, perhaps even predict, fluctuations in moods, feelings, energies, and sensitivities—and you will not spend time and energy trying to relate energy fluctuations in mood to flaws in your personality. Understanding your natural biological rhythm can be a technique of avoiding or minimizing the frequency of stress by having your social clock tick in rhythm with your biological clock.

Another social engineering strategy involves a conscious concern with the foods that we eat. The conscious manipulation of diet as a strategy for reducing stress is called *nutritional engineering*. The food you eat can have an effect on your reaction to stressors, as certain foods can deplete the body's ability to react to stressful situations. Some foods may increase lethargy and irritability, causing you to react with stress in normally unstressful situations. Finally, some foods can actually strengthen the body's ability to handle stress. The manipulation of nutritional habits in order to facilitate the body's ability to cope with stress can be another effective, yet underused social engineering strategy.

Analysis of biorhythms and nutritional engineering are but two types of social engineering. In Chapter 9 you will find a comprehensive plan from which you can develop your own personal social engineering strategies for modifying or avoiding the sources of stress which normally arise from the environment and from social interaction.

Personality Engineering

To a large degree the amount of stress caused by society and the environment depends upon what information is taken in and what is blocked—upon how the information is perceived, evaluated, and given meaning, and what effect this whole process has on mental and physical activity.

Our attitudes—the way we "look" at things, the meanings and values we give to various events in our lives—in combination with our characteristic ways of behaving (behavioral patterns), can be referred to as an individual's *personality*. The personality has the awesome capacity of transforming a normally neutral aspect of life into a psychosocial stressor. Few events are innately stressful, but we make them stressful by the way in which we perceive them. A person may alter these stress-causing attitudes by first becoming aware of how we form such attitudes and then working to change the process through *personality engineering*. This strategy, which is examined in depth in Chapter 10, is shown at its intervention point in Figure 3.4. If personality engineering is effective, the way you perceive a particular event will be changed to the point where there will be little or no physical arousal.

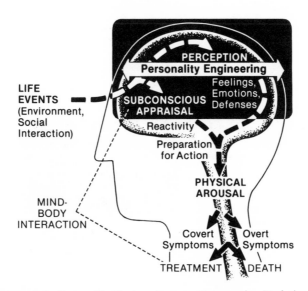

Figure 3.4 Personality Engineering as an Intervention Technique

TECHNIQUES TO MINIMIZE THE INTENSITY OF THE STRESS RESPONSE AND REDUCE EMOTIONAL REACTIVITY

In Figure 3.5 it can be seen that the information being sensed is actually alerting the central nervous system by two distinctly different pathways. (The central nervous system will be discussed more thoroughly in the next chapter.) One is the *subconscious* appraisal pathway, discussed earlier. This system, the *autonomic nervous system,* prepares the body for any potential action which might be needed. However, action or responses themselves are *conscious* and occur only after the appropriate part of the brain—the other pathway—perceives and evaluates the situation. Thus, the stress response, which is physical arousal, can be elicited by conscious, voluntary action or by subconscious, involuntary (autonomic) activation which keeps the body in a state of readiness. The constant state of readiness to respond with the fight or flight response when such a response is unwarranted is called *emotional reactivity.* If the body remains in this state for long periods, the organ systems become fatigued and the result is often organ system malfunction.

Relaxation training along with various other techniques that we will describe in Chapters 11–14—*meditation, biofeedback*-aided relaxation, and *neuromuscular* and *autogenic relaxation*—help reduce emotional reactivity. Not only does relaxation training promote voluntary control over some central nervous system activities associated with arousal, it

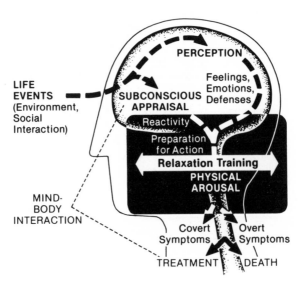

Figure 3.5 Relaxation Training as an Intervention Technique

promotes a quiet sense of control which eventually influences attitudes, perception, and behavior. Relaxation training will foster interaction with your inner self, and you will learn by actual feeling (visceral learning) that what you are thinking influences your body processes and that your body processes influence your thought processes. You will come to know your feelings and emotions as a part of your thinking experience. Your behavior will come more from what is within you, rather than merely be responses triggered by the people and the environment around you.

TECHNIQUES TO USE STRESS AND PROMOTE BODY CONSCIOUSNESS

The primary stress response is the fight or flight response. This reaction has helped ensure our survival and continues to do so; no amount of relaxation training can ever diminish the intensity of this innate reflex. Stress is physical, intended to enable a physical response to a physical threat; however, *any* threat—physical or symbolic—can bring about this response. Once the stimulation of the event penetrates the psychological defenses, the body prepares for action. Increased hormonal secretion, cardiovascular activity, and energy supply signify a state of stress, a state of extreme readiness to act as soon as the voluntary control centers decide the form of the action, which in our social situation is often no "action" at all. Usually the threat is not real, but holds only symbolic significance. Our lives are not in danger, only our egos. Physical action is not warranted and must be subdued, but for the body organs it is too late: what took only minutes to start will take hours to undo. The stress products are flowing through the system and will activate various organs until they are reabsorbed back into storage or gradually used by the body. And while this gradual process is taking place, the body organs suffer.

The solution, very simply, is to use the physical stress arousal for its intended purpose—physical movement. In our cultured society, which does not include killing a saber-toothed tiger nor allow us to physically abuse our neighbor, the most efficient use of the physical arousal is physical exercise. The increased energy intended for fight or flight can be used simply in running or swimming or riding a bike. Thus, one can accelerate the dissipation of the stress products, and if the activity is vigorous enough, it can cause a rebound or overshoot after exercise into a state of deep relaxation.

One note of caution! Exercise is itself a stressor, and competition adds substantially to that arousal level; and while the stress of the exercise is usually absorbed by the exercise, the stress of competition often sets in motion thoughts and feelings which linger beyond the event and become

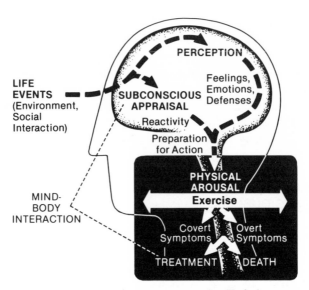

Figure 3.6 Exercise as an Intervention Technique

the stimulus for prolonged emotional arousal. We often confuse recreation with relaxation; they are not necessarily the same, and for most people they are usually not the same. Recreation, while fun, can be stressful, and if competitive, can produce stress that lingers with the rehash of missed points, social embarrassment, and self-doubt. Exercise to reduce stress should not add stress which lingers after the exercise. Ideally, it should be exercise which is devoid of ego involvement. Though strenuous, it should be a time of peace and of the harmonious interaction of mind and body. And in that sense, it may be the most natural of the stress reduction techniques. Reducing stress through physical activity is covered more fully in Chapter 15.

TREATMENT OF OVERT SYMPTOMS, SURGERY, AND DRUGS

Physical arousal may be considered a symptom of potential malfunction, but it remains hidden, because most people do not know enough about how disease develops and are not sufficiently aware of their bodies. It is not until they have overt symptoms of pain and dysfunction—our society's conception of disease—that they seek treatment. Our health care system is in reality a disease care system. The least desirable alternative is treatment with surgery and drugs; unfortunately, that is where our society places most of its energies and resources. The emphasis is on treatment because of the fixed concept that disease is treatable only *after* symptoms of malfunction or damage are observed. If we change the basic concept from psychosomatic illness to psychosomatic health, we can take positive intervention steps and formulate educational experiences which bring us closer to optimal health.

4

Systems That Control Stress Arousal

THE NERVOUS SYSTEM

Every system of the body is involved in the stress response at some time by nervous stimulation of an organ or through nervous stimulation of the endocrine glands. But the central nervous system (CNS), or brain, is always involved, and thus becomes the logical starting point in the analysis of the stress response. Brain function is divided into two parts: a voluntary system and an automatic system (the autonomic nervous system).

It may help to use an analogy made by Dr. Paul Maclean, noted researcher at the National Institute of Mental Health. He likens the brain to an archeological site revealing three distinct layers, each layer not only representing a stage in evolutionary development, but also representing a different function. Each of these layers also represents a different type of stress the body is capable of exhibiting.

In terms of evolution, the oldest part of the brain is found in the lower centers, nearest the spinal cord. For the sake of simplicity, we will refer to this as the *brainstem* or *hindbrain*, although our discussion is concerned more with the *function* of the various parts than with the physical

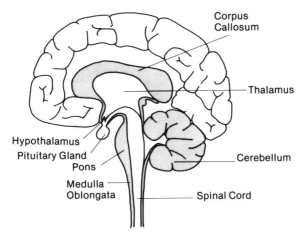

Figure 4.1   The Brainstem or Hindbrain

boundaries usually shown in anatomy textbooks (see Figure 4.1). These are simple structures (if there is such a thing in the brain) in the sense that their activities are reflexes, their primary function being to preserve the self and the species. These structures include the spinal cord, the cerebellum (center of muscle coordination), the medulla oblongata (which controls the heart rate, circulation of blood, and breathing), the pons (a network that sends nerve impulses to various parts of the brain), the thalamus (the switchboard that sends incoming signals to proper brain areas), and the hypothalamus (which regulates hunger, thirst, body temperature, rage, pain, and pleasure).

If humans have any resemblance to other animal species, then it is due to basic programs stored within these lower centers. The actions or behavior governed by these centers are natural, direct, and open, without learned inhibition. Activities centered on keeping alive and reproducing —preparing a homesite, establishing and defending territory, hunting, homing, hoarding, mating, forming simple social groups, and doing routine daily activities—are instinctive and exist in lower animals as well as in humans.

Perhaps to ensure survival, a new layer of brain tissue evolved or appeared in so-called higher animals, enabling them to modify or refine the basic instincts. This new layer, called the *limbic system* (Latin for "border"), wrapped around the old layer. It is often referred to as the *interbrain* as it has structures which communicate with both the higher and lower brain centers. The limbic system consists of two primary parts, an upper and lower. The various sections of the interbrain can be seen in Figure 4.2.

29

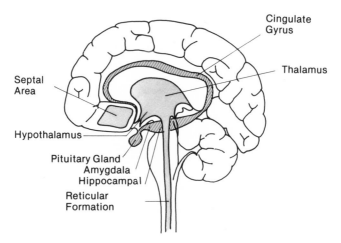

Figure 4.2 The Interbrain

Animals with the second layer, or limbic system, had not only the basic survival instincts, but also a measure of freedom from the stereotyped behavior of their ancestors. They could think and act on emotion and approach new situations with additional abilities. Primarily, the limbic system added feeling and emotion. These further assured attendance to basic survival activities, ostensibly by making some activities pleasurable and others unpleasurable. Researchers have been able to locate pleasure and unpleasure centers in the limbic system. Feelings such as fear, anger, and love attached to certain situations guided behavior toward that which protected and away from that which was threatening. Understandably, two of our major neural pathways (those governing eating and reproduction) have intricate connections to the pleasure and unpleasure centers of the limbic system. The concepts of reward-pleasure and punishment-unpleasure are important to the development of stress.

The brain continued to develop with the addition of a third layer called the *cortex, neocortex,* or *forebrain* and reached the zenith of development in humans. (See Figure 4.3.) The addition of the vast number of cortical cells allowed the development and storage of analytical skills, verbal communication, writing ability, empathy, fine motor control, additional emotion, memory, learning and rational thought, as well as more sophisticated problem-solving and survival abilities. New dimensions were added to oral and sexual behaviors and vision replaced smell as the primary sense. Reactions could be more than reflex responses. For better or for worse, an individual's reality could be determined by his or her own perceptions. Behavior could be weighed against possible outcomes. Symbolism, goals, motivation, and anticipation became part of the functioning human being.

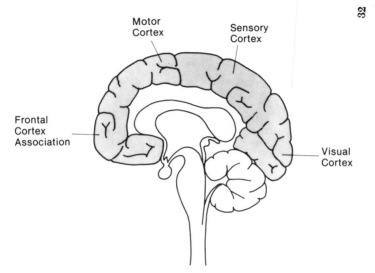

Figure 4.3 The Cerebral Cortex

Even though the brain developed in three stages, the three areas do not function independently. It is true that lower centers deal mainly with biological survival and the higher centers permit the existence of complex society, but we cannot view the lower centers as primitive or negative, requiring control by the higher thought centers. We must understand the function of each of these specific nervous system structures in order to understand stress and how to overcome it. At the same time, keep in mind that we cannot think of stress as anything but total brain integration.

To help us understand the concept of upper-center lower-center integration, let's examine the action of the *reticular system*, often referred to as the reticular activating system or *R.A.S.* This system is a network of nerve cells (or *neurons*) that extends from the spinal cord up through the thalamus (lower brain centers) and that is responsible for waking and alerting the brain (higher centers). The R.A.S. is neither sensory (connected to the sense organs) nor motor (connected to the muscles), but links both sensory and motor impulses. Thus, it is a two-way street, carrying impulses from brain to body and body to brain.

What is unique about the messages that pass through the R.A.S. is that they are general as well as specific. In the process of hearing, for example, once a sound is perceived by the auditory mechanism, it sends both specific and nonspecific impulses through the appropriate parts of the R.A.S. The specific arousal alerts the brain for increased attention to the sounds; at the same time, the nonspecific impulses will cause a general arousal of the cortex. Even before the cortex appraises the potential threat of the sound, this general arousal stimulates the limbic system (which, you will recall, is the seat of emotions such as fear) and the hypothalamus (which regulates such things as body temperature and heartbeat); they in turn prepare the body for potential action. Increased muscle tension, hormonal and metabolic action take place *before* the cortex identifies the source of the stimulus. The increases in various bodily functions are sensed by the R.A.S., which further alerts and arouses the system. If action occurs, the arousal was purposeful and the stress products are utilized. If the sound is never consciously appraised or if no action is pursued, then the system becomes stressed for no reason and stress products must circulate until they can be reabsorbed or otherwise used up. The process is illustrated in Figure 4.4.

The R.A.S. has the capacity for reverberation (prolonged vibration) of an impulse and will also prolong a response. This means that the R.A.S. can maintain a resting level of activity which is reflective of the general state of the other brain structures. A high level of resting activity increases and prolongs arousal, whereas a lower level of resting activity inhibits and shortens potential arousal. If you live a stressful life and find that you are stressed many times during the day, chances are that the parts of the brain that become aroused to deal with that stress also effect the R.A.S., which adapts to frequent arousal by staying aroused. It is as if the R.A.S. is saying, "Well, if you are going to be aroused so often I might as well just stay aroused and save the time and energy of going up and down." The R.A.S. also has the capacity to recruit impulses from other brain structures and it will adapt to stimuli. It is partly because

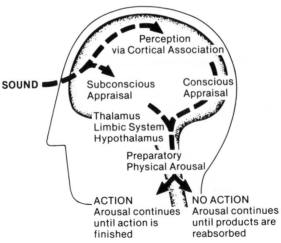

Figure 4.4 Specific and General Arousal in Response to Stress

of this ability to adapt that repeated situations cause less stress than novel experiences and the noise of the city is less stressful for the permanent resident than for the visitor.

In order to understand the stress response it is also necessary to learn about that part of the central nervous system called the *autonomic nervous system*. As the name implies, the autonomic system is primarily automatic or involuntary. It controls basic, elementary body processes such as hormone balance, metabolism, body fluid regulation, vascular (blood vessel) activity, and reproduction. It also has centers which influence feelings of pleasure and pain. Even though these activities can be influenced by the higher conscious centers, the day-to-day operation of the body goes on without much conscious thought.

One of the major areas of the brain which regulates the activities of the autonomic nervous system is the *hypothalamus*, a pea-size collection of nerve cells located at the base of the brain. The hypothalamus influences the stress response mainly by providing what might be termed "background action" to prepare the body for action. This was already demonstrated in the discussion of the R.A.S. Consider the example of the response to noise. The noise was first perceived by the lower centers before it was registered in the conscious cortex. Once the hypothalamus is stimulated, it prepares for possible action by increasing the discharge of hormones, increasing the availability of energy, preparing the cardiovascular (heart and circulatory) system by shifting blood flow to essential organs, and at the same time tensing the muscles. The conscious cortex may ultimately prevent the action, but the body is prepared for any eventuality and is technically in a state of stress. It is the hypothalamus, with its intimate relationship to the pituitary gland, which provides the link between the nervous system and the endocrine system. This will be explained further in the next section.

The impulses that arise from the autonomic nervous system are carried to the body through two major subdivisions called the *sympathetic* and *parasympathetic* systems. The sympathetic system has become famous for its lifesaving "fight or flight" capacities. All parts of the sympathetic system react with a mass discharge to accomplish a common purpose—to allow the body to act above and beyond its normal everyday function. For example, in a fight or flight situation, the body needs more blood, more oxygen, and more energy. Let's see how the sympathetic system accomplishes that. The action of the heart is increased: there are more beats per minute and more blood pumped per beat. At the same time, the body makes more efficient use of the available blood supply by constricting blood vessels in organs that are not essential to the stress response, such as the gastrointestinal tract. This decreases the function of the unneeded organ and allows an increased flow of blood to go to essential organs such as the heart and skeletal muscles. In the lungs, the bronchials (which carry the air) expand, and breathing becomes deeper, faster, and generally more efficient. The pupils of the eyes enlarge, improving visual sensitivity. The rate of salivary secretion decreases. The adrenal glands secrete adrenalin, which reinforces and prolongs the sympathetic effect and stimulates the liver to release more glucose to fuel the action. Thus, stimulation of the sympathetic system increases the activity of the organs that are needed for the fight or flight response and inhibits the organs that are not essential. Here again, prolonged stimulation or inhibition of organs can result in malfunction of the organ and promote a stress-related illness.

The parasympathetic system, by contrast, is not a system in the sense that there is no *mass* reaction to stimulation. It is responsible for day-to-day functioning of organs and is relatively specific, acting on specific organs. Parasympathetic stimulation also can increase the action of some organs while inhibiting the action of others, and this system works in contrast to the sympathetic system. In the previous example, parasympathetic stimulation of those same organs would slow down the action of the heart. At the same time it would expand most blood vessels and increase the functions in the gastrointestinal system. Bronchials in the lung would constrict, as would pupils of the eyes. The rate of salivary secretion would increase.

Most organs in the body work with both the sympathetic and parasympathetic systems acting on them. Some organs, however, are stimulated by only one of those nervous systems. In this case, it is the fluctuation between the two systems that determines whether the organ is activated or inhibited.

The fight or flight response is by no means the *only* contributor to the stress response. Actually, there are many emotional situations that can alter the body's function, and different emotions bring about different physical states. When we feel anger, we are full of energy, become flushed, and are excited. Wolf and Wolff (1947) have reported that in anger situations mucous membranes of the nose and stomach redden, swell, and become congested to the point of hemorrhage. Often gastritis can be traced to this cause. When we are afraid, we tremble, our knees feel weak, and we often have difficulty speaking. During fear, the mucous membranes of the nose and stomach become pale and shrunken.

However, it is difficult to generalize about how the nervous system affects stress-related disorders. For one thing, either stimulation or inhibition can lead to body malfunction. Also, the action of the nervous system is influenced by the action of the other control system of the body: the endocrine system.

THE ENDOCRINE SYSTEM

The *endocrine system* consists of the glands within the body that secrete substances called *hormones* into the bloodstream. These various hormones influence a great many body activities. The glands we are most concerned with in this section are the pituitary gland and the adrenal glands, although all the glands are involved to some extent in the stress response.

We have already mentioned that there is an intimate relationship between the hypothalamus and the pituitary gland. As various areas of the hypothalamus are stimulated, it in turn stimulates corresponding areas in the pituitary, and thus thoughts, anticipations, and nervous system responses in general can become hormonal actions. Some portions of the hypothalamus stimulate the parasympathetic nervous system and inhibit the stress response. Other areas of the hypothalamus activate the sympathetic nervous system and increase the stress response.

Although all the endocrine glands are involved, the adrenal glands are responsible for most of the physical responses to stress arousal, such as increased heart rate and others just discussed. There are two adrenal glands, one sitting over each kidney. The adrenal consists of two parts: the inner section, called the *medulla,* and the outer layer, called the *cortex.* Figure 4.5 shows the medulla surrounded by the adrenal cortex.

The medulla is connected to the hypothalamus by sympathetic nerves which extend into the medulla. When the hypothalamus is stimulated, the impulse is carried into the medulla, and this area of the gland immediately releases the hormone *epinephrine* (also called *adrenalin*). The effects of this hormone were outlined in the description of the fight or flight response. It is primarily the cardiovascular system that is affected.

The adrenal cortex is related to the hypothalamus not directly through nerve impulses, but by means of a hormone secreted by the pituitary

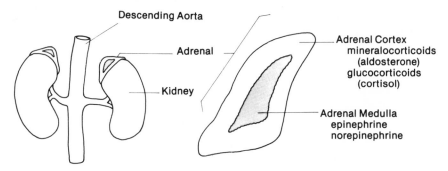

Figure 4.5 Adrenal Glands and Hormones

gland. It works as follows. The pituitary gland secretes the hormone *ACTH* (adrenocorticotrophic hormone) into the bloodstream. Through the bloodstream it circulates to its target gland, the adrenal cortex. Once the adrenal cortex is stimulated, it in turn secretes hormones into the blood, and to a large extent, these hormones constitute the stress response. The two primary secretions of the adrenal cortex are the *glucocorticoids* (primarily *cortisol*) and the *mineralcorticoids* (primarily *aldosterone*).

Cortisol affects metabolism (that is, the total body processes) by increasing energy, either for the stress response or for recovery from an extreme period of overactivity. Cortisol also increases, as much as tenfold, a metabolic process of the liver called *gluconeogenesis*; through this process the body forms glucose. This assures the body of an adequate supply of the most efficient energy source (blood glucose) for use during the accelerated period of activity. During the process of gluconeogenesis, cortisol mobilizes both fats and proteins in the blood. The mobilization of protein reduces the stores of protein in all body cells except in the liver and gastrointestinal tract, which is where the process takes place. If the process is maintained for a long period because of a prolonged stress response, there may not be enough protein available for the formation of mature white blood cells and antibodies. In this way, prolonged stress can promote muscular wasting and impair the immunity system. In the case of mobilizing the fats, taking fat from the fat cells is not in itself detrimental, but circulating it through the bloodstream can be. High levels of fatty tissue in the blood appear to promote atherosclerosis. Furthermore, during the process of gluconeogenesis, cortisol decreases the use of glucose by muscles and fatty tissue, probably by making the system insulin resistant, thus producing a mild diabetic effect.

Aldosterone is also secreted in increased amounts during the stress response. As a result, the body makes certain adjustments to prepare itself for increased muscular activity and better dissipation of heat and waste products. The body retains extra sodium (salt), resulting in increases in water retention, blood volume, blood pressure, and the amount of blood the heart pumps out with each beat.

5

The Body's
Response to Stress

Harold G. Wolff, one of the first proponents of psychosomatics in the United States, considered stress as an internal or resisting force which is usually stirred to action by external situations or pressures which appear as threats—not so much physical as symbolic (that is, involving values and goals). However, mobilizing our *physical* defenses (which were originally for the purpose of battling physical threats) in response to *symbolic* sources of threat (social or psychological) produces a response which is inappropriate. To determine if a response is appropriate, we have to consider the outcome. Physical arousal to physical threat is appropriate: it is usually short-lived and is usually dissipated with action. Physical arousal to symbolic threat is inappropriate: it tends to be of longer duration and is not as easily dissipated. Such action is not warranted, is not performed, and the reaction is therefore physically detrimental to the system.

We can categorize the damaging effects of stress as either (1) changes in the physiological processes that alter resistance to disease, or (2) pathological changes, that is, organ system fatigue or malfunction, that result directly from prolonged overactivity of specific stress organs. Noted stress researcher Hans Selye, who exposed laboratory animals to various stressors over a period of time, observed these detrimental effects of arousal. He found enlargement of the adrenal glands, atrophy or shrinkage of the spleen, thymus, and lymph nodes, disappearance of a specific kind of white blood cell, and the development of bleeding ulcers in the lining of the stomach. These varied physical responses led Selye to conceptualize stress as a syndrome, that is, the same complete pattern of physiological processes occur in response to a wide variety of stimuli.

To Selye, stress was more than a response, it was a process that enabled the body to resist the stressor in the best possible way by enhancing the functioning of the organ system best able to respond to it. He described this reaction in 1936 as a syndrome which was produced by a variety of agents. This syndrome became known as the three-stage General Adaptation Syndrome. The three stages are: (1) the alarm reaction stage, (2) the stage of resistance, and (3) the stage of exhaustion, described not only as a stress response, but as an adaptability to stress.

In the *alarm reaction stage*, characterized by increased ACTH secretion, which stimulates the adrenal glands (see Chapter 4), the body shows generalized stress arousal, but with no specific organ system being affected.

The second stage, that of *resistance*, is marked by decreases in ACTH, and what is called "specificity of adaptation" occurs. This means that the stress response is channeled into the specific organ system or process most capable of dealing with it or suppressing it. However, it is this adaptation process which contributes to stress-related illness. The specific organ system eventually becomes aroused, and may fatigue and start to malfunction. Chronic resistance can eventually diminish the ability of the system to function, and as the system deteriorates, specific problems such as skin ailments or gastrointestinal problems occur, depending upon the system affected.

Adaptation energy is limited, and exhaustion may eventually occur. During the *exhaustion phase*, the organ system or process that is dealing with the stress breaks down. Again, ACTH secretion increases and the response takes on the generalized character of the alarm reaction stage.

In the stage of exhaustion, disease or malfunction of the organ system or even death may occur. Sometimes exhaustion of one weakened system will shift the resistance to a stronger system, forcing that system into the adaptation process. To illustrate the damage that can be caused by adaptation, let's consider hypertension as a response to stress. The body can adapt to high blood pressure without constantly eliciting an alarm reaction, but the increased pressure is promoting kidney and heart damage which can eventually kill the individual if the situation is allowed to continue. Adaptation may be a lifesaving process, but it must be recog-

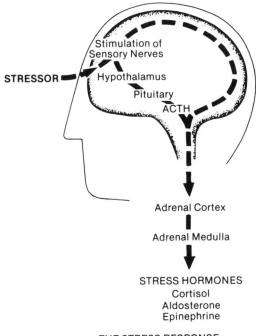

Figure 5.1 The Stress Response Pathway

nized also as a type of disease process. In fact, Selye often referred to stress-related diseases as "diseases of adaptation."

Figure 5.1 illustrates the flow of stress arousal from the brain to the stress response. This process was explained in more detail in Chapter 4.

THE MUSCLES' RESPONSE

The muscles are our only means of expression. We cannot move toward pleasure or away from danger without muscle movements. Speech, facial expression, eye movements, every mode of expression, of feeling and of resolution of an emotion are all achieved through muscle movement. Yet the muscles are under the command of the will, awaiting orders and obligingly obeying them. Oddly enough, many of the orders are given subconsciously, are counterproductive, and contribute significantly to stress and tension because: (1) chronically tense muscles complete a feedback loop and further stimulate the mind, resulting in greater stress states, and (2) chronically tense muscles result in numerous psychosomatic disorders including headache, backache, spasms of the esophagus and colon (the latter resulting in either diarrhea or constipation), posture problems, asthma, tightness in the throat and chest cavity, some eye problems, lockjaw, muscle tears and pulls, and perhaps rheumatoid arthritis.

It is important here to emphasize the word *chronic*. Stress disorders are caused by chronic, long-term overactivity. Acute, even violent, muscle contractions are not as harmful to the body as are slight or moderate contractions sustained over a long period of time.

Muscles have only two states: contraction and relaxation, although there are varying degrees of contraction, called *tension*. When relaxation occurs, there is an absence of muscle contraction or tension. Although it has been mentioned before, it is important enough to restate that the common use of the term "relaxation" (as in the sentence, "I am going to the movie to relax") is better termed "recreation." Movies may be recreational, but seldom do they produce muscle relaxation.

A muscle is actually a mass of millions of muscle cells which have the ability to shorten when stimulated by nerve impulses. This shortening moves bones, skin, or some organ, and work is accomplished. Often an incomplete or partial contraction occurs, tension develops, but no work is done. It is this situation which is referred to as "muscle tension" and is linked with the psychosomatic disorders mentioned above. Pain probably develops because a partially contracted muscle closes the vessel, and so an inadequate amount of blood is delivered to the tissues. Pain can also develop when a chronically shortened muscle exerts an abnormal pulling pressure on a joint; or from the tearing of fibers when a chronically shortened muscle is overexerted; or just from the disruption of the proper function of an organ, which is the case in the smooth muscle disorders such as diarrhea, constipation, or esophageal spasms.

It is possible to measure the strength of a muscle contraction, or muscle tension, by placing electrodes on the muscle before it is contracted. This is accomplished through use of an instrument called an *electromyograph* (EMG). The electrical activity of the muscle is sensed, amplified (electric potential of muscle fibers is measured in *microvolts*, or millionths of volts), integrated, and recorded. The signal can be converted to a light or a sound, and then fed back to the subject, so the EMG becomes a biofeedback device. Any muscle in the body can be measured in this manner, and thus keying into muscle tension is a relatively simple process. Muscles of the back would be most indicative of backache, while certain muscles of the head and neck are indicators of general muscle tension associated with mental work, stress, and frustration.

Even though muscles maintain their own resting level of contraction, purposeful movement is under the control of the central voluntary parts of the brain, primarily the cerebellum and motor cortex. The most specific and exacting control comes from the motor cortex of the brain, which contains specific areas corresponding to particular areas of the body, such as fingers, leg area, neck area, and so on. Stimulation of any one of these areas in the brain results in movement of muscles in the corresponding body area. When the brain finally decides on an action, impulses are directed from the motor cortex and the muscle contracts.

Now remember that muscles receive only two commands, *contract* or *relax*—this is the limit of their capabilities. A finely coordinated action involves an unbelievable number of "contract and relax" commands whose sequence must be learned, practiced, and stored in the memory. Even then a coordinated movement is impossible without constant feedback of the result of the contraction. This allows you instantly to approve and refine the muscle action until your brain can accomplish the act without your conscious control. You have just to think, "Pick up the pencil," and not figure out how to accomplish the act.

Let's consider this now in relation to stressful muscle tension. Imagine a potentially threatening situation in which you are contemplating some defensive action. You think defensive, you prepare to move, and you automatically assume a defensive posture. Whether you were correct in interpreting the situation as a threat is not important. What is important is that you have *engrams* (learned patterns) for this type of reaction which can be assumed without your consciously thinking about it. The muscle action for bracing, defensive posturing, or preparing for action can be completed even though your conscious mind is not actively considering such action. So you can see how hidden fears or anger can result in chronic stressful muscle tension.

While anticipation is necessary for preparation, it has been found that muscle tension develops and remains until the task is completed or the mind is diverted to a new thought process. Interestingly enough, successful completion of a task results in more rapid resolution of muscle tension than does failure at the task. Also, if you imagine a muscle movement or an action (for example, a defensive posture) the same preparatory muscle tension will occur as when you are actually engaging in the activity. This perhaps explains why highly anxious people who are often in a high state of expectation often prove to have a great amount of muscle tension.

Impulses from the motor cortex are normally carried to the muscles via the spinal cord and a cable of neurons called the *pyramidal tract.* However, another pathway, called the *extrapyramidal motor system,* also sends signals from the hypothalamus and upper limbic area to the muscles. Stimulation through this pathway causes a variety of unconscious postures and rhythmic movements. This system seems to be both specific and nonspecific, as was the reticular formation discussed in Chapter 4. Nonspecific activation may result in what is referred to as *nonspecific tonus,* or increased general tension in the system. This hidden state of tension may last over a period of time and could augment a "voluntary" bracing action or cause a muscular overreaction. Either situation results in chronic muscle tension which could lead to illness. Of course, the opposite can also exist, if the inherent rhythm is dominated by a low-arousal, tranquil rhythm. That is the purpose of the exercises in the later sections of this book.

THE GASTROINTESTINAL RESPONSE

When Hans Selye conducted his classic experiments on stressed laboratory animals, he found ulcerations of the stomach lining to be one of the responses. One might wonder why the gastrointestinal (GI) system would be involved. It serves no function in the fight or flight response, and logically should not be controlled by the parts of the brain that anticipate or interpret possible threats. Yet, GI disorders are responsible for filling more hospital beds in this country than any other body system, and science has clearly established that many GI disorders have psychological roots.

The gastrointestinal system, as seen in Figure 5.2, is responsible for accepting food, mechanically breaking it down by churning it in the stomach, moving it through the intestines by a rhythmic movement called *peristalsis,* and supplying enzymes that will finally digest the small food particles into blood sugar, simple fatty acids, or amino acids which the body uses for energy or building tissue. The GI system has an inherent rhythm and is governed by numerous automatic reflexes to control its movements, its emptying, and its secretion of enzymes. The GI system is also associated with the motivation system in that hunger must lead to food-gathering behavior. The centers that control hunger and appetite are located in the hypothalamus and are closely related to pleasure and unpleasure (see the discussion of the limbic system in Chapter 4). Hunger and satiety are definitely emotional states, so perhaps this structure and process have opened Pandora's box and allowed other emotions to likewise affect the functioning of the GI system.

The GI system responds to emotional situations in a manner more

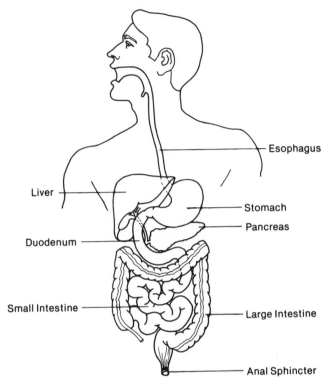

Figure 5.2 The Gastrointestinal System

complex than the typical sympathetic versus parasympathetic process described in the preceding chapter. And the GI system dispels the good guy/bad guy stereotype of those two divisions of the autonomic nervous system, for overstimulation of each can result in disease.

Response to stress arousal can be measured in every structure along the alimentary canal, starting with the mouth. Since Pavlov's classic studies it has been clearly demonstrated that emotional states influence the flow of saliva. You may have had the experience of getting up before an audience to deliver a speech and finding your mouth dry. This occurrence has been so long used as a measure of fear that in ancient China suspected criminals were made to chew rice, and the lack of a mucous wad was taken as an indication of guilt. Yet, seeing the dentist preparing to drill a tooth often turns on saliva to the point where the dentist must continuously vacuum it away.

The emotions have been known to induce spastic contraction of muscles in the esophagus, which leads to the stomach. This disrupts peristalsis (the rhythmic movement that carries food through the digestive system), and makes swallowing difficult and in some situations impossible.

The stomach too has been recognized as part of the emotional response system. Most anxiety tests take into consideration the state of the stomach. Statements such as "I have no appetite," "I have a gnawing feeling in the pit of my stomach," and "I feel nauseated" are the most often described physical symptoms of anxiety and emotional arousal. Ulcers have even been associated with professionals and executives in high-pressure positions of decision making.

Doctors have been able to observe the activity in the stomach linings of patients. They have noted that in situations producing anger, resentment, and aggression, the lining of the stomach increased its secretions of hydrochloric acid and various enzymes and became engorged with blood. The membrane became so frail that eruptions would occur spontaneously and ulcerations would develop. Situations described as producing fright, depression, listlessness, and being overwhelmed to the point of withdrawal produced the opposite reaction—it functioned below its normal level. But even that situation is not without problems: decreasing the blood flow to the secreting glands lessens the natural protection of the area against certain harsh substances, such as hydrochloric acid, which helps break down food in the stomach.

In the intestines, similar patterns have been observed. Stress arousal has also been shown to alter peristaltic rhythm. This alteration in normal peristalsis in both small and large intestines is responsible for two of the most classic stress responses: diarrhea, if movements are too fast and normal drying through water absorption does not take place; and constipation, if movement through the intestines is very slow and there is excessive drying. Chronic constipation can further lead to more severe intestinal blockage. Blockage of the bile and pancreatic ducts as well as inflammation of the pancreas (pancreatitis) have been linked with stress arousal, although little research has been conducted in this area.

THE BRAIN'S RESPONSE

Even though we discussed the brain in Chapter 4 as part of the control system, we can also view it as a response system because its electrical activity can be analyzed. First we should understand how the nerve cells function. These neurons contain constantly exchanging *ions*, which are atoms that carry tiny electrical charges. This activity forms wave patterns and the patterns can be followed through the use of an *electroencephalograph* (EEG). This instrument measures the frequency or rate of the wave patterns in *Hz*, or cycles per second. Unlike the muscles, which remain electrically inactive until they are stimulated to action, the cells of the brain emit a constant electrical rhythm.

The dominant, quiet rhythm of the brain has been designated by the Greek letter *alpha*. It describes a wave pattern that fluctuates at the rate of 8 to 13 Hz, and it emits energy that typically varies from 25 to 100μv (microvolts). An increase in the activity of the brain changes the basic alpha rhythm, producing a wave pattern that is higher in frequency, 13 to 50 Hz, but emits less energy. This faster wave of lesser voltage has been designated as *beta*. Another common wave pattern, designated *theta*, fluctuates between 4 and 7 Hz, and an even slower wave pattern, *delta*, fluctuates at less than 4 Hz and is usually observed only during sleep.

The analysis of complex brain wave patterns has been used to diagnose abnormal brain states. More recently, the practice of referring to wave patterns to describe various activation states has become popular. The alpha wave has been associated with the absence of meaningful cause-and-effect thinking: this is a quiet state of mind in which stress arousal is at a minimum. The beta pattern is characterized by a focusing of attention, problem solving, and relating the self to the external world. While this is not necessarily a stressful state, stress arousal is more possible in the beta state. Less is known about the mental state associated with the theta pattern, although researchers report that the thought patterns are directed internally and are less related to specific external events. Daydreams, fantasies, and what some researchers term "creative images" are more likely to occur during the theta state. More on the brain wave and associated mental states will be presented in the chapters on meditation and biofeedback.

Apart from the more measurable physical responses of the brain to stress, there are psychological or mood responses as well. During rest and relaxation, the psychological nature of the brain is said to be in *homeostasis*. That means that the subjective moods of the individual are in harmony, promoting a healthful relationship between mind and body. However, during stress the psychological mechanisms of the mind are thrown into turmoil. A "mood disturbance" is often one characteristic of the stress reaction. During stress it is common to have feelings of confusion, fear, extreme emotional sensitivity, and ego-threat. Many researchers feel that schizophrenia, a severe state of being out of touch with reality, results as a compensation for the excessive traumas of life. The schizophrenic simply becomes unable to cope with the stresses of reality through the traditional coping mechanisms and therefore unconsciously decides to remove him/herself from reality as an escape from stress. In support of this theory, there has been some success in returning these people to reality by providing warm and supportive environments.

THE CARDIOVASCULAR RESPONSE

Not all diseases are psychosomatic, and not all of the psychosomatic diseases can be considered psychogenic (see the description of psychosomatic diseases in Chapter 2). However, in the case of cardiovascular disease, it is almost impossible to completely rule out the role of stress. The only real question is exactly how much of a contributor stress is in relation to the other risk factors. The answer is obscured by the indirect nature of stress and the long-term development of this chronic disease.

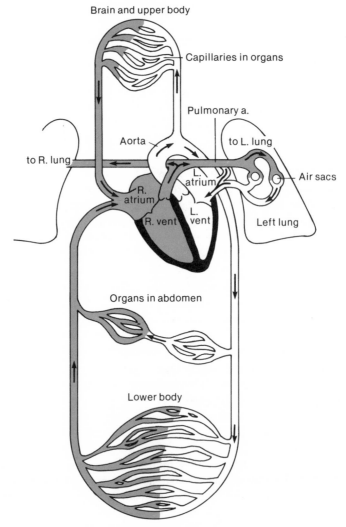

Figure 5.3 The Cardiovascular System

Diseases of the cardiovascular system (shown in Figure 5.3) include problems related to the heart itself (its basic structure and rhythm), to systemic blood flow and blood pressure, the structure of the blood vessels, and the constituency of the blood. It is obvious that each cannot be considered separately from the others, as they are all intricately related, and malfunction of one affects the others.

The work of the heart is to pump blood to the cells of the body. The blood contains oxygen and energy-producing substances, which are the basic necessities for the life of the cell. To accomplish the pumping task, the heart, which is a cavity surrounded by muscle, must contract. As the muscle contracts, the cavity becomes smaller. This increases the pressure of the blood within the chamber. When the pressure in the cavity is greater than that outside of it, the blood is ejected into the miles of blood vessels, arteries and veins, that travel to every part of the body. Each blood vessel contracts in a similar manner, thus helping to maintain the pressure and aiding the movement of the blood traveling through the system. Once ejected, the blood is pushed along under pressure, which in the average adult male is about 120 mmHg (slightly less for females). When the heart completes its contraction phase, it relaxes and the pressure in the system drops to about 80 mmHg in the average adult male, and again slightly less for females. These pressure indications (120/80) are used to express one's blood pressure and this is easily measured by a cufflike instrument called a *sphygmomanometer*. You should have your blood pressure taken regularly and be sure what it is.

It should be obvious that the fewer times a heart must contract or beat to accomplish the necessary supply functions, the more rest it will get. The heart has an inherent rhythm which is determined by the membrane potential of a special area in the right atrium called the pacemaker. Even when the heart is denied nervous stimulation, it is capable of independent action; however, the heart is constantly receiving impulses from the brain, and its inherent rhythm is continually influenced by the central nervous system. The heart receives impulses from both the sympathetic and parasympathetic nervous systems (see Chapter 4). Thus, it is under moment-to-moment control by various centers of the brain which are in touch with metabolic and physiological demands of the body. In addition to neural regulation, the heart can also be influenced by the hormone epinephrine, which can increase the contractability of the heart muscle (the *myocardium*), increasing the speed and strength of the contraction.

A significant survival mechanism of the cardiovascular system is that the heart is capable of anticipating physiological and metabolic demands by increasing action of the heart before it is actually required. However, as we've seen before, very often the anticipation of such a demand increases the activity of the system, but then the final action is thwarted by the conscious cortex. In this case the cardiovascular system response is to no avail. Similarly, many psychological states increase cardiovascular activity when no action is actually required. A new or unusual experience frequently elevates heart rate, as does fear, anger, anxiety, and most situations which threaten the ego. You will recall Harold Wolff's definition of stress as a physical response to a psychological or symbolic threat leading to responses that are inappropriate in kind and intensity. In our complex society, stressors are usually symbolic, requiring no physical action. But our response is nevertheless physical. Thus, a chronically stressed person often has a chronically overworked heart.

Another cardiovascular problem related to stress is chronically elevated blood pressure, or *hypertension*. It has been estimated that perhaps 15 to 20 percent of the adult population suffers from hypertension, usually considered to be a pressure above 160/95. Approximately 90 percent of the cases are called "essential hypertension," meaning it is of unknown origin. Since the primary work of the heart is to overcome the pressure in the arteries to which the blood must flow, increasing blood pressure greatly increases the work of the heart and contributes to cardiovascular problems.

Like the heart, the blood vessels have an inherent tone which can be altered moment to moment by both parts of the autonomic nervous system (sympathetic and parasympathetic systems) and by hormones (epinephrine and norepinephrine) to reflect the physiological demands placed on the system. Anticipation and psychological states such as fear, anger, and anxiety will alter the diameter of vessels, producing a physical response to symbolic or imagined threats.

A third problem area concerning the cardiovascular system relates to the destruction of the vessels by the infusion of fatty plaques, called *atherosclerosis*. The relationship between stress and vascular problems appears to lie in the fact that during stress arousal, the hormones epinephrine and cortisol mobilize fats and cholesterol for use by the muscles and these circulate in the bloodstream until they are used or reabsorbed. This process was described in Chapter 4. Although there are many factors that contribute to the development of atherosclerosis, constantly saturating the system with unneeded fats through the stress mechanism can only exacerbate the problem. It is well known that these plaques contain cholesterol, triglycerides, and other fatty tissues.

An artery infused with such plaques will eventually lose elasticity and harden, producing *arteriosclerosis* (an advanced form of atherosclerosis). This disease is directly responsible for over half a million deaths annually in the United States.

When an artery in an advanced state of disease loses its elasticity, it elevates the blood pressure, thus contributing to hypertension and disease of the heart itself. In addition, atherosclerotic plaques which narrow the diameter of the blood vessels diminish oxygen delivery and may bring on a *myocardial infarction*, or heart attack, if the coronary arteries are affected.

There are many factors which contribute to the development of atherosclerosis and hypertension, including a diet high in cholesterol and saturated fats (which adds to the amount of potential fatty deposits in the blood vessels); lack of exercise (which decreases the utilization of these nutrients); smoking (which mimics sympathetic nervous system stimulation, narrowing the blood vessels and increasing the heartbeat); obesity; sex (being a male); age; heredity; and of course, stress, which underlies many of the others.

Another vascular problem which has been associated with stress is the vascular headache, also known as the migraine headache. Migraines are thought to be caused by an exaggerated constriction of blood vessels in and around the brain, followed by a reflex dilation or enlarging of those vessels, which causes the release of toxic chemicals which irritate local nerve endings and add to the pain. The root of this type of attack is complex and seems to involve, in a headache-prone individual, a psychogenic trigger of the sympathetic nervous system which causes the initial constriction of the blood vessels. This phase, known as the *prodromal* phase, is characterized by nausea, increased irritability, and an unusual sensitivity to noise and light. Physiologically, this phase seems to deplete the system of the hormone *serotonin*. It may be the loss of this hormone that causes the reflex dilation of the vessels and the accompanying intense pain.

Little is known of the actual underlying cause of migraine. The migraine-prone individual may have abnormal metabolism of serotonin or may be deficient in an enzyme which oxidizes this hormone. Recent clinical investigations have shown that certain types of migraine headaches can be alleviated by learning control of the central nervous system through elaborate relaxation training. This points not to an alleviation of any chemical imbalance, but to a control over the initial psychogenic trigger.

THE SKIN'S RESPONSE

It is sometimes difficult to think of the skin as a separate system capable of responding to stress arousal, but its complex function and intricate nervous control make it a sensitive response system, and its accessibility makes it a convenient window into the body. When you observe the stress response of any body system, you are looking through that system into the mental activity responsible for the response.

The skin has two basic response patterns which show the world what is going on in the body and the mind. One is often referred to as "electrical language" because it seems to speak if you have the proper listening device. Each of the millions of cells that make up the skin system contains chemicals that have an electrical nature. As the body expresses itself, the chemical activity of the skin cells changes, producing different patterns of electrical activity. This electrical activity can be measured on the skin surface. The constant but ever changing activity of the skin appears as "chatter," and although it is complex and sometimes difficult to interpret, it is used by police authorities in most lie detector systems, and by health professionals to help understand your emotions, your motivations, and your problem-solving techniques.

The second basic response system of the skin is its temperature. There are small blood vessels under the skin that change in response to emotion. During tense, anxious periods they shut down and allow less blood to pass, causing the skin to appear pale and the skin temperature to decrease. At other times the blood vessels open and allow the skin to flush with blood, increasing the skin temperature.

With this type of response pattern, it is not hard to visualize how prolonged emotional responses could change the activity of the skin long enough to result in malfunction and disease. Certain skin conditions or illnesses have been found to have roots in our psychological response patterns. For example, eczema, a skin lesion characterized by redness, swelling, itching, and fluid discharge, has been associated with emotional stimulation. The reddening and itching are indicative of abnormal blood flow into the area, while the fluid discharge is indicative of an increased rate of fluid production by the skin cells. Laboratory studies have established that in eczema-prone individuals emotional arousal increases the amount of fluid exuded by the skin cells, whereas relaxation diminishes it. Eczema patients have been classified as restless, impatient, and unduly irritable, but the relationship of these characteristics to the skin condition has not been clearly established.

Similar preliminary work has been done with patients suffering from urticaria (hives), psoriasis, and acne, but these investigations are still in their infancy.

part II

What Causes Stress and What Is Your Stress Profile?

Introduction

This section will explore the factors that trigger the stress response. One of the most important stages in coping with stress is the recognition of what aspects of your life contribute to excessive stress. In this section you will learn about the various causes of stress and will take several self-assessment tests in order to gain some insight into how you are affected by each of these potential causes. A total stress profile is provided at the end of this section to help you summarize your level of vulnerability to the stressors discussed.

By definition, stress is an arousal reaction to some stimulus—be it an event, object, or person. This stress reaction is characterized by heightened arousal of physiological and psychological processes. The stimulus that causes this arousal reaction is the *stressor*, which is the object of our investigation here.

A major source of confusion which makes the study of origins of stress difficult is the tendency to lump all stressors together because they may all result in the same general reaction called stress. The categorization of stressors in Table II.1 should help alleviate some of this confusion. This classification is based upon the external nature of the stressor, that is, upon the fundamental basis or cause of the stress reaction. From this we see that stressors may be divided into three general classes:

1. *Psychosocial causes.* These stressors are a function of the complex interaction between social behavior and the way our senses and our minds

Table II.1

MAJOR CAUSES OF STRESS

Psychosocial	
Adaptation	Overload
Frustration	Deprivation
Bioecological	
Biorhythms	Noise
Nutrition	
Personality	
Self-perception	Anxiety
Behavioral patterns	

interpret those behaviors. In other words, much of our societal stress is determined by the meanings that we assign to the events in our lives. Different individuals are likely to interpret differently, or to assign different meanings to, the same situation. This explains why each person's pattern of societal stress is unique.

2. *Bioecological causes.* These stressors basically are biologically related and may arise out of our relationship with our environment. They are only minimally subject to differing interpretations.

3. *Personality causes.* These reflect the dynamics of an individual's self-perception and characteristic attitudes and behaviors which may somehow contribute to excessive stress.

6

Psychosocial
Causes of Stress

This chapter examines what may be referred to as the basic "psycho-social" origins of the stress reaction. These stimuli are capable of inducing the stress response in many human beings; therefore, the stimuli are, by definition, labeled as stressors. The psychosocial stressors originate as a result of a complex interaction that exists between socialization and perception. That is, they are sociological events which we may perceive as undesirable on the basis of our past experiences or other learning processes.

There are four psychosocial processes that appear to be most connected to stress: (1) adaptation; (2) frustration; (3) overload; and (4) deprivation. We will examine these potential sources of distress and look at examples of how each touches our daily lives. Before you read each section, be sure to complete the self-assessment exercise that precedes it.

STOP!!

Self-Assessment Exercise 1 [1]

Below are listed events which occur in the process of living.[2] Place a check in the left-hand column for each of those events that have happened to you during the *last 12 months*.

	Life Event	*Point Values*
_____	Death of Spouse	100
_____	Divorce	73
_____	Marital separation	65
_____	Jail term	63
_____	Death of close family member	63
_____	Personal injury or illness	53
_____	Marriage	50
_____	Fired from work	47
_____	Marital reconciliation	45
_____	Retirement	45
_____	Change in family member's health	44
_____	Pregnancy	40
_____	Sex difficulties	39
_____	Addition to family	39
_____	Business readjustment	39
_____	Change in financial status	38
_____	Death of close friend	37
_____	Change to different line of work	36
_____	Change in number of marital arguments	35
_____	Mortgage or loan over $10,000	31
_____	Foreclosure of mortgage or loan	30
_____	Change in work responsibilities	29
_____	Son or daughter leaving home	29
_____	Trouble with in-laws	29
_____	Outstanding personal achievement	28
_____	Spouse begins or stops work	26
_____	Starting or finishing school	26
_____	Change in living conditions	25
_____	Revision of personal habits	24
_____	Trouble with boss	23
_____	Change in work hours, conditions	20
_____	Change in residence	20

[1] Holmes and Rahe, 1967.
[2] If you are a full-time student or under 25, use the Student Questionnaire which appears on the next page. If you are borderline between these two life phases, take both and use the higher score.

Exercise 1 (cont.)

Life Event	*Point Values*
___ Change in schools	20
___ Change in recreational habits	19
___ Change in church activities	19
___ Change in social activities	18
___ Mortgage or loan under $10,000	17
___ Change in sleeping habits	16
___ Change in number of family gatherings	15
___ Change in eating habits	15
___ Vacation	13
___ Christmas season	12
___ Minor violations of the law	11

Score: _____

After checking the items above, add up the point values for all of the items checked. Then read the section that follows concerning *adaptation* to interpret your score.

Student Questionnaire

Below are listed events which occur in the life of a college student. Place a check in the left-hand column for each of those events that have happened to you during the *last 12 months*.

Life Event	*Point Values*
___ Death of a close family member	100
___ Jail term	80
___ Final year or first year in college	63
___ Pregnancy (to you or caused by you)	60
___ Severe personal illness or injury	53
___ Marriage	50
___ Any interpersonal problems	45
___ Financial difficulties	40
___ Death of a close friend	40
___ Arguments with your roommate (more than every other day)	40
___ Major disagreements with your family	40
___ Major change in personal habits	30
___ Change in living environment	30
___ Beginning or ending a job	30

Exercise 1 (cont.)

Life Event	Point Values
_____ Problems with your boss or professor	25
_____ Outstanding personal achievement	25
_____ Failure in some course	25
_____ Final exams	20
_____ Increased or decreased dating	20
_____ Change in working conditions	20
_____ Change in your major	20
_____ Change in your sleeping habits	18
_____ Several-day vacation	15
_____ Change in eating habits	15
_____ Family reunion	15
_____ Change in recreational activities	15
_____ Minor illness or injury	15
_____ Minor violations of the law	11

Score: _____

After checking the items above, add up the point values for all of the items checked. Then read the section that follows on *adaptation* to interpret your score.

ADAPTATION

> We are simultaneously experiencing a youth revolution, a racial revolution, a sexual revolution, a colonial revolution, an economic revolution, and the most rapid and deep-going technological revolution in history.[3]

This description of the massive process of change was true in 1970 and is even more in evidence today. The single most descriptive phrase that could be used to describe the twentieth century is the "era of change."

Most of us have been reared with the feeling that change is good and desirable, as it usually denotes an easier and more productive life. However, in his book *Future Shock*, Alvin Toffler suggested that even though change is a necessary element in societal behavior, if it occurs at too intense a rate or on too massive a scale, the participants may cease reaping the rewards of change and begin realizing how devastating change can be. Though Toffler spoke somewhat as a philosopher and social critic, the scientific literature strongly supports his contentions.

[3] Alvin Toffler, *Future Shock* (New York: Random House, 1970), p. 186.

Your health and even your very survival are based largely upon your body's ability to maintain a healthy balance of mental and physical processes. This state of equilibrium is called *homeostasis*. It has been suggested that excessive change is harmful to your health because it acts to destroy homeostasis and forces the body to restore homeostasis through adaptation.

Homeostasis. The state of the body in which there exists a stable equilibrium of internal functions.

Adaptation. The tendency of the body to fight to restore homeostasis in the face of forces which upset the natural bodily balance.

In the early 1960's Thomas H. Holmes and Richard H. Rahe attempted to discover if change did have major effects upon human health. *Generic change*—that is, change resulting in either positive or negative consequence—was the focus of their research efforts. Based on earlier work by Adolph Meyer with "life charts," which was a paper and pencil tool for creating a medical biography, Holmes and Rahe compiled a list of positive *and* negative life events which seemed to contribute to the stress reaction. From these efforts emerged the Social Readjustment Rating Scale (SRRS), first published by Holmes and Rahe in 1967. This scale originally listed 43 specific life events and each item carried with it a weighting indicative of the amount of stress to be attributed to that item. The weightings are determined by the sample populations being tested. The weighting units were called Life Change Units (LCU's). The most highly weighted life event was the death of a spouse (100 LCU) and the lowest weighted event was minor violations of the law (11 LCU). Interestingly enough, outstanding personal achievement was weighted with 28 LCU, only one point less than trouble with in-laws! This points to one of the more important and interesting aspects of this study of life events: the fact that it concentrated on generic change, a force which causes stress through the destruction of homeostasis.

Remember, it is change, the disruption of homeostatic equilibrium, that produces stress and adaptation, regardless of whether the event is desirable or undesirable. Negative or distressful events are usually the most harmful, as they are more disruptive for a longer period of time. They stimulate negative thoughts which linger in the mind, producing a secondary effect by stimulating fear, self-doubt, and catastrophic imaginings. However, positive events can likewise be stressful in that they also initiate change which necessitates adaptation; but usually positive change does not produce the secondary effect of the negative event, and thus it is given fewer points in the weighting of life events.

One question that always arises in regard to the concept of life change events is: "Doesn't a specific event exert differing amounts of stress on different individuals?" The answer is technically yes, because everyone's perception of the events in their lives differs. How you perceive an event in your life is tempered by your past experiences. For example, knowing what to expect is a great help in overcoming stress. Someone who has not lived through an event will anticipate the event as being more stressful than will someone who has actually experienced the event before. Novelty is always stress-arousing, but that new situation becomes tempered through subsequent experiences. Nevertheless, some events are stressful no matter how many times you experience them, and as such they are only minimally less stressful through experience.

Take moving, for example. The first time a person moves is the most difficult, and one becomes more efficient with experience, but each moving experience still requires much adaptation. If you own a house, then the process of finding a realtor, negotiating prices, being displaced during showings, trying to live in a perpetually clean house for weeks or months, finding a new residence, securing new loans, and countless details are constant stressors. Packing, accumulating records, the move itself, finding a new physician, dentist, stores, schools, and friends are all stressors to the move, also. Thus, even if the event is positive, such as moving to a better job in a nicer place, and even if moves have been made before, there is much change, much adaptation, and thus moving is considered a stressful event.

With this concept of generic change as a stressor in mind, Rahe and Holmes amassed data from their Social Readjustment Rating Scale (SRRS). The SRRS is administered by asking the individual to indicate how many of the 43 items he/she has experienced over the past 12 months. A total LCU score is then obtained by adding up the LCU's for all of the items that have been checked. This scale has proven to be a remarkable predictor of physical and mental illness for a two-year period after the accumulation of the stressors.

The original SRRS, which is provided at the beginning of this section, has undergone several revisions, two of the later versions being the Life Events Inventory and the Life Change Events Scale, which are among the most popular instruments in use today. These scales were made to be used with adults and do not include events which are known stressors for other populations. For this reason, numerous other life events inventories have been created. The life events concept has been additionally validated with military personnel (Rahe, 1967), teenagers (Marx, 1975), and children (Coddington, 1972), and has been validated across cultures (Rahe, 1971).

As new classifications of stressors are identified for particular populations, new event scales will be developed to increase the accuracy of prediction. While the scales and populations change, the basic process of Rahe and Holmes remains the same—compile a list of stressful events unique to a certain population, have that specific group determine the stressfulness of the items, and conduct arduous studies on correlations between the cluster of events and subsequent illness. The items in the student form at the beginning of this section were formulated to measure life events of college students, so the weighting of the events were established by that specific group. It is still too soon to present any definitive statistics regarding that test, since it is a relatively new one, but it is expected that the correlations between life change and subsequent illness will be similar to those of the other tests.

It is important to remember that no one event has ever been related to illness, but rather it is the accumulation of the effect of numerous events occurring in a concentrated period which is predictive of illness. Thus, it is not the event, but rather the numerical score accumulated by the cluster of events which becomes the focus for analysis. Those individuals who accumulate higher scores seem most susceptible. In most of the previously published scales, "high" equaled 300 or more points, "low" equaled 150 or less, and "moderate" susceptibility was in between those extremes.

An important word here is *susceptibility*. A high score does not mean that the individual will *definitely* become ill. It means that they are more susceptible to illness, more likely to become ill than those with lower scores. There are many intervening variables—the most important of which might be the stress intervention techniques currently being practiced by the individual.

If you have not yet done so, go back and add up your score on Exercise I. If your total score for the year was under 150 points, your level of stress, based upon life change, is low. If your total was between 150 and 300, your stress levels are borderline; you should minimize other changes in your life at this time. If your total was more than 300, your life change levels of stress are high; you should minimize any other changes in your life and work more vigorously at instituting some of the stress intervention techniques presented in Part III of this book.

Now that you have determined your life change score, let us see how life change may lead to illness. First remember that change, whether favorable or unfavorable, requires adaptation. Change disturbs the equilibrium, inducing a temporary destruction of homeostasis. Such disequilibrium is met by the body with attempts at restoring homeostasis, and the restoration of homeostasis is called *adaptation*. Selye (1976) pointed out that adaptation stressed the body by requiring a concerted effort on the part of the body to restore the body's balance. This effort at restoring homeostasis requires energy—"adaptive energy"—and unfortunately, we have only so much adaptive energy available. It will eventually diminish if the disequilibrium becomes highly intense or chronic. When the person's adaptive energy becomes drained, dysfunction can occur on a localized or specific level. When the body is totally depleted of adaptive energy, general bodily exhaustion may result in death.

The fact that excessively intense disequilibrium (change) can result in death is supported by the studies of George Engle (1977), who found that in over 250 cases of sudden death, the deaths usually occurred within minutes or hours of a major event in the person's life. Of added interest is the fact that most of these people were in good or fair health before the death.

Engle looked for patterns to the sudden death phenomenon, and his investigations supported Holmes' contention that favorable as well as unfavorable change can be stressful. While the leading category of "sudden deaths" was those deaths preceded by some "traumatic disruption of a close human relationship," another major category consisted of people who died suddenly during moments of great triumph or personal satisfaction. Engle noted the example of a 55-year-old man who died during a joyous reunion with his 88-year-old father after a twenty-year separation. The father then dropped dead as well.

In summary, change can be a positive force for growth or it can be a negative force of mental and physical deterioration. The key lies not in the positive or negative valence of the change, but rather in how intense or chronic that change is. There is a considerable amount of research evidence which suggests that such excessive change does make a significant contribution to the onset and course of mental and physical illness.

STOP!!

Self-Assessment Exercise 2

Choose the most appropriate answer for each of the 10 statements below as it usually pertains to you. Place the letter of your response in the space to the left of the question.

_____ 1. When I can't do something "my way," I simply adjust to do it the easiest way.

    (a) Almost always true   (b) Often true
    (c) Seldom true   (d) Almost never true

_____ 2. I get "upset" when someone in front of me drives slowly.

    (a) Almost always true   (b) Often true
    (c) Seldom true   (d) Almost never true

_____ 3. It bothers me when my plans are dependent upon the actions of others.

    (a) Almost always true   (b) Often true
    (c) Seldom true   (d) Almost never true

_____ 4. Whenever possible, I tend to avoid large crowds.

    (a) Almost always true   (b) Often true
    (c) Seldom true   (d) Almost never true

_____ 5. I am uncomfortable having to stand in long lines.

    (a) Almost always true   (b) Often true
    (c) Seldom true   (d) Almost never true

_____ 6. Arguments upset me.

    (a) Almost always true   (b) Often true
    (c) Seldom true   (d) Almost never true

_____ 7. When my plans don't "flow smoothly," I become anxious.

    (a) Almost always true   (b) Often true
    (c) Seldom true   (d) Almost never true

_____ 8. I require a lot of room (space) to live and work in.

    (a) Almost always true   (b) Often true
    (c) Seldom true   (d) Almost never true

_____ 9. When I am busy at some task, I hate to be disturbed.

    (a) Almost always true   (b) Often true
    (c) Seldom true   (d) Almost never true

_____ 10. I believe that "all good things are worth waiting for."

    (a) Almost always true   (b) Often true
    (c) Seldom true   (d) Almost never true

Scoring: 1 and 10: a = 1, b = 2, c = 3, d = 4   Score: _____
       2–9: a = 4, b = 3, c = 2, d = 1

After you complete this exercise, total your score, then read the section that follows concerning *frustration* to interpret this scale.

FRUSTRATION

Have you ever gotten up-tight because the car in front of you was going too slowly? Have you ever stood in a long line and become anxious because it didn't move fast enough? If you've experienced these or similar situations, then you know what it is like to be frustrated.

> *Frustration.* The thwarting or inhibiting of natural or desired behaviors and goals.

Frustration occurs when we're blocked from doing what we want to do, whether it is a certain behavior we wish to perform or a goal we wish to attain. Emotionally, we respond to frustration with feelings of anger and aggression and with the nervous and hormonal responses that accompany these emotions. Frustration, then, causes the stress response, and in a highly technological, urban society this source of stress should be recognized so that it may be dealt with. Four major sources of everyday frustration in urban and suburban America are overcrowding, discrimination, economic conditions, and the bureaucracy. These serve as examples of psychosocial causes of stress.

Overcrowding

Perhaps the major psychosocial factor contributing to frustration is overcrowding. As our cities slowly grow into mass urban corridors, called megalopolises, social scientists wonder about the effects of such increasing human density upon the overall quality of life. Unfortunately, reports on the impact of crowding on health and happiness are conflicting or at least inconclusive.

The essence of the confusion surrounding the crowding/urbanization issue seems to be in the definition of the term "crowding." According to Freedman (1975), crowding is the *space* allotted per organism, or the *sensation* or *perception* of being crowded. The latter part of the definition makes the way we perceive a situation the determinant of whether crowding does or does not exist. Crowding, then, becomes a function not solely of space and people, but of your perception or feeling of being crowded, when the presence of other people inhibits your natural or desired behavior or keeps you from attaining your goal. Such a perception is highly relative. Three could be a crowd in one situation and 33 might not be a crowd in a different situation. If you perceive yourself as being crowded (inhibited by the presence of others), then overcrowding exists, and it is a psychosocial stressor for you.

In a variety of experiments with animals, it has been shown that crowding produces excessive stress hormone secretion, excessive adrenalin secretion, atrophy of the thymus gland (which involves the immunity system) and of secondary sexual characteristics, and elevated blood pressure. Researchers at the National Institute of Mental Health have concluded that "there is abundant evidence that among animals, at least, crowded living conditions and their immediate consequence . . . impose a stress that can lead to abnormal behavior, reproductive failure, sickness, and even death." [4]

While the animal research seems conclusive, there is still doubt as to whether these findings apply to human beings. The problem in human research is that a feeling of crowding depends on our perception, which is a function of complex sensory and thought processes in addition to the more basic lower brain processes which we share with the so-called "lower animals." In addition, this complex integration of perceptual processes may be different for different types of people. However, in general, research supports the theory that when individuals feel inhibited or frustrated due to overcrowding, the stress response results.

For instance, Tanner studied train commuters in Stockholm and found that the first passengers on a commuter train experienced less stress than those who boarded the train after the halfway point. This was true despite the fact that the earlier boarders had to tolerate the crowding for twice the time period. He concluded that the resultant stress was not a function of crowding alone, but came more from the fact that the later arrivals were inhibited from gaining a seat and from stowing their coats and briefcases. Singer (1975) studied New York City commuters and came to similar conclusions. He found that the commuters boarding after the halfway point had higher secretions of stress-related hormones (such as epinephrine) than those who boarded earlier.

Finally, in studies of crowding in penal institutions, it has been found that inmates confined to cells with many other prisoners exhibit higher blood pressure levels than those in less crowded cells. The highly crowded cells created an atmosphere of insecurity and depersonalization which was more frustrating and inhibitive than the less crowded cells.

Discrimination

Crowding is not the only source of psychosocially induced frustration in this country. Prejudice and discrimination are also sources of psycho-

[4] National Institute of Mental Health, *The Mental Health of Urban America* (Washington, D.C.: U.S. Government Printing Office, 1969) p. 20.

social stress. In fact, discrimination may be the most widely destructive form of stress by frustration. Discrimination refers to the unfavorable actions taken against others based upon such things as religion, race, social status, sex, physical characteristics, national origin, or even general lifestyle. Although it is widely denounced as un-American and inhumane, it appears to be ingrained into much of our social fiber. Such arbitrary discrimination has been the basis of many social and occupational attitudes and practices.

The effect of prejudice and discrimination upon its victims can be the stifling of anything from simple day-to-day activities to long-range goals and dreams. A National Institute of Mental Health report (1969) suggested that the effects of prejudice and discrimination, particularly upon children, were the retardation of intellectual functioning and a decreased probability of healthy personality development. The NIMH report similarly indicted prejudice as a potential cause for increased violent tendencies and a general distrust of democratic institutions and systems. Finally, it was concluded that prejudice negatively influenced the development of self-concept in children.

It seems that so-called reverse discrimination has appeared in the United States as a compensatory mechanism for equalizing the injustices of the past, but this, like its predecessor is, in fact, discrimination and involves essentially the same stress reactions for those discriminated against. Therefore, reverse discrimination is just as harmful to a person's health as were the preceding discriminatory practices it was designed to correct.

Socioeconomic Factors

In addition to the stress caused by overcrowding and prejudice, stress may also be caused by frustration due to socioeconomic elements. Inflation, unemployment, excessive taxation, and general economic recession/depression can create stress on massive societal scales, as was apparent in the Great Depression of the 1930's. During periods of economic turmoil, your ambitions may be shattered. Maintaining financial security may become a day-to-day endeavor. The dreams of sending your children to college, of retiring early, of owning a home—all of these aspirations may be frustrating when the capability to fulfill them is blocked by financial insecurity. The stress of such realities can be as detrimental to the health of the frustrated individual as it is detrimental to his/her finances. It has been shown that during socioeconomic hardship, a significant increase in mental disorders, suicide, crime, and disease occurs, and family and marital relationships seem to be strained during such periods as well.

The effects of poverty upon those at the lowest levels of the socioeconomic structure may lead to personal insecurity. Many of those living at the poverty level have a sense of powerlessness and hopelessness, and many suffer from a general personality disorientation in which they believe themselves to be playing a meaningless role in life. Such conditions are clearly harmful to the health of these people and to society in general.

Bureaucracies

If you feel "trapped" in a job that is unrewarding or without a future you might search for reasons why. One possible explanation may be that you are caught in the tentacles of a massive bureaucracy. Large bureaucratic entities seem to promote stress from frustration. Large bureaucracies are almost inherently frustrating because of their complexities, "red tape," and impersonal nature. The bureaucracy often dampens individual initiative and motivation and decreases job satisfaction. There is an increasing demand for job satisfaction on the part of today's workers, and jobs that offer self-esteem and education as part of the work functions are high in demand. It is clear that money is no longer the sole determinant of job satisfaction. The bureaucracy cannot seem to meet these job satisfaction demands of the new enlightened worker of today.

Those served by the bureaucracy are often victims of stress, also, when they are frustrated by the inefficiencies and impersonalization of the immense bureaucratic structure. The growth of the consumerism movement may reflect, to some degree, the frustration and anger of those who feel at the mercy of corporate policies they do not understand or agree with.

Summarizing frustrational stress, it is found that overcrowding, prejudice and discrimination, socioeconomic elements, and large bureaucratic structures are a few of the elements capable of causing, or at least contributing to, the inhibition of human behavior. Such inhibition is capable of producing psychophysiological stress reactions which are expressed in the forms of anger, aggression, increased sympathetic nervous activity, and an increased incidence of mental trauma.

Having reviewed some of the causes of frustrational stress, go back now and look at Exercise 2, which examined the perception of being frustrated. Statements 1 and 10 show your flexibility and patience. Items 2 through 9 indicate frequent perceptions or feelings of frustration. The highest score possible is 40 and the lowest score is 10. The higher your score, the greater your perception of frustration and the more stressful frustration would appear to be for you. General guidelines are: 26–40 = High frustration/high stress; 20–25 = Moderate frustration/moderate stress; 10–19 = Low frustration/low stress.

Since frustration is characteristically inhibitive or thwarting, it appears that the way to alleviate stress due to frustration is to find equally rewarding alternatives to the original goals or behaviors. Chapter 9, Social Engineering, will show you how to find such alternatives as an aid to combatting frustration-linked stress.

STOP!!

Self-Assessment Exercise 3

Choose the most appropriate answer for each of the 10 statements below and place the letter of your response in the space to the left of the question.

How often do you . . .

_____ 1. Find yourself with insufficient time to complete your work?
(a) Almost always   (b) Very often
(c) Seldom   (d) Never

_____ 2. Find yourself becoming confused and unable to think clearly because too many things are happening at once?
(a) Almost always   (b) Very often
(c) Seldom   (d) Never

_____ 3. Wish you had help to get everything done?
(a) Almost always   (b) Very often
(c) Seldom   (d) Never

_____ 4. Feel that people around you simply expect too much from you?
(a) Almost always   (b) Very often
(c) Seldom   (d) Never

_____ 5. Feel overwhelmed by the demands placed upon you?
(a) Almost always   (b) Very often
(c) Seldom   (d) Never

_____ 6. Find your work infringing upon your leisure hours?
(a) Almost always   (b) Very often
(c) Seldom   (d) Never

_____ 7. Get depressed when you consider all of the tasks that need your attention?
(a) Almost always   (b) Very often
(c) Seldom   (d) Never

_____ 8. See no end to the excessive demands placed upon you?
(a) Almost always   (b) Very often
(c) Seldom   (d) Never

Exercise 3 (cont.)

_____ 9. Have to skip a meal so that you can get work completed?
   (a) Almost always   (b) Very often
   (c) Seldom   (d) Never

_____ 10. Feel that you have too much responsibility?
   (a) Almost always   (b) Very often
   (c) Seldom   (d) Never

Scoring: a = 4, b = 3, c = 2, d = 1   Score: _____

After you complete this exercise, total your score, then read the section that follows concerning *overload* to interpret this scale.

OVERLOAD

Have you ever felt that the pressures of life were building up so that you could no longer meet their demands? Perhaps you felt as though there simply wasn't enough time in the day for you to accomplish all of the things that needed to be done. During this time you may have noted a decline in your social life and more of a "self-centeredness." Perhaps you lost sleep, and so became tired and irritable. You may have even become more susceptible to colds and flu. If any of these things sound familiar, chances are you were a victim of overload.

Overload, which means the same as overstimulation, refers to the state in which the demands around you exceed your capacity to meet these demands. Some aspect or aspects of your life are placing *excessive* demands upon you. When these demands exceed your ability to comply with them, you experience distress. Overload is perhaps better explained by the analogy of a telephone operator deluged with 75 calls all at once, each of which must be connected by hand. Like that operator, the brain can process only a limited number of incoming messages. Forcing the brain to exceed its natural processing capabilities, as during a period of overstimulation, will lead to a breakdown of the system, just as the operator will break down from exhaustion if pushed too far beyond his/her limitation.

> *Overload.* A level of stimulation or demand that exceeds the capacity to process or comply with those demands; overstimulation.

The four major factors which contribute to the excessive demands of overload are: (1) time pressures, (2) excessive responsibility or accountability, (3) lack of support, and/or (4) excessive expectations from yourself and those around you. Any one or a combination of these factors can result in stress from overload.

Overload is perhaps the most pervasive of the psychosocial stressors in our country. It encompasses the cities, the occupational environment, school, and even the home.

Urban Overload

Visitors to large cities often comment on the unfriendly or impersonal ways of urban life in contrast to the more personal suburban or rural lifestyles. Many scientists are at a loss to explain such events as the rape of one female in a large northern city, witnessed by over a dozen people who neglected to make any attempts to help her. Such shocking lack of concern for the welfare of others and the blatant egocentric attitudes that seem to fester in many large cities is of concern to us all. Social psychologist Stanley Milgram developed the concept of overload to explain the impersonal attitude of many urban dwellers. He viewed the large urban center as a vast collection of potential stressors—mass media, mass transportation, vast technological innovations, intense interpersonal stimulation, a deadline-oriented society, excessive and diverse responsibilities. These all combine in the city to form an aggregation of potential stressors. In light of these facts, Milgram explained the development of the impersonal attitudes via the overload concept. He suggested that such a lack of interpersonal concern is actually a coping mechanism by which urbanites cope with the bombardment of excessive social stimuli (overload) prevalent in most large cities. Therefore, impersonality is a defense mechanism that protects the urbanite's psychological well-being by shielding that person from all but the most necessary environmental demands placed upon him/her.

Occupational Overload

Within the work environment such things as deadlines (time pressure), excessive responsibility and accountability, lack of managerial or subordinate support, and excessive role expectations from self, supervisor, or subordinates can all create overload. Task overload occurs when the work environment places demands upon the individual beyond that person's available resources. In our time- and money-oriented society, it is not surprising that many jobs are deemed to be more stressful than is healthy for the employee. This is especially true in this age of increased organizational accountability. Think of the tasks that are creating (or have created in the past) overload stress for you. Make a list of them for future reference as you read the intervention section of this book.

To demonstrate the effects of time pressure on workers, Friedman, Rosenman, and Carrol (1958) studied tax accountants at the peak season (just prior to April 15). Analysis of blood samples revealed significant increases in serum cholesterol and blood coagulation times. Both of these signs indicated that these individuals were experiencing excessive stress which might eventually contribute to the development of heart disease.

Perhaps the best example of the concept of occupational task overload is seen in studying air traffic controllers (ATC's). These individuals are faced with a combination of excessive time pressures, life and death responsibility, often insufficient support (be it managerial or technical), and a virtually damning expectation for perfection from themselves and all others involved. Research concerning these workers clearly demonstrates the stressful outcome of task overload. For example, at Chicago's O'Hare Field researchers found that ATC's were under greater stress than pilots having to fly extended, ten-hour flights in simulators. This conclusion was reached by measuring secretions of the adrenal medullae and the adrenal cortex (the main stress hormones). When compared to telegraphists, ATC's showed considerably stronger stress reactions on the job, based on analysis of their blood. Research has revealed that ATC's are occupationally predisposed to certain stress-related diseases, the most significant of which is hypertension, followed by peptic ulcers, and finally, diabetes. The highly stressful jobs of the ATC's must certainly contribute to the fact that 32.5 percent of those examined in one research study suffered from either gastric or duodenal ulcers (Grayson, 1972).

These studies demonstrate the devastating effects of task overload as a stressor. The important point here is not that work is stressful, but rather that certain intrinsic elements of a job task may be highly stressful if the occupational demands are hyperstimulating and exceed the individual's available resources.

Academic Overload

Overload doesn't stop in the urban milieu or on the job, it reaches into the classroom as well. Teachers are experiencing increased demands for accountability and are expected to contribute to the search for knowledge (research) and serve the community in a professional manner in addition to excelling in teaching skills. These demands are often coupled with such sidelights as advising, collecting milk money, parent-student counseling, and other tasks, upon which salary increase, promotion, and/or tenure often depend.

The academic environment is also becoming increasingly stressful for students. This society's demand for higher education has created a highly competitive academic environment reaching back into even the primary grade levels. Children are pressured to do well academically to ensure college admission. Once in college, the student is exposed to the possibility of graduate or professional schooling, but many graduate and professional schools demand "honors" status for a student to even be considered for admission. Added to the grade battle is the admissions testing procedures which are stressors in themselves. Little wonder that anxiety in the face of testing is becoming a major problem in the academic world. Test anxiety may lead to inaccurately low evaluations of a student's scholastic achievement or potential.

For many students the academic grind has led to dropping out of school, poor self-concept, and more severe mental disturbances (the most severe of which has been suicide). In response to the growing pressures of education, many schools have increased funding for counseling and mental health services, and this is especially true in higher education. Schools have initiated programs to help students learn to study, reduce test anxiety, and generally improve coping skills.

Domestic Overload

The home has always been capable of being a source of overload stress. The small, comparatively low-cost "first home" of many couples with children is easily outgrown and space is at a premium. In addition to a perceived crowding, there are now a multiplicity of electronic gadgets around the home—television, radios, record players, and tape cassettes—that contribute to overload stress. Never-ending home repair, yard work, and everyday household chores round out a picture of the home as an overload stressor.

Unfortunately, it seems that no matter where you go or what you do, you become a prime candidate for this society's far-reaching stressor: overload.

Self-Assessment Exercise 3 was designed to assess your level of stress due to overload. Total your points and see how stressed you are by overload. Roughly speaking, a total of 26 to 40 points is indicative of a high stress level; such an excessive level could be psychologically and physiologically debilitating if steps are not taken to reduce this level. A total of 20 to 25 points is indicative of moderate stress, and 10 to 19 points indicates low stress due to overload. You can get further insight into the specifics of overload stress by analyzing the specific items. Items 1, 2, 6, and 9 pertained to time demands placed upon you. Items 4, 5, 7, and 8 concerned expectations from superiors, family, and self. Finally, items 3 and 10 looked at how much support you have in facing your stress. Are you disproportionately high or low in any of these areas? If so, you may want to work specifically to diminish the stress of that one aspect. Part III of this book should help you in all these dimensions.

STOP!!

Self-Assessment Exercise 4

Indicate the most appropriate response to the following 10 statements in the space provided.

_____ 1. I have trouble paying attention during lectures that last over 20 minutes.
    (a) Almost always true   (b) Often true
    (c) Seldom true   (d) Almost never true

_____ 2. When I know I will have to wait for someone, I usually bring something to keep me busy.
    (a) Almost always true   (b) Often true
    (c) Seldom true   (d) Almost never true

_____ 3. I dislike repetitive tasks; I would rather work on something different every time.
    (a) Almost always true   (b) Often true
    (c) Seldom true   (d) Almost never true

_____ 4. I get anxious when I don't have anything to keep me busy.
    (a) Almost always true   (b) Often true
    (c) Seldom true   (d) Almost never true

_____ 5. I relax best by keeping busy.
    (a) Almost always true   (b) Often true
    (c) Seldom true   (d) Almost never true

_____ 6. Moving away from family and friends is very undesirable for me.
    (a) Almost always true   (b) Often true
    (c) Seldom true   (d) Almost never true

_____ 7. I find it difficult to throw away old clothes, furniture, and other mementos.
    (a) Almost always true   (b) Often true
    (c) Seldom true   (d) Almost never true

_____ 8. I get homesick when I'm in a new place for even a short time.
    (a) Almost always true   (b) Often true
    (c) Seldom true   (d) Almost never true

Exercise 4 (cont.)

_____ 9. I hate to be alone.
(a) Almost always true   (b) Often true
(c) Seldom true   (d) Almost never true
_____ 10. I make a point of belonging to some social group.
(a) Almost always true   (b) Often true
(c) Seldom true   (d) Almost never true

Scoring: a = 4, b = 3, c = 2, d = 1   Score: _____

After you complete this exercise, total your score, then read the next section concerning *deprivational stress* to interpret your score.

DEPRIVATIONAL STRESS: THE EFFECTS OF BOREDOM AND LONELINESS

The idea that overstimulation of your mental and emotional processes can result in stress and ill health probably did not surprise you, but now consider the notion that understimulation of these very same processes can result in the same stress response and the same deterioration of your health. We call this state *deprivational stress.*

Deprivational Stress. The psychophysiological stress response caused by states of boredom and/or loneliness.

Deprivational stress has been defined as "the internal bodily reaction to cognitive understimulation," that is, our bodies' response to boredom (the reaction to monotonous, unchallenging tasks) and to loneliness (a state of emotional deprivation) (Galdston, 1954).

In affluent societies advanced technology relieves humans from many tasks, but the human time and interest in those tasks are often replaced with the boredom of watching a machine do the work. Highly repetitive or insufficiently challenging tasks can result in a state of distress.

Boredom appears to prey quite heavily upon American adolescents. Some psychologists suggest that as many as 20 percent of American adolescents are psychologically handicapped by boredom and depression. Such a handicap may lead to loss of self-esteem and eventually to self-destructive behaviors such as drug abuse and even suicide. The fact that suicide has risen to be one of the leading causes of adolescent death appears to support this contention. As a result, billions of dollars are spent each year on specialized entertainment and diversions for adolescents. All of these signs appear to indicate that, through massive technological advances, we are literally boring many Americans to death!

In a similar vein, loneliness can also be a devastating stressor. Children who are not given adequate, caring attention are known to suffer from stimulus deprivation. Such emotionally deprived children may suffer a decreased production of growth hormone, so growth and development may be retarded; but, when these children are placed in an emotionally supportive environment, their growth returns to normal. Nevertheless, psychological scars may persist for a lifetime.

James Lynch's book (1977) on the subject of loneliness demonstrates how stressful loneliness can be. Lynch noted that for the major causes of death in this country (heart disease, cancer, and automobile accidents), death rates were higher among single, widowed, and divorced individuals for all races and both sexes, than for married individuals. Similarly, in the United States unmarried men between the ages of 45 and 54 have a 123 percent greater death rate than married men. Lynch concluded that "in a number of cases of premature coronary disease and premature death, interpersonal unhappiness, the lack of love, and human loneliness seem to appear as the root causes of the physical problems." [5] These suggestions are further underscored by the fact that the health status of married people seems to be improving, while the health of nonmarried individuals is not.

How well do you tolerate deprivational stress? Self-Assessment Exercise 4 was designed to find out. If your score is 26 to 40, you are vulnerable to deprivational stress; you seem to need stimulation to avoid distress. If your score is 20 to 25, you are average. If your score is 10 to 19, you have a high tolerance for low stimulation. More specifically, items 1 to 5 deal with boredom, and items 6 to 10 deal with loneliness. Did you find one outweighed the other, that you are more vulnerable to boredom than to loneliness or vice versa? Such insight may help you better utilize the interventions to be discussed in Part III.

CONCLUSIONS

This chapter has examined four major sources of stress: adaptation, frustration, overload, and deprivation. Adaptation is stressful because it requires "adaptive energy" in order to allow the body to regain homeostasis. When this energy is depleted, the health of the person suffers. Frustration as

---

[5] J. J. Lynch, *The Broken Heart: The Medical Consequences of Loneliness* (New York: Basic Books, 1977), p. 68.

an aspect of stress can be caused by numerous aspects of modern life. Overcrowding, prejudice, socioeconomic elements, and organizational bureaucracies can all inhibit human behavior and as such are frustrating. Overload, that is, the state in which environmental input exceeds the ability to process and/or respond to that input, is another form of stress. Overload is common on the job, but can also be found at home or at school. Finally, deprivation is another source of stress. In this instance, stress results from the inability to receive enough meaningful stimulation. Thus, considering all of these stress origins, stimulation becomes a continuum and either extreme is capable of producing stress.

7

Bioecological Causes of Stress

The term "bioecological stressor" refers to stimuli, arising out of our relationship with our environment, that produce a stress response in most individuals through an innate biological mechanism. This type of stressor is only minimally colored by an individual's higher perception and thought processes. This point separates the bioecological stressors from the other two major categories (psychosocial causes and personality causes of stress).

Three classes of stimuli which are biologically relevant and which may play a role in distress are: (1) biological rhythms, (2) nutritional habits, and (3) noise pollution. We will discuss each of these in this chapter.

BIOLOGICAL RHYTHMS

Time has always been recognized as perhaps our greatest stressor. Most people usually just think of meeting deadlines as the stress imposed by time. However, that is only one aspect of time that is stressful. The natural world also runs on time: solar or light time, lunar time, and seasonal time are but a few examples. The human body also runs on time: temperature time, metabolism time, energy time, hormonal time, to mention a few. Social, cultural, technological man has arrogantly ignored his biological time or rhythm for convenience and conformity. We try to synchronize work and recreation schedules with what is socially and economically efficient. We utilize artificial light and we speed through time zones. All of these things and more act to change the body's natural tempo and rhythm. The result of being out of phase with your body may be undue irritability, emotional instability, and increased susceptibility to illness.

Someday, synchronization of internal rhythm or body time may dictate work and social schedules, but for the time being, increasing your personal knowledge of your own body rhythm will at least allow you to better understand, expect, and even predict fluctuations in moods, feelings, and sensitivities. It may save you the anguish of self-psychoanalysis, trying to find flaws or triggers in your social interactions and self-directions. Stress arousal can be diminished by your understanding and expecting fluctuation in body weight, muscle tone, energy, strength, hunger, sleep, excretion demands, motivation, attention, and productivity.

Biological rhythms are naturally recurring cycles of biological activities governed by the nervous and hormonal systems. Some of these activities are completely internal, stubbornly resisting change; others are greatly influenced by external stimulation, such as exposure to light. Still others, such as eating, adapt themselves to clock time and social activities. Biological rhythms recur in periods of time which may be minutes, hours, days, or years. Each completes a cycle which graphically appears as a sine wave as shown below:

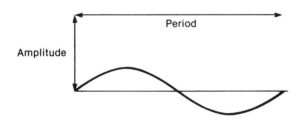

Each cycle has a beginning and an end. Each has a *zenith*, a maximal level or peak of the cycle, and a *nadir*, a minimal level or low point of the cycle. A *cycle* is one complete revolution about a given point. The *amplitude* is the amount of deviance from baseline, and the *frequency* is the number of cycles in a given period of time.

Circadian Rhythms

The most researched cycle is the 24-hour cycle, called the *circadian* (Latin: "about a day") rhythm. Some of the body processes that fluctuate in a circadian rhythm are body temperature, blood pressure, respiration rate, blood sugar, hemoglobin levels, adrenal hormone level, amino acid levels, and urine production. As these fluctuate, so do energy levels, attention span, and motivation. As strength changes, so do vulnerabilities. Drugs taken at one time of the day may produce a mild effect, whereas the same dose taken later in the day produces a more profound effect.

Body temperature fluctuations seem to reflect psychophysiological changes occurring during the circadian period: the highest temperature, which coincides with one's most productive hours of the day, is usually in the early afternoon, and it usually reaches its nadir in the early hours of the morning. Many illnesses become terminal around 2 to 3 o'clock in the morning when vitality is at its lowest; and more children are born when strength to resist labor contractions diminishes. The zenith of the temperature rhythm is often associated with increased attention and muscle coordination. This is perhaps the best time to take both psychological and physiological tests.

Just as temperature fluctuates rhythmically throughout the day, so too does metabolism. Proteins are utilized differently and calorie counters may find that identical calories taken in the morning are burned up more quickly than those taken later in the day. The list seems endless. Hormones of the adrenal glands reach a peak level just before morning rising time and fall to their nadir at night. The male hormone, testosterone, is at zenith around 8 or 9 A.M. Liver enzymes, which are responsible for the breakdown of the basic unit of body energy, adenosine triphosphate (ATP), fluctuate throughout the day, increasing during more active periods.

Our ability to perform is certainly different at different times during the day. Biologically and behaviorally, we are different people between 10 and 12 in the morning and 10 and 12 at night.

Ultradian Rhythms

The term *ultradian rhythm* has been given to cyclical rhythms that occur in periods shorter than a day. Most current research is centered around the 90- to 100-minute rest-activity cycle. It has long been known that sleep is characterized by rhythmical patterns of dream or REM (rapid eye movement) sleep occurring every 90 minutes. More recently it has been found that while we are awake, our attention appears to wax and wane in 90- to 100-minute cycles also. Increased vigilance gives way to altered states of consciousness and daydreaming. We have all had the experience, while reading or studying, of suddenly realizing that nothing on the last three pages was at all familiar. There you sat, reading the words, turning the pages while your mind was in another world. The next time that happens, jot down the time and see if the sequence is rhythmical.

Another situation which spontaneously occurs is that all of a sudden we find ourselves standing in front of the opened refrigerator door. It is not lunch time and we did not consciously plan to be eating at this time, but here we are! We find this especially true on days when activity is lowest, and we repeat food-finding behavior about every 90 minutes. It seems that about every 90 minutes we experience stomach contractions and exhibit more intense oral activity. As was mentioned earlier, these basic biological rhythms stubbornly resist change, although it was found that extreme boredom and/or stress shorten the 90-minute oral cycle to 60 minutes or less. This may be the causal link between stress arousal and weight control problems.

Thus, the basic 90-minute ultradian rhythm during sleep and during consciousness may explain fluctuations in drive, motivation, and attention which, if expected, can be planned for and adjusted to rather than fought.

In order to identify any pattern of behavior, record-keeping is a necessity, so take some time now and start your record-keeping by filling out the Biological Rhythms Form A that follows. This form can be photocopied for subsequent recording, or you can just record your answers on a blank sheet of paper. Observing your own biological and psychological patterns may help you understand some of your behaviors and reactions to stress. Pay particular attention to sleeping patterns, not only for quality of sleep, but time required to fall asleep once you go to bed; that is a good indicator of tension. Whether or not you need an alarm to wake up is a good indicator of whether your sleep cycle is synchronized with social demands. The same goes for hunger and eating patterns. You may find that you are forcing your body to perform at times when energy levels are down. You may find the same with enthusiasm and/or intellectual functioning levels. Most importantly, you may find your patterns of behavior are a reflection of natural cycles of your body, not responses to social and environmental circumstances.

BIOLOGICAL RHYTHMS FORM A

Circadian and Ultradian Rhythms

Choose four different times of the day, at least two hours apart, starting upon arisal (exclude times that fall within one hour after physical activity), and answer the following questions at each of these times. Repeat this daily, using the same time periods each day.

1. Heart rate: _____ beats per minute

2. Body temperature: _____ degrees

3. Body weight: _____ pounds

Circle one of the following numbers according to how you feel now.

4. Alert	7 6 5 4 3 2 1	Dull
5. Energetic	7 6 5 4 3 2 1	Sluggish
6. Happy	7 6 5 4 3 2 1	Sad
7. Self-assured	7 6 5 4 3 2 1	Doubtful
8. Tranquil	7 6 5 4 3 2 1	Anxious, tense, rushed
9. Outgoing	7 6 5 4 3 2 1	Withdrawn
10. Exhilarated	7 6 5 4 3 2 1	Depressed
11. Hungry	7 6 5 4 3 2 1	Sated
12. Weather good	7 6 5 4 3 2 1	Weather poor
13. Sexual feeling heightened	7 6 5 4 3 2 1	Sexual feeling depressed
14. Concentration good	7 6 5 4 3 2 1	Concentration poor, daydreaming a lot

Presence of specific pain or illness symptoms, i.e., headache, diarrhea:

15. _____ present

16. _____ present

17. _____ present

At the end of the day record the clock times for:

18. Meals, including snacks _____ _____ _____ _____

_____ _____

Form A (cont.)

19. Urination _____ _____ _____ _____ _____ _____
_____

20. Bowel movements _____ _____ _____ _____ _____
_____

21. Drug intake, including coffee, tea, cigarettes _____ _____
_____ _____

22. Awakening _____

23. Going to sleep for the night _____

24. Naps _____ _____ _____

25. Was sleep good or poor? _____

26. Most productive time of day: _____
Least productive: _____

27. Overall, today was: good _____ average _____ poor _____

Infradian Rhythms

Another rhythm or cyclic variation which has received much attention in recent years is the *infradian,* or longer than circadian, rhythm. These cycles may last for days, weeks, or even months. The most used of all infradian cycles is the female menstrual cycle, which describes hormonal, structural, and functional changes that occur in stubbornly systematic manner, month after month. Because of its practical application as a birth control device, it has been thoroughly researched and written about until it has become common knowledge to most adults in the world. More recently, this cycle has been used also to describe ebbs and flows of emotional responses and moods and it has been related to fluctuations in motivation, hunger, and performance.

Other less practical, thus less researched, infradian rhythms include the possibility of a four- to six-week fluctuation in the emotion, moods, motivation, and thus the productivity of men. Another example is a condition termed "arctic winter madness," a short period of dramatic change in emotionality often resembling psychosis, which occurs in people living at polar latitudes. This may be related to endocrine fluctuations resulting from a lack of sunlight-formed vitamin D. There may be countless other undetected infradian cycles which could account for the periodic fluctuations in weight, appetite, stability of sleep, alertness, work output, creativity, irritability, and emotionality that we all experience.

Biological processes, especially hormonal secretions, do fluctuate rhythmically, and since hormone stability influences most of the aforementioned psychophysiological processes, we are fairly safe in assuming the existence of inherent rhythms. However, research of infradian rhythm is a most difficult undertaking and scientific verification will be slow in coming. But, if you are sufficiently motivated and persevering, you can conduct some personal research by religiously charting your responses to Biological Rhythms Form A over an extended period of time. After you have recorded your ultradian and circadian rhythms four times daily for several weeks, choose one of the times of the day and chart the scores for one or all of the responses over the period. You will produce a chart or charts that will look similar to the one on page 83.

By charting several factors on one chart with different symbols or colored pencils, you can instantly see any relationships that develop. Look for cycles or rhythms, or relationships between, for example, moods and feelings of hunger or sexual desire, or between moods and menstrual cycle, or any other combination. Those responses which do not appear as cycles are usually influenced by social or environmental factors. Do not discount factors such as the weather. If nothing else, the activity will serve to get you in touch with yourself and you may be surprised to find that personal interactions and social activities exert a profound influence over you.

Charting Biorhythms

The popular notion of charting infradian rhythms, commonly referred to as *biorhythms*, stems from the work of Wilhelm Fliess, who in 1887 published a formula for the use of biological rhythms. His theory was based on cyclical changes in the engorgement of the mucosal lining of the nasal passageways and correlations with observed fluctuations in emotion, sensitivity, intuition, and "performance." Fueled by Sigmund Freud, the basic theory has been expanded in bits and pieces by extrapolating from similar studies information concerning endocrine fluctuations as related to physical, emotional, and intellectual abilities. The currently popular charting of biorhythms focuses on three theorized infradian cycles:

1. A 23-day *physical* cycle. This is thought to be related to muscle protein levels, muscle tone, and the metabolism of various neurohormones. It governs physical strength, endurance, energy, and resistance.
2. A 28-day *emotional* cycle, based on hormonal levels, this is thought to exist in both men and women. It governs nervousness, sensibilities, feelings, moodiness, cheerfulness, general temperament, and creative abilities.
3. A 33-day *intellectual* cycle. This cycle varies with hormonal changes and

BIOLOGICAL RHYTHMS FORM B

Infradian Rhythms

Alertness–Dullness for the Month of April

Your Response	1	2	3	4	5	6	7	8	9	10	11	12	13	14	15	16	17	18	19	20	21	22	23	24	25	26	27	28	29	30
7																														
6																				x	x	x	x							
5								x			x	x	x		x	x	x		x					x						
4			x		x	x	x		x	x				x				x							x	x				
3	x	x		x																							x	x		x
2																													x	
1																														

is thought to be related to intelligence, memory, mental alertness, logic, quickness, reasoning power, and ambition.

All three cycles are theorized to start at birth and to continue rhythmically throughout.

While the theoretical basis for biorhythms is sound, the mathematical analysis is speculative and based on the assumptions that all three cycles start at birth and that if there is any illness or other event that alters the cycle, it must somehow reregulate itself. As yet there is little conclusive scientific evidence to either support or refute those assumptions, so as an academic exercise to get into the concept of infradian rhythm, and as a motivator to use biological rhythms to better understand yourself (and to save the price of another book, kit, specialized calculator, or wristwatch), here is a simplified method of calculating these three most popular biorhythms. Remember that they are best used as a possible explanation of past behavior, rather than a teller of future and fortune.

First you have to determine the number of days you have lived. The easiest way to accomplish this is to multiply the years you have lived as of your last birthday by 365.25. To that, add the days, including today, since your last birthday. If you do not have a calendar handy, remember:

> Thirty days hath September,
> April, June, and November,
> Thirty-one have all the rest,
> 'Cept for February with birthdays blessed
> It has twenty-eight so fine,
> Till leap year brings it twenty-nine.

If you were born before March 1 of a leap year, add one day to your total.

EXAMPLE	YOUR CALCULATIONS
Age: 20 years old	Age: _____
Birthday: March 13	Birthday: _____
Today's date: May 14	Today's date: _____
Days since last birthday: 62 (March 13–May 14)	Days since last birthday: _____
Calculation of days lived:	Calculation of days lived:
$20 \times 365.25 = 7305 + 62 = 7367$ days	_____

Next you want to find how many cycles you have lived through. Since the cycles are 23, 28, and 33 days long, divide the days in each into the total days lived (carry to 2 decimal places).

EXAMPLE	YOUR CALCULATIONS
$7367 \div 23 = 320.30$	Days lived: _____ $\div$ 23 = _____
$7367 \div 28 = 263.11$	_____ $\div$ 28 = _____
$7367 \div 33 = 223.24$	_____ $\div$ 33 = _____

The individual in the example has lived 320 complete physical cycles and is .30 into the present one. To convert .30 to days, multiply it by the days in the cycle (in this case, 23 days). Do this for each cycle.

EXAMPLE	YOUR CALCULATIONS
$.30 \times 23 = 6.9$, rounded up to 7	_____ $\times$ 23 = day ____ of cycle
$.11 \times 28 = 3.0$, rounded down to 3	_____ $\times$ 28 = day ____ of cycle
$.24 \times 33 = 7.92$, rounded up to 8	_____ $\times$ 33 = day ____ of cycle

The next step is to plot all three cycles on a chart. Time and frustration can be saved by using graph paper. From today's date prepare a calendar on a single line that is long enough to go back at least 1 month and ahead 3 months to a year. You will have to join several sheets together to accomplish this, but be creative!

Now you find and plot a starting point of where you are in each cycle on this date (May 14 in this example). You determined above that the 23-day cycle is 7 days old today, so if May 14 is day 7, May 13 would be day 6, and so on, and May 8 would be day 1. From the zero day (May 7) to the zenith of the cycle would be 5.75 days (which is one-quarter of the 23-day cycle). The first quarter always goes up. Another 5.75 days would see a return to baseline. The next quarter (5.75 days) drops to the nadir, and from there the cycle returns to baseline, 23 days from the onset of the cycle. Day 23 is the same cyclical day referred to as day 0 above, so a new day 1 will follow and the physical cycle will begin again, rising to its zenith.

With a different colored pencil do the 28-day emotional cycle in a similar manner. Here the quarters are 7 days. In the example here, the individual is on day 3 of this cycle (determined by dividing, above) so in 4 days he or she will be at the zenith. Seven days later the cycle will be at baseline, in 7 more it will be at nadir, and 7 more will bring the cycle back up to baseline.

With a third color, draw in the 33-day intellectual cycle, which has 8.25 days per quarter. In the example here, the cycle is at its zenith on May 14, and returns to baseline in 8.25 days, and so on.

The height or amplitude of the cycles is entirely optional, but choose one height and use it with all three cycles.

Now go back and compare your biorhythms with Form B, your infradian rhythm of choice. How do these rhythms compare with the questions indicating physical prowess? There are several questions (6, 7, 8, 9, and 10) which indicate mood states; how do these compare with the 28-day cycle just calculated? Look for other possible comparisons.

What Determines Biological Rhythms?

Biological rhythms can be viewed as natural fluctuations in body processes which promote survival by automatically dictating that periods of high energy be interspersed by periods of restorative rest. Generally speaking, biological rhythms are fixed by generations of genetic programming, but they have a built-in flexibility to allow maximum adaptation, thus increasing survival. As the seasons change, so does the amount of heat and light imposed on the body, so metabolic and hormonal adaptation is required. The biological rhythm that controls these processes has the ability to change—probably using the changing light as a trigger, although the exact mechanism is not known for certain.

It has long been known that biological rhythms in lower animals are responsive to light. Numerous experiments which control and systematically alter the natural light pattern have confused animals to the point where they will change their estrous cycle (or period of heat), thus mate in an unusual time of the year and fly south in the spring. In humans the artificial light studies are much more difficult to conduct. The most successful studies were done with highly motivated volunteers who descended into darkened caves for weeks or months at a time. In almost all such experiences, alteration in the normal biological rhythms were found. Most subjects without light changes, clocks, or anything to tell date and time go into what is called a free-running state in which their feelings dictate their behavior. Most went naturally to a slightly longer day—between 24.5 and 26 hours. Time sense was altered and subjects would grossly underestimate the time they spent in isolation. In one situation, the urine excretion cycle went to 25 hours, but was subsequently shortened when lights were turned up. In another cavern situation where the only illumination was the light from a miner's cap, the usually normal 29.4-day menstrual cycle of one woman dropped to 25.7 days and subsequently returned to normal within a year of living in bright lights and a normal 24-hour day. Another study also concluded that diminished light stimulates menstrual activity; it found that girls are more likely to enter menarche in winter and that girls born blind reach menarche at an earlier age than do sighted girls.

It would be beyond the scope of this book to cite all the different physiological processes that are influenced by light, but most, if not all, biological rhythms can be slightly changed by changing light. While this basic fact is known, the exact mechanism is still theoretical. Most of this research centers around the *pineal gland*, a tiny structure buried deep in the brain between the two cerebral hemispheres. The pineal gland has been recognized as a controller of activity for thousands of years and appears by this or other names in most of the yoga and meditative literature. It was thought by Indian mystics to be the vestigial third eye. The pineal gland has indirect connection with the outside world through nerve tracts which, by a very indirect route, are connected to the optic tract. Like the hypothalamus, the pineal gland receives neural impulses and gives off hormonal responses. The pineal gland also is controlled by the sympathetic nervous system hormone norepinephrine, and a complex interaction of the hormones serotonin and melatonin.

Through the pineal gland the body does have a demonstrated system of adapting to various environmental lighting situations. This is important not only for adapting to the changing seasons, but for adapting to socially imposed environmental changes such as light, travel, and shift work. The industrial revolution, maximal production efficiency, war, and around-the-clock police, fire, and medical attention have all prompted the shift or night-working concept. The few studies that have been conducted on shift workers have shown an increase in accidents between 2 and 4 in the morning, accompanied by a decrease in work performance. Police officers during these hours are more apt to sleep on duty. Tests on airline pilots have shown they exhibited their quickest reaction time and best psychomotor coordination between 2 and 4 in the afternoon and the poorest performance between 2 and 4 in the morning. Radar operators are more likely to make errors and to have a harder time staying awake during the hours when normally they would be asleep (have you ever wondered why the airlines have reduced rates for overnight flights?).

It is not that the body cannot adjust to changes in lighting or time zones, but rather that the body cannot make the necessary adjustment in the short time usually allowed. For example, a night worker's body temperature cycle would be expected to be opposite that of a day worker's; yet it usually is not so unless the night shift schedule is maintained for several weeks—long enough for the body to adapt to a new schedule. In many companies a worker may continually rotate shifts each week—

one week working nights and the next week working days—giving the worker inadequate time to adapt to the change.

The recent interest in jet lag or jet fatigue has spurred several studies which found a syndrome of symptoms accompanying the lag: headache, gastrointestinal problems including loss of appetite, increased sweating, blurred vision, and alteration of sleep patterns (nightmares, insomnia), with the addition of menstrual difficulties for female flight attendants. This seems to be the price one must pay for making several phase shifts in a short period of time. These studies have shown that adaptation differs with each biological rhythm. Some examples from specific cases show that it takes five days for urinary electrolytes to adjust, eight days for heart rate, ten days for urinary steroids, and six days for temperature to adjust to a new schedule.

Concerned and forward-looking companies have increased layover time for airline crews and business travelers, correctly reasoning that the extra cost of room and board is a good investment when weighed against the potential costliness of accidents, poor business decisions, or illness.

In summary, we now have enough information regarding the health aspects of biological rhythms to realize that they may hold the explanations to some mood and behavior fluctuations, changes in immunity, incidences of illness, variances in toxicity of drugs, changes in body weight, appetite, motivation, activity levels, sexual interest and performance, sensitivity to stress and, in general, to the development of psychosomatic disease. Knowledge of biorhythms may eliminate the tension of uncertainty by explaining and perhaps predicting fluctuations, thus reducing the frustration and self-doubt which often accompany normal fluctuations in mood and performance.

STOP!!

Self-Assessment Exercise 5

Choose the most appropriate answer for each of the statements below and place the letter of your response in the space to the left.

_____ 1. I usually eat pastries or other foods high in quick energy as my only lunch:

    (a) 2 times/week or less   (b) 3–4

    (c) 5–6   (d) Every day

_____ 2. I drink _____ cola beverages (12-oz. portion) per day.

    (a) 2 or less   (b) 3–4

    (c) 5–6   (d) 7 or more

Exercise 5 (cont.)

_____ 3. I drink at least _____ cups of coffee or tea per day (excluding herbal tea).

(a) 2 or less   (b) 3–4

(c) 5–6   (d) 7 or more

_____ 4. I use _____ teaspoons of refined sugar per day.

(a) 4 or less   (b) 5–8

(c) 9–15   (d) 16 or more

_____ 5. I add salt to my food at meals (total shakes of a table salt shaker):

(a) 10 or less   (b) 11–20

(c) 21–30   (d) 31 or more

_____ 6. I eat chocolate (average-sized bar, 1 oz.):

(a) 1 bar or less/day   (b) 2–3 bars/day

(c) 4–5 bars/day   (d) 6 or more bars/day

_____ 7. I eat a doughnut or pastry as my only breakfast food other than a beverage:

(a) 2 times/week or less   (b) 3–4

(c) 5–6   (d) Every day

_____ 8. I smoke tobacco.

(a) Never   (b) Less than 1 pack/day

(c) 1–2 packs   (d) More than 2

_____ 9. I am exposed to the sidestream smoke of others around me:

(a) Not at all   (b) Less than 1 hr./day

(c) 2–4 hrs./day   (d) More

_____ 10. When I am around even minimal cigarette or cigar smoking my eyes or nose become irritated.

(a) Never true   (b) Seldom true

(c) Often true   (d) Always true

Scoring: a = 1, b = 2, c = 3, d = 4   Score: _____

The following section on nutrition and the stress-prone diet will aid in interpretation of your score.

NUTRITION: THE STRESS-PRONE DIET

Everyone knows that good nutrition contributes to healthful living, but it may surprise many to know that certain nutritional habits can actually contribute to distress. The consumption of certain foods can add to the stress of everyday life, either by stimulating the sympathetic stress response directly, or by contributing to its stimulation by creating a state of fatigue and increased nervous irritability. Either condition greatly lowers your tolerance to the common stresses of day-to-day living. There are numerous nutritional habits that may be involved in stress, some of the more common ones will be examined in this section. Collectively they are referred to as the "stress-prone diet."

Sympathomimetic agents are chemical substances which mimic the sympathetic stress response. Many foods naturally contain these sympathomimetic substances. When you consume them, they trigger a stress response in your body, and the severity of that response will depend upon how much of the chemical you consumed.

The most common of these sympathomimetic stressors in the American diet is caffeine, a chemical that belongs to the *xanthine* group of drugs. Xanthines are powerful amphetamine-like stimulants that increase metabolism and create a highly awake and active state. They also trigger release of the stress hormones which, among other actions, are capable of increasing heart rate, blood pressure, and oxygen demands upon the heart. Extreme, prolonged stress hormone secretion can even initiate myocardial necrosis, that is, destruction of heart tissue.

Coffee (*coffea arabica*) is the most frequently consumed source of caffeine in the American diet. Americans over the age of 14 consume an average of 3 cups of coffee a day! The average brewed 6-ounce cup of coffee contains about 108 milligrams of caffeine. Caffeine consumption of more than 250 milligrams per day is considered excessive and will have an adverse effect upon the human body. A lethal dose of caffeine could be consumed in the form of 20 cups of coffee, if drunk all at once! Frequent side effects of excessive coffee drinking are anxiety, irritability, diarrhea, arrhythmias (irregular heartbeats), and the inability to concentrate, in addition to a host of other symptoms characteristic of the stress response. Coffee may also stimulate the secretion of the digestive enzyme, pepsin, within the stomach. In an empty stomach, this enzyme combined with the natural oils in coffee can irritate the stomach lining. All in all, not a very good way to start the day.

Additional sources of the xanthine stimulants are tea (*camelia theca*), cola beverages, chocolate, and cocoa. A 6-ounce cup of tea contains about 90 milligrams of caffeine, as well as the other xanthines: theobromine and theophylline. Yet tea does not contain the irritating oils found in coffee. Various cola beverages and sodas that include the name "Pepper" (e.g., Dr. Pepper) contain 50–60 milligrams of caffeine per 12-ounce can or bottle. Finally, a 1-ounce chocolate bar contains about 20 milligrams of caffeine.

As colas, cocoa, and chocolate are foods favored by children, parents should seriously consider the inadvisability of making them available in the home, especially since a child's body is far less tolerant of chemical agents than is the adult body. The fact that such foods are highly desirable to most children will make their restriction difficult. Yet, it has been clearly shown that such foods in excess can adversely affect the child by increasing anxiety and decreasing their learning effectiveness. Many teachers are aware of the hyperactive effect that caffeine may have on children.

Generally speaking, 6 to 8 ounces of coffee can have a hypermetabolic effect on children—that is, excessively stimulate the metabolic system— and anything in excess of 3 cups of coffee within one hour for adults will adversely affect their behavior, as well as increase the possibility of stomach upset or irritation. For the child, anything in excess of 2 to 3 cola beverages may be excessive, while for the adult anything over 4 to 5 would be excessive during the course of an average day. While chocolate has less caffeine, it has other drawbacks which make it undesirable (for example, high calorie, no nutritional value); therefore, more than 2 average servings of chocolate a day would be excessive for a child and 4 to 5 would be considered excessive for an adult. These general limits were computed by considering the effects of other food intake as well. Check your responses to items 2, 3, and 6 on Self-Assessment Exercise 5 to determine your level of caffeine intake.

In searching for alternatives to coffee or tea, many people have found herbal beverages such as winterberry or mint teas enjoyable. Unless they are mixed with common tea, their caffeine content is zero. Herbal teas do not irritate the stomach lining as does coffee, and some of the herbs (such as camomile) actually have a calming effect as opposed to the stimulation caused by regular tea. To find out about herbal teas, browse through the tea shelf of your local natural food store or supermarket section.

The second factor at work in the stress-prone diet is that of *vitamin depletion*. Especially during stressful times, high levels of certain vitamins are needed to maintain properly functioning nervous and endocrine systems: These are vitamin C and the vitamins of the B complex, particularly vitamin B-1 (thiamine), B-2 (riboflavin), niacin, B-5 (pantothenic acid), B-6 (pyridoxine hydrochloride), and choline. These B-complex vitamins are important components of the stress response in that deficiencies of vitamins B-1, B-5, and B-6 can lead to anxiety reactions, depression, insomnia, and cardiovascular weaknesses, while vitamins B-2 and niacin deficiencies have been known to cause stomach irritability and muscle weakness. Their depletion lowers your tolerance to, and ability to cope with, stressors.

Vitamins also play important roles in the actual mechanics of the stress response. Vitamins B-1, B-2, and niacin are used up at far greater rates during the stress response because of their roles in carbohydrate metabolism and gluconeogenesis (the process whereby the body forms glucose for more energy; see Chapter 4). Furthermore, vitamins B-5, C, and choline are necessary elements in the producing of adrenal hormones secreted during the stress response. Therefore, excessive stress over prolonged periods of time will deplete these vitamins and render you highly prone to the stress-predisposing factors and side effects caused by B-complex deficiencies.

A major dietary component implicated in the depletion of the necessary B-complex vitamins is refined white sugar. Sugar—and therefore sugar products such as cakes, pies, cookies, and candy (see Table 7.1)—is a good source of energy but has no other redeeming feature. In order for sugar to be utilized for energy, however, the body must have B-complex vitamins. Most foods that need these vitamins for their metabolism do contain the necessary vitamins, but since sugar contains none of them, it must "borrow" the vitamins from other food sources. This creates a B-complex debt in the body. If this borrowing occurs frequently and if the body does not have sufficient sources of B vitamins from nutritious foods or supplements, the result is a B vitamin deficiency, and symptoms such as anxiety, irritability, and general nervousness will appear. This vitamin depletion may be exacerbated by stress because of their increased utilization in the production of stress hormones.

Another food that has been implicated in vitamin B depletion is

Table 7.1

HIDDEN SUGAR IN COMMON FOODS

Food	Portion	Tsp. Sugar *
Chocolate bar	1 average size	7
Chocolate fudge	$1\frac{1}{2}''$ square	4
Marshmallow	1 average	$1\frac{1}{2}$
Chocolate cake	1/12 cake (2 layer, icing)	15
Angel food cake	1/12 cake	6
Doughnut, plain	3'' diameter	4
Brownies	$2'' \times 2'' \times \frac{3}{4}''$	3
Ice cream	$\frac{1}{2}$ cup	5–6
Sherbet	$\frac{1}{2}$ cup	6–8
Apple pie	1/6 medium pie	12
Cherry pie	1/6 medium pie	14
Pumpkin pie	1/6 medium pie	10
Sweet carbonated beverage	12 oz.	9
Ginger ale	12 oz.	7

* 100 grams sugar = 20 teaspoons = $\frac{1}{2}$ cup = $3\frac{1}{2}$ ounces = 400 calories

processed flour. Most of the flour used in this country is processed by using steel rollers which crush the wheat grains into a fine powder. This powder is then bleached into the common white flour used for baking and turned into the various flour products such as macaroni, spaghetti, or white bread. Rosenberg suggested that with the advent of mechanized grain processing came the decline of the American diet. The various processing procedures appear to remove "at least 22 known essential nutrients, including most of the entire B-complex of vitamins, vitamin E . . . and necessary minerals such as calcium, phosphorous, potassium, and magnesium." [1]

The actual degree to which white flour products contribute to stress is controversial due to the fact that most such processed flour products are "enriched" with some of the vitamins and minerals that were lost during processing. The degree to which this enrichment process restores the foods' natural integrity is still under investigation, but as Rosenberg notes: "(even if enriched) they rob the body of B vitamins, disrupt calcium and other mineral metabolism, cause obesity . . . and have a damaging effect on the nervous system." [2]

Despite this controversy, one way to assure that you get enough of the essential vitamins is to eat balanced meals which include a high intake of natural (rather than highly processed) foods. Some find this difficult, however, and resort to a vitamin supplement. There exist many excellent multivitamins on the over-the-counter market, and many are reasonably priced. Synthetic vitamins appear to be just as useful to the body as the more expensive "natural" vitamin sources. There is no need to invest in exotic vitamin regimens. It has been suggested that the American urine is the most expensive in the world because of its high concentration of excessive vitamins. Also it is important to realize that excessive consumption of some vitamins can be toxic, specifically the fat-soluble vitamins— A, D, E, and K—because they can be stored in the body. However, if you feel that your diet lacks sufficient vitamins or that you are under extreme stress, vitamin supplements may be a consideration. Some companies have even marketed a specific "stress vitamin" capsule which is high in the vitamins depleted by the stress reaction. It is always a good idea, however, to consult a knowledgeable physician before taking any dietary supplement or drastically altering your diet.

Table 7.2 lists the adult Recommended Daily Allowances (RDA) average ranges for selected nutrients that are depleted from the body during excessive stress reactions.

[1] H. Rosenberg, *The Book of Vitamin Therapy* (New York: Berkley Windover Books, 1975), p. 25.
[2] Rosenberg, p. 28.

Table 7.2

ADULT RDA FOR STRESS-RELATED VITAMINS
(in milligrams)

Thiamine	1–1.5
Riboflavin	1.3–1.7
Niacin	13–18
Pantothenic Acid	0.5–10
Pyridoxine HCl	1.5–1.8
Choline	unknown
Vitamin C	45–60

Table 7.3 lists the usual supplementary ranges for those same selected nutrients.

While toxic values for the supplements in Table 7.3 are not known, you should always consult a knowledgeable physician before exceeding the RDA for any vitamin.

The third way in which diet may predispose an individual to distress is through a *hypoglycemia phenomenon.* Hypoglycemia is a state of low blood sugar. Symptoms may include anxiety, headache, dizziness, trembling, and increased cardiac activity. These symptoms may cause normal stimuli to become severely acute stressors by making the individual highly irritable and impatient. In effect, they lower the individual's stress tolerance. This is routinely seen in people who get "crabby" when they are hungry.

Although there are numerous causes for hypoglycemia, we are most interested in two that are directly related to dietary behaviors. *Reactive hypoglycemia* is a form of hypoglycemia caused by high intake of sugars

Table 7.3

DAILY SUPPLEMENTARY RANGES FOR STRESS-RELATED VITAMINS
(in milligrams)

Thiamine	2–10
Riboflavin	2–10
Niacin	50–5000
Pantothenic Acid	20–100
Pyridoxine HCl	4–50
Choline	100–1000
Vitamin C	250–5000 *

* Intake above 5000 mg. a day may produce some undesirable effects.

within a limited amount of time. Eating a meal high in sugars or even snacking on foods high in sugars may cause the hypoglycemic reaction in individuals prone to this disorder. *Functional hypoglycemia* occurs when meals are missed, and it may be exacerbated by sugar intake which, over a period of time, results in a lower overnight (or fasting) blood sugar level than what would be considered normal.

The process by which such dietary behaviors lead to hypoglycemia is somewhat paradoxical because the hypoglycemia is preceded by a state of high blood sugar (*hyper*glycemia). What happens is that the high intake of sugar first raises the sugar level in the blood. This high blood sugar level stimulates the release of insulin (within one or two minutes), which allows the excess sugar to enter all the tissues of the body. Therefore it is not selectively saved for the central nervous system, whose function and vitality depend on blood sugar. Generally, if blood sugar levels drop below 60 milligrams of glucose per 100 milliliters of blood, symptoms such as irritability, anxiety, and fatigue occur.

In extreme cases of high sugar intake, the symptoms of hypoglycemia may occur within a short period of time and may be so severe as to cause nausea, staggering, slurred and mixed speech, and fainting. Extreme hypoglycemic shock can result in coma and death, but in this situation there is generally some underlying disease such as a pancreatic tumor or the insulin shock seen in a diabetic.

Whether due to perpetual high sugar intake or other physiologic conditions, a low blood sugar level due to hypoglycemia may be responsible for the "mid-morning slump" and continuous feelings of hunger that seem to be sated only with sugar products such as cookies, crackers, candy bars, or soft drinks. As many Americans eat only a jelly roll, doughnut, or bowl of highly sweetened cereal for breakfast, it is to be expected that low mid-morning blood sugar will bring about increased response to stress situations and diminished ability to perform. The same situation may occur in mid-afternoon or any other time of day after high sugar intake—or merely from starvation.

The best way to avoid the stresses of hypoglycemia and its glucocorticoid stress response is to eat well-balanced meals (the size of which should be determined by the energy demands for the next few hours) which contain a minimum of sugar and processed foods.

The fourth and final mechanism to be discussed in the stress-prone diet concerns consumption of *salt*. Salt (sodium chloride) is the mineral most responsible for regulating the body's water balance. The sodium ion of salt causes a retention of water within the body, and therefore high levels of table salt or of foods naturally high in sodium may result in excessive fluid retention. Excessive fluid retention has the effect of increasing nervous tension (through *edema,* an abnormal accumulation of fluid) of the general nervous tissue and cerebral tissue.

Excess fluid retention will also usually lead to higher blood pressure. In many people, increased blood pressure is the most common manifestation of the stress reaction. However, if a person's blood pressure is already high due to excessive fluid retention, the pressure elevation during distress may reach a danger point. It may become enough to increase the risk of stroke, heart attack, or perhaps to become chronically elevated.

The body has the ability to store salt; therefore the daily survival needs are relatively low (less than 1 gram). Most people consume 4 to 8 grams per day. It's easy to see why this consumption is so high when you consider an average shake of salt from the salt shaker is 100 milligrams. Since everyone's dietary needs are different, however, you should not drastically restrict your sodium consumption without consulting a physician.

Table 7.4 lists foods high in sodium, and Table 7.5 lists seasonings low in sodium that may be used as substitutes for table salt. Also, there are many salt substitutes that are becoming popular, the most frequently used one being potassium chloride. You can switch to one of the com-

Table 7.4

FOODS HIGH IN SODIUM

Most canned:	*Pork products:*	*Snack foods:*
meats	ham	pretzels
soups	bacon	popcorn
stews	sausage	potato chips
sauerkraut	hot dogs	
Cheeses:	*Seasonings:*	
processed cheese	prepared mustard	
cheese dips	catsup	
snacking cheese spreads	Worcestershire sauce	
	soy sauce	
Most quick-order foods at	pickles	
drive-in restaurants	relishes	
	meat tenderizers	
	peanut butter (Most brands are heavy in sodium additives.)	

Baking soda (Sodium bicarbonate contains about 1000 mg. of sodium per level teaspoon.)

As a rule, processed foods contain more sodium than do fresh foods.

Table 7.5

SEASONINGS THAT MAY BE USED IN LOW-SODIUM DIETS

almond extract	ginger	paprika
bay leaf	lemon	parsley
caraway seed	lime	pepper
chili powder	maple extract	pimiento
chives	mint	sage
cinnamon	mustard (dry)	sesame seeds
cloves	nutmeg	thyme
coconut	orange extract	vanilla extract
curry	oregano	vinegar

mercial substitutes and derive some of the same taste benefit without risking the stress factors.

The conscious manipulation of nutritional behavior to control stress is called *nutritional engineering*. When used as one of the social engineering strategies, it can prove to be a powerful addition to the holistic pattern for stress control. You can use the suggestions in this section and expand on them to create your own program for controlling stress through diet.

The final consideration under this topic concerns *smoking*. It may seem out of place in a section on nutritional habits, but for many people eating and smoking share many characteristics. In addition, smoking also calls for greater intake of vitamins E and C for the smoker, and perhaps also for the person who is exposed to a good deal of smoke daily.

There have been massive volumes written on the harmful effects of smoking. It is not the purpose of this book to dissuade you from that practice, but merely to outline how smoking contributes to distress.

Tobacco contains nicotine. Like caffeine, nicotine is a sympathomimetic chemical, and as such, it is capable of all the adverse reactions of the sympathetic nervous system noted earlier. Thus it can cause a stress response.

Nicotine may enter the body by your actually smoking tobacco, by inhaling the tobacco smoke of others, or by chewing tobacco. Nicotine stimulates the adrenals, releasing hormones which elicit the stress response—increased heart rate, blood pressure, and respiration rate, and stimulation of the release of fatty acids and glucose into the blood, among other body reactions.

Smoking represents a stressor in that the stress response is elicited physiologically, but there is no actual psychosocial factor present. In other words, the smoker and the person facing any one of the numerous psychosocial stressors discussed in the preceding chapter would exhibit the same physiological state. One difference is that the chronic smoker's body is continuously elevated to the point where this arousal state becomes the "normal" state. Being without the stimulating effect of nicotine creates a mild depression and general uneasy feeling which lead to the desire for additional nicotine for the pickup.

As the chronic smoking habit develops, the stress tolerance to nicotine is increased and the adverse stress-related effects become somewhat reduced, but the constituents of the smoke continue to affect the respiratory system of the smoker, and they also affect the nonsmoker. As the nonsmoker has not developed any tolerance to nicotine, the smoke itself can cause decreases in work performance. A smoky working area can cause an irritation of the eyes and nose of the nonsmoker, thus impeding finely detailed work, concentration, and tolerance for more difficult work tasks. Smoky conditions can even result in increased absenteeism for the nonsmoker.

Thus, smoking can result in physical as well as adverse psychological reactions to the smoker that are detrimental to the health and performance of both the smoker and the nonsmoker. Questions 8, 9, and 10 on Exercise 5 examined smoking.

A total score of 30 to 40 on Exercise 5 indicates habits which are conducive to stress, 20 to 29 indicates moderate stress levels, and a total score below 20 indicates low stress.

STOP!!

Self-Assessment Exercise 6

Listed on page 99 are the noise levels of common activities that we are exposed to almost every day. These are measured in decibels (dB) on the A audiometric scale.

Calculate your average hourly noise level exposure for a typical 8-hour day, using the following procedure. Choose your busiest 8-hour interval, whether it be during the day, evening, or night. Estimate how many hours, or fractions of one hour, you spend exposed to the listed activities during this period. Then multiply the hours by the dB(A) provided for each activity. Add up the column to get a total. Then divide that total by 8 to get your average hourly exposure level to noise.

If you don't find exactly the right activity in the list provided, estimate a dB(A) value based on those sounds that may be similar. Once you have obtained your average hourly noise level, determine where you fall on the scale in Figure 7.1.

Activity	dB(A)	Hrs./Day	
Rocket engine	180 ×		=
Jet plane takeoff	150 ×		=
Police/fire sirens at 100 feet	138 ×		=
Pneumatic (air) drill at 5 feet	125 ×		=
Live rock concert	125 ×		=
Loud rock music (recorded)	115 ×		=
Boiler room	110 ×		=
Train passing at 10 feet	108 ×		=
Heavy manufacturing plant	100 ×		=
Riveting gun at 35 feet	100 ×		=
Large truck at 90 feet	98 ×		=
Household appliances	90 ×		=
10-hp outboard motor at 50 feet	88 ×		=
Heavy freeway or city traffic at 5 feet	85 ×		=
Bus ride	85 ×		=
Stenographic room	75 ×		=
Average assembly line	75 ×		=
Inside average automobile	70 ×		=
Department store	65 ×		=
Average office	65 ×		=
Classroom	64 ×		=
Conversation at 3 feet	63 ×		=
Average residential street	55 ×		=
Air conditioner	55 ×		=
Average domestic noises	48 ×		=
Quiet radio at home	42 ×		=
Library	38 ×		=
Quiet auditorium	30 ×		=
Whisper at 5 feet	20 ×		=

Add 10 minutes for each time a noise or sound annoys you or disrupts your concentration on a task.

Total noise level = _____

Total noise level ÷ 8 = _____

This is your average hourly noise level.

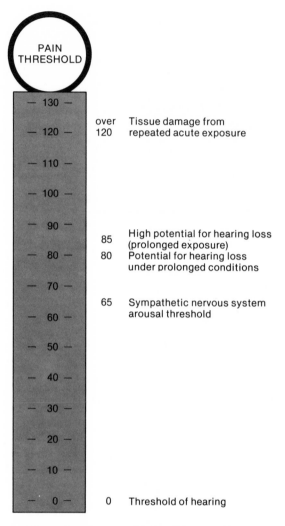

Figure 7.1 Average Hourly Noise Level Scale

NOISE

The study of noise as a stressor is somewhat complex, as noise, more so than the other bioecological stressors examined in this section, has a strong psychosocial component as well as being biological. Noise can produce a stress response in one or more of the following ways:

1. By causing physiological reaction, that is, by stimulating the sympathetic nervous system.

2. By being annoying and subjectively displeasing.

3. By disrupting ongoing activities.

First let's look at the anatomical structure of the ear. There are two neural pathways that go from the ear to the brain. One pathway ends in the auditory cortex as information on what the sound means to the individual, while the other one ends in the Reticular Activating System. You will recall that the R.A.S. is responsible for general arousal of the brain (see Chapter 4). It is this neural pathway from the ear to the R.A.S. that allows the alarm clock to awaken you from even the deepest sleep. Constant bombardment of environmental noise stimulates the R.A.S., causing ongoing autonomic (sympathetic) nervous system arousal. As was the case with nicotine, chronic exposure will result in a tolerance which somewhat diminishes but does not eliminate the effect of noise. However, part of the adaptation process is loss of hearing, which is one effective method of reducing the impact of noise on the central nervous system.

Research has demonstrated that the frequency and amplitude of noise can have a harmful physiological effect upon a person's hearing mechanisms. This physiological discomfort, which may occur anywhere in excess of 85 dB(A) (decibels on the A audiometric scale), will also result in a generalized stress response throughout the body. If the noise level exceeds 120 dB(A), it is considered acute and actual tissue damage may occur.

Noise also has a psychological aspect: the sound may be perceived as unwanted or somehow inappropriate. This reaction—and the accompanying stress response—can occur at any frequency level, because it depends upon the particular situation. For example, a conversation at a distance of 3 feet generates only about 60 dB(A), far below the pain threshold; yet if you are trying to figure out your income tax or study for a final exam, this conversation could be highly stressful because it disrupts your activity. Similarly, what may be music to you may be noise to someone else. Thus, the music which one person plays every day and finds relaxing might be very annoying, and thus stressful, to another.

Whether the noise has a predominantly physical or psychological effect, it is clearly capable of producing the stress response. Research has demonstrated that noise can produce cardiovascular changes. Let us briefly review some of the research findings which warrant that conclusion. Studies on the effects of noise upon blood circulation found that acute exposure to moderately high noise frequencies was capable of decreasing circulation to the arms, legs, hands, and feet. A more recent study discovered that repeated exposure to noise may result in a permanent rise in blood pressure due to structural adaptation of the heart and blood vessels. Finally, studies in an industrial environment demonstrated that workers exposed to moderate and high levels of noise had higher blood levels of the stress hormones.

Such research assurance that noise is capable of creating the stress response prompted the National Institute for Occupational Safety and Health to go on record stating that noise is capable of stimulating changes in essential physiologic functioning suggestive of a general stress reaction.

Noise not only seems to affect physiological functioning, but also seems to produce evidences of stress in our behavior as well. This case is perhaps most strongly supported by the studies of Glass and Singer (1972). While researching the effects of noise on work, these researchers discovered that workers under noisy conditions tended to suffer from shorter concentration and a lower frustration threshold.

Glass's team also studied the effects of chronic noise upon the learning rates of families living in a 32-story apartment building constructed directly over a 12-lane New York City expressway. The results indicated that after four or more years of exposure to the constantly noisy environment, children living on the lower (noisier) floors of the building had incurred a significant impairment in their ability to learn to read.

In recognition of the stressful effects of noise upon human behavior, the U.S. Department of Labor has stated that government employees should not be exposed to steady noise levels in excess of 90 decibels per 8-hour day.

Finally, we should consider adaptation to noise. In a review of the effects of noise on man, Kryter (1970) cited studies which clearly demonstrated that human beings have certain capabilities which allow them to adapt to excessive noise stress. These studies concerning adaptation have mistakenly been interpreted as minimizing the harmful effects of noise. On the contrary, adaptation requires energy and therefore can deplete the body of biological and psychological stamina. Selye (1976) noted that while humans can adapt to stressors, they ultimately pay the price in biological depletion and, should the exposure become chronic, in eventual breakdown. The scientist/philosopher Dubos (1968) noted that adaptation could have "indirect," "deleterious" costs to the individual on a psychological level.

It appears quite clear, then, that prolonged exposure to noise can have physiologically and psychologically deleterious effects on the human organism.

CONCLUSIONS

This chapter has examined biological rhythms, nutrition, and noise as bioecological stimuli which are capable of contributing to the distress that a person experiences in day-to-day existence.

The study of biological rhythms points out that human behavior should be synchronized, whenever possible, with the naturally occurring rhythms that surround us. In this chapter you were given a method for determining possible innate rhythms, so that you might better synchronize your behavior with these natural rhythms.

An examination was made of how certain nutritional habits may contribute to stress. You should now be acutely aware of how sympathomimetic agents (such as caffeine and nicotine), vitamin-depleting foods, hypoglycemic foods and habits, and sodium may all affect the stress response. It was pointed out how the sympathomimetic and irritational factors of smoking contribute to distress as well.

Finally, the complex topic of noise pollution was discussed. Noise consists of biological and psychosocial components—both capable of causing distress. Regardless of certain adaptive characteristics, noise in excessive quantity or quality is distressful.

8

Personality Causes
of Stress

> *Personality* may be thought of as the summation of the
> characteristics, attitudes, values, and behavioral pat-
> terns that individuals manifest in interacting with their
> environment.

No discussion of stress, much less any aspect of human behavior, would
be complete without some mention of the elusive and complex construct
of personality. What we think of ourselves and the way we behave and
react are elements of our personality which are important determinants
of stress. This chapter examines these aspects under the broad umbrella
classification of *personality*. First we will consider how self-concept can
affect stress and disease. Next we will look at the role that consistent
patterns of behaving play in the onset of stress and the development of
disease. Finally, we will examine how the manner in which a person
responds to a threatening situation may, indeed, affect the stress response
and the eventual development of psychosomatic disease. Once again,
each section is preceded by a self-assessment exercise; complete each one
before reading about the topic relating to it.

Self-Assessment Exercise 7

Choose the alternative that best summarizes how you generally behave, and place your answer in the space provided.

_____ 1. When I face a difficult task, I try my best and will usually succeed.
   (a) Almost always true   (b) Often true
   (c) Seldom true   (d) Almost never true

_____ 2. I am at ease when around members of the opposite sex.
   (a) Almost always true   (b) Often true
   (c) Seldom true   (d) Almost never true

_____ 3. I feel that I have a lot going for me.
   (a) Almost always true   (b) Often true
   (c) Seldom true   (d) Almost never true

_____ 4. I have a very high degree of confidence in my own abilities.
   (a) Almost always true   (b) Often true
   (c) Seldom true   (d) Almost never true

_____ 5. I prefer to be in control of my own life as opposed to having someone else make decisions for me.
   (a) Almost always true   (b) Often true
   (c) Seldom true   (d) Almost never true

_____ 6. I am comfortable and at ease around my superiors.
   (a) Almost always true   (b) Often true
   (c) Seldom true   (d) Almost never true

_____ 7. I am often overly self-conscious or shy when among strangers.
   (a) Almost always true   (b) Often true
   (c) Seldom true   (d) Almost never true

_____ 8. Whenever something goes wrong, I tend to blame myself.
   (a) Almost always true   (b) Often true
   (c) Seldom true   (d) Almost never true

_____ 9. When I don't succeed, I tend to let it depress me more than I should.
   (a) Almost always true   (b) Often true
   (c) Seldom true   (d) Almost never true

_____ 10. I often feel that I am beyond helping.
   (a) Almost always true   (b) Often true
   (c) Seldom true   (d) Almost never true

Scoring: 1–6: a = 1, b = 2, c = 3, d = 4   Score: _20_
        7–10: a = 4, b = 3, c = 2, d = 1

Total your score, and to interpret it, read the following section on *self-perception.*

SELF-PERCEPTION

The origin of much of your personal stress may lie within your concept of yourself. Psychologists have been pointing to the individual's self-concept as perhaps the single most influential factor in determining behavior. It would logically follow that self-perception plays an important role in personal stress and stress management also.

Self-perception, or self-concept, refers simply to the image that you hold of yourself. You form this image by evaluating your power and self-worth, based upon input from your family, friends, and other people who hold significant places in your life. At a very early age (perhaps even before you begin to speak) you begin to accumulate information about yourself from these sources, and slowly but surely you form your self-concept. This formation may stop as early as the age of 5 or 6 or may continue until death.

What is your image of yourself? Self-Assessment Exercise 7 was designed to provide some insight into your self-concept. If you scored from 10 to 19 points, you have a strong self-concept. A score of 20 to 25 indicates a moderate self-concept. If you scored between 26 and 40, your self-concept appears to be in need of bolstering.

Researchers and clinicians have known for years that if in a given situation a person devalues himself, perceives himself as helpless and certain of failure, this perception will virtually ensure failure in that situation. This concept has been referred to as the "self-fulfilling prophecy": the likelihood of your failure at some task will be greatly increased if you imagine yourself as failing even before the task in question has begun. The converse of this relationship is true as well: that is, if you imagine yourself succeeding at your task, your probability of success will be greatly enhanced.

Just as self-perception affects task behavior, it can greatly affect the stress response and the eventual course of disease. Lazarus (1966) theorized that the greater degree to which persons perceive themselves in control of a situation, the less severe their stress reaction. This suggests that feeling helpless and feeling a lack of sufficient power to change one's environment may be a fundamental cause of distress.

This point was clearly demonstrated during World War II. Psychiatrists observed that soldiers who could actually return the enemy's fire when attacked suffered fewer mental disorders than did those who could not return the fire but had to simply take shelter and hope that they were not harmed by the enemy's assault.

Similarly, it has been shown by Geer and colleagues (1970) that just the expectation of control over your stressors can be effective in reducing stress. In their studies, one group of students was deceived into believing that their reaction times to shock could reduce the frequency of the shocks, that is, the faster the reaction to push a lever, the fewer the shocks that would be received. The experimenters then reduced the number of shocks for all subjects, regardless of their reaction times. The group that was told that they were, indeed, controlling the reduction experienced a decrease in their level of distress, measured by skin conductance. A similar group that received an equal number of shocks, yet was told that they had no control over them, experienced an increased stress response. Thus, anything that adds to the feeling of self-control is likely to reduce the severity of the stress reaction. This has been one of the more lauded advantages of biofeedback; that is, the learning of skills that allow a person to control the autonomic nervous system appears to greatly increase self-concept and a positive attitude as well.

Go back to Self-Assessment Exercise 7 and look at items 1, 4, 5, and 8. How did you score on feeling in control of situations?

Not only is self-perception important in the severity of the stress response, self-perception (especially the devalued, helpless, and hopeless image of self) may similarly play a significant role in the eventual onset of disease. One of the more intriguing aspects of the role of a devalued self-image in disease emerges from the study of cancer.

The bulk of personality research done with cancer patients concluded that there may, indeed, be such a thing as a "carcinogenic personality." This cancer-prone personality is characterized by gross self-devaluation, helplessness, and feelings of hopelessness. In effect, this personality sees itself in a totally passive and dependent role within its environment.

According to W. W. Meissner of the Harvard Medical School (1977), cancer patients are relatively "selfless" individuals. They often display signs of great sacrifice and self-effacement. Finally, most exhibit feelings of "hopelessness" and "helplessness," which is typical before the onset of cancer.

As early as 1955, clinical observations by Lawrence LeShan led him to conclude that one of the major personality correlates of cancer was a severe degree of poor self-expectation coupled with self-dislike. Similar research by Simonton and Simonton verified LeShan's conclusions. The Simontons' observed that a very pessimistic outlook on life characterized many cancer patients. More importantly, those with the lowest self-perceptions eventually succumbed to the disease, whereas those patients who maintained optimism and the conviction that they could "win" over cancer survived.

Once these researchers began to realize the significance of the cancer patients' self-perception, they designed counseling methods to help improve these self-perceptions and used this counseling as an adjunct to the more traditional cancer treatment. Reports by Simonton and Simonton (1975) and LeShan (1977) showed progress was made when self-perception enhancement was used as a treatment for cancer.

In summary, certain points should be underscored. First, the perceptions of helplessness and self-devaluation can lead to increased stress. Second, a poor self-concept may not only lead to increased stress, but may also play a significant role in the onset of various diseases, the most dramatic of which may be cancer. It may be that a poor self-concept generally increases one's susceptibility to many disease forms. Third, by improving your perception of control and self-worth, you may begin to reduce and eliminate stress. You may find that as an added benefit, you begin to see your "luck" in all endeavors change as well. Specific strategies on how to improve your self-perception will be discussed in Chapter 10, Personality Engineering. Finally, it is important to note that Self-Assessment Exercise 7 was *not* designed to give any predictive insight into cancer; the exercise was merely to give you some feedback concerning your self-perception.

STOP!!

Self-Assessment Exercise 8

Place your answer to each of the following questions in the space provided before each number.

_____ 1. I hate to wait in lines.

   (a) Almost always true   (b) Often true
   (c) Seldom true   (d) Almost never true

_____ 2. I often find myself "racing" against the clock to save time.

   (a) Almost always true   (b) Often true
   (c) Seldom true   (d) Almost never true

_____ 3. I become upset if I think something is taking too long.

   (a) Almost always true   (b) Often true
   (c) Seldom true   (d) Almost never true

_____ 4. When under pressure I tend to lose my temper.

   (a) Almost always true   (b) Often true
   (c) Seldom true   (d) Almost never true

_____ 5. My friends tell me that I tend to get irritated easily.
   (a) Almost always true   (b) Often true
   (c) Seldom true   (d) Almost never true

_____ 6. I seldom like to do anything unless I can make it competitive.
   (a) Almost always true   (b) Often true
   (c) Seldom true   (d) Almost never true

_____ 7. When something needs to be done, I'm the first to begin even though the details may still need to be worked out.
   (a) Almost always true   (b) Often true
   (c) Seldom true   (d) Almost never true

_____ 8. When I make a mistake it is usually because I've rushed into something without giving it enough thought and planning.
   (a) Almost always true   (b) Often true
   (c) Seldom true   (d) Almost never true

_____ 9. Whenever possible I will try to do two things at once, like eating while working, or planning while driving or bathing.
   (a) Almost always true   (b) Often true
   (c) Seldom true   (d) Almost never true

_____ 10. I find myself feeling guilty when I am not actively working on something.
   (a) Almost always true   (b) Often true
   (c) Seldom true   (d) Almost never true

Scoring: a = 4, b = 3, c = 2, d = 1   Score: _____

Total your score and then read the discussion of stress and behavior patterns that follows to interpret your score.

PATTERNS OF BEHAVIOR

We have known for years that specific patterns of behavior can adversely affect your health. The prime example of such behavior patterns is the now-famous list of cardiovascular risk factors which include smoking, lack of exercise, obesity, and high fat diets. It has been clearly demonstrated that the consistent practice of one or more of these behaviors will increase your susceptibility to premature heart disease.

It is possible that far more general behavioral traits could affect your health. Could it be that the way in which you *generally* interact with your environment may predispose you to stress and related disease? The answer is a definite yes! Evidence strongly suggests that the manner in which you choose to interact with your surroundings can play a major role in determining whether you develop premature heart disease.

Two cardiologists, Myer Friedman and Ray Rosenman, in the normal course of treating their patients, noticed some recurring behaviors among patients, especially in relation to how they dealt with time. They noticed an extreme anxiousness of the patients in the waiting room, and the fact that their conversations constantly centered around time, work, and achievement.

From their contact with coronary patients, Friedman and Rosenman formulated a construct of action-emotion behavior patterns that seemed to embody the coronary-prone individual. They referred to this construct as the Type A Personality, and it included the following characteristics:

1. An intense sense of time urgency; a tendency to race against the clock; the need to do more and obtain more in the shortest possible time.

2. An aggressive personality that at times evolves into hostility; this person is highly motivated, yet may lose his/her temper very easily; a high sense of competitiveness, often with the desire to make a contest out of everything; the inability to "play for fun."

3. An intense achievement motive, yet too often this "go for it" attitude lacks properly defined goals.

4. Polyphasic behavior, that is, the involvement in multiple and diverse tasks at the same time. [1]

During a series of impressive research studies known as the Western Collaborative Studies, the Type A behavior pattern was shown to precede the development of coronary heart disease in 72 to 85 percent of the 3,411 men tested. These results strongly suggest that a Type A personality may be predictive of the eventual onset of premature heart disease.[2]

It should be remembered that Type A behavior is not a stress response nor a stressful situation, but a style of behavior which constantly elicits the stress response (which to a large extent consists of cardiovascular system arousal). Therefore, quite simply, Type A behavior seems to be harmful because it leads to a psychophysiological condition which compromises the integrity of the cardiovascular system.

The next logical question is: what makes a Type A person behave in that particular manner? Studies on both male and female twins do not suggest that heredity has much impact on the A behavior characteristics. That leaves child-rearing practices and the general influence of the social-

[1] M. Friedman and R. Rosenman, *Type A Behavior and Your Heart* (New York: Alfred A. Knopf, 1974).
[2] R. H. Rosenman *et al.*, "Coronary Heart Disease in the Western Collaborative Group Study: A Follow-up Experience of 2 Years," *Journal of the American Medical Association*, 195:86–92, 1966.

cultural environment as the basis. Parental expectations and high standards with frequent urging and criticism of actions, as well as an intensely competitive atmosphere, may all be involved.

Cultural influences in general must be considered as important contributions, especially the underlying value of our culture, which motivates and rewards hard work and achievement. However, one can be a hard worker without necessarily being hard-driving and competitive. So it is not only the underlying value of the culture, but also how the members of that culture perceive the methods for achieving what they value.

This idea points to an interesting phenomenon about the Type A behavior pattern: those who exhibit it feel comfortable with it, value it, and reinforce it. They describe themselves as challenged and eager to meet the competition. They are happy with their work and wish they had more time to do more work. The Type A personalities are confident and do not fear losing the struggle with life and work tasks. They are aggressive, ambitious, and competitive, are not fearful or anxious, and do not as a rule suffer neurotic states. On the contrary, they usually are striving to control their environment and exert power over other people. Generally, they view their behavior as positive and they receive rewards through their behavior. Thus, not only does society condition the behavior pattern, but it reinforces it as well. The Type A behavior pattern must be operationalized, that is, it can exist only in an environment which stimulates it and allows it to function. Our fast-moving competitive society does not lack challenges for those who would seek them out.

Self-Assessment Exercise 6 sampled your Type A behavior. Items 1, 2, and 3 dealt with time urgency. Items 4, 5, and 6 concerned themselves with aggressiveness. Items 7 and 8 looked at the tendency to rush into things without properly defined goals. Finally, items 9 and 10 sampled polyphasic behavior, the act of thinking and doing several things at the same time. A total score of 26 to 40 indicates a Type A-like behavior. A total score of 20 to 25 is moderate, and scores below 20 are very low for the Type A construct.

The evidence points to the Type A behavior pattern as being a learned behavior. As such, it can be unlearned or at least modified. Stress-reducing techniques, both specific to Type A behavior and general, are presented in Part III.

STOP!!

Self-Assessment Exercise 9

Choose the alternative that best summarizes how you usually react during anxious moments and place your response in the space provided.

When I'm anxious I . . .

_____ 1. Tend to imagine all of the worst possible things happening to me as a result of whatever "crisis" made me anxious to begin with.
   (a) Almost always true   (b) Often true
   (c) Seldom true   (d) Almost never true

_____ 2. Do everything I can to resolve the problem immediately; if I don't it will drive me crazy worrying about it later.
   (a) Almost always true   (b) Often true
   (c) Seldom true   (d) Almost never true

_____ 3. Will relive in my mind the crisis over and over again even though the crisis may be over and resolved.
   (a) Almost always true   (b) Often true
   (c) Seldom true   (d) Almost never true

_____ 4. Will be able to picture the crisis clearly in my mind as long as a week after it's over.
   (a) Almost always true   (b) Often true
   (c) Seldom true   (d) Almost never true

_____ 5. Can feel my heart pounding in my chest.
   (a) Almost always true   (b) Often true
   (c) Seldom true   (d) Almost never true

_____ 6. Feel my stomach sinking and my mouth getting dry.
   (a) Almost always true   (b) Often true
   (c) Seldom true   (d) Almost never true

_____ 7. Notice that I sweat profusely.
   (a) Almost always true   (b) Often true
   (c) Seldom true   (d) Almost never true

_____ 8. Notice my hands and fingers trembling.
   (a) Almost always true   (b) Often true
   (c) Seldom true   (d) Almost never true

_____ 9. Have difficulty in speaking.
   (a) Almost always true   (b) Often true
   (c) Seldom true   (d) Almost never true

_____ 10. Can feel my muscles tensing up.

    (a) Almost always true   (b) Often true

    (c) Seldom true   (d) Almost never true

Scoring: a = 4, b = 3, c = 2, d = 1   Score: _____

Total your score and read the following discussion on *anxious reactivity* to interpret the score.

THE ANXIOUS REACTIVE PERSONALITY

Anxiety is a basic component of stress. As we discuss it here, keep in mind that anxiety is not only a *symptom* or manifestation of stress, but also a *cause* of further stress.

Based upon the observations of people who suffer from chronic anxiety and seem to complain of stress-related disorders, we've identified another personality type that appears to create excessive, chronic stress. We call this personality type the "anxious reactive" personality. If you are one of these people, you suffer from anxiety to a far greater degree than most people because your reaction to a stressor results in a form of anxiety which seems to perpetuate itself. Therefore, the characteristic that makes you different from other people lies in the feedback mechanisms involved in the anxiety reaction. Most people experience an anxious moment and it quickly ends when the stressor is removed. The "anxious reactive" individual experiences stress that seems to persist, or increase, even after the stressor is gone.

Before describing the specific mechanism involved in this anxious reactive personality, and its role in excessive stress and disease, a description of anxiety in general seems in order. Anxiety may be thought of as one thinks of fear, and in effect, may be used synonymously. The anxiety reaction process begins with the point at which you perceive a stimulus (person, place, or thing) as challenging or threatening. This perception occurs in the higher (neocortical) regions of the brain and entails your interpretation, or assigning a meaning to the stimulus which makes you become insecure or perhaps apprehensive. These feelings of insecurity are transformed into physiological arousal of the endocrines and sympathetic nervous system. So now not only are your thought processes aroused, but also your bodily processes. Fortunately, this hyperaroused condition usually subsides shortly after the stimulus has been removed.

Most individuals suffer from this form of arousal. It is quite common in this society to be occasionally faced with things that make us insecure and result in generalized anxiety. Ordinarily, the anxiety reaction represents no major threat to mental or physical health. Yet, the more severe form of anxiety reaction of the anxious reactive personality does seem to represent a significant challenge to health and well-being.

This self-perpetuating anxiety reaction—which persists or increases even after the original stimulus has been removed—is important to our discussion of stressors because a person prone to this reaction can become mentally and physically incapacitated by exposure to even the mildest of stressors. Furthermore, these personality types are highly prone to the development of chronic psychosomatic disorders.

The anxious reactive personality is hypersensitive to the feedback mechanisms at work during the stress reaction. This means that the anxious individual suffers from an anxiety feedback "loop" that perpetuates the anxiety reaction. The basis of this anxiety feedback loop is as follows. Any arousal response to some perceived stressor can eventually assume the role of a stressor itself and, in turn, cause further arousal. Thus, an automatic feedback loop is created when the arousal response becomes a stressor and brings on anxious behavior.

The feedback messages that will further increase arousal can come in three forms: cognitive, visceral (smooth muscle), and musculoskeletal (striated muscle).

The first and perhaps the most volatile feedback during stress reaches the body in the form of thoughts (*cognition*) concerning the nature of the stressor and the possible outcomes. Fear-laden thoughts that follow the stressor are capable of inducing visceral arousal by way of the autonomic nervous system, and further thoughts may increase musculoskeletal reaction indicative of a stress response. These cognitions are perhaps the most harmful of the three feedback forms. Many individuals engage in what may be called "catastrophizing," that is, always perceiving the stressor event as far worse than it really is. The catastrophizer often views all psychosocial stress as "life or death" in urgency and severity. This tendency to overreact consistently may result in severe mental and physical incapacitation and trauma during a stress reaction and may help bring on psychosomatic disease at an early age. Items 1 and 2 on Exercise 9 concerned themselves with your catastrophizing tendencies. How did you score?

Another type of sufferer from cognitive feedback is the person who relives any and all crises over and over in his/her mind for days or weeks after the incident is over. This "reliver" suffers from distress every time he/she relives the incident. Do you tend to relive stressful events? Items 3 and 4 on Exercise 9 dealt with that aspect. The "catastrophizer" and the "reliver" are both forms of the anxious reactive personality demon-

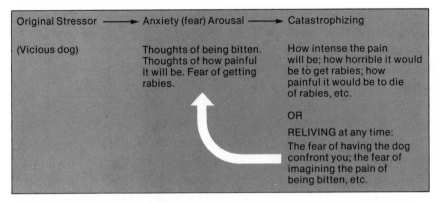

Figure 8.1 Cognitive Activity in the Anxiety Feedback Loop

strated by prolonged cognitive feedback about the stressful event. These mechanisms are depicted in Figure 8.1.

The second form of feedback involved in anxious behavior and the stress reaction is that of visceral, or smooth muscle activity. These involve the heart, stomach, gastrointestinal tract, etc. The awareness of smooth muscle activity, such as heart pounding or stomach gurgling, can increase stressful cognitive processes. In this way, visceral awareness can perpetuate further visceral activity. How responsive are your visceral mechanisms? Items 5, 6, and 7 examined this issue.

Finally, anxiety feedback can occur in the musculoskeletal system. This involves overt movement of the striated muscles, those attached to tendons and bones. In our own observations and research with public-speaking students, we found that the awareness of trembling hands, awkward speech, or muscle tension could produce increased visceral activity (heart rate). Increased musculoskeletal activity has been found to lead to further increases in the same system. Items 8, 9, and 10 dealt with how reactive this system is during stress. Figure 8.2 is a diagram of the anxiety feedback loop at work in the visceral and musculoskeletal reactions.

In summary, the anxious reactive personality is one who is hypersensitive to stress reactions. These reactions may occur on cognitive, visceral, and/or musculoskeletal levels. Once these reactions have been perceived by the individual, they form an automatic feedback loop which perpetuates and, in some cases, worsens the severity of the stress reaction. Perhaps the most severe form of this anxiety feedback is the catastrophizing individual, who consistently perceives problems (stressors) in the worst possible context. For these people stress is a constant companion which affects their daily behavior; they are vulnerable to incapacitation from the slightest stressor and also vulnerable to psychosomatic disease.

A total score of 26 to 40 on Exercise 9 would indicate a high degree of

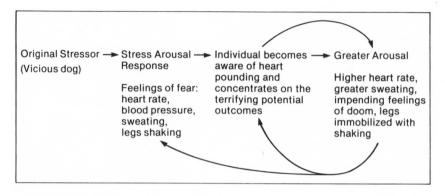

Figure 8.2 Visceral and Musculoskeletal Activity in the Anxiety Feedback Loop

anxious reactivity. A score of 20 to 25 is average, and a score below 20 indicates low reactivity.

SUMMARY

This chapter isolated three aspects of personality and showed how they are implicated in stress and disease. Of most importance to us were the areas of self-concept, consistent behavioral patterns (Type A), and anxious (fear) reactivity.

One can readily see that the concept of self is one of the most important determinants of stress and psychosomatic disease yet uncovered. Poor self-expectation will likely lead to failure at behavioral tasks. Hence, we can understand the desire to "psyche up" athletes before contests, the need for an entertainer or a speaker to face the audience confidently, and the need for a student to face an exam with confidence. Self-devaluation in such situations usually results in the tendency to "freeze in the clutch," more specifically, to play below one's potential in athletics, to suffer from stage fright, and to be incapacitated by "test anxiety" during an exam. Such poor self-image has been more tragically linked with serious mental and physical diseases as well.

In examining behavior patterns, we found that they are also highly implicated in the stress-disease continuum. The Type A personality, or the coronary-prone personality, is a characteristic pattern of goal-oriented, ego-involved behavior that is highly correlated with coronary heart disease.

Finally, we examined how the anxiety reaction is part of a feedback loop perpetuating and augmenting the stress response and lowering performance.

Of course many abnormal personality traits may be changed only through intensive psychotherapy; however, there is sufficient evidence to suggest that education can be used for self-awareness and ultimate positive personality change. These techniques for change will be outlined in the chapter on personality engineering.

CONCLUSION: CAUSES OF STRESS

In Part II we classified the numerous origins of the stress reaction into three meaningful groups. In Chapter 6 we examined how one's perception interacts with the socialization process to produce psychosocial stressors, and we looked at some of the most frequently encountered sources of psychosocial stress. In Chapter 7 we examined sources of stress that are fundamentally biological in nature and therefore less affected by subjective perceptions. Finally, in Chapter 8 we analyzed how personality characteristics, perception of self and others, can play a significant role in the stress response.

At this point, you can get a total picture of your own stress vulnerability by transferring each of your scores from the nine Self-Assessment Exercises to the Personal Stress Profile Sheet on page 120. After you have filled in your scores on each of the scales, connect all of the points. You have now plotted a graph indicative of your stress profile. Although there is no linear relationship between the exercises, the line forms a visual graphic which will help you assimilate the total profile and will be most helpful when you compare results from retests at some later date. Knowing the source of your stress can be a valuable tool in managing that stress.

Now, armed with a summary of your sources of stress, you can go on to Part III, which deals with stress interventions. Using the information about yourself that you have gained from this section, you can formulate your own individualized strategy for stress management, using the techniques you will learn in Part III. At a later date you may want to come back and retake the self-assessment exercises, formulating a second, third, or fourth profile as a record of progress.

A final note: You may be quite vulnerable to stress from a specific determinant even though your score was low on the assessment test in which it occurred. The reason for this is simply that several of the exercises consisted of two or three aspects under the same general heading. For example, you may be a "catastrophizer" of the greatest magnitude and this fact may cause your life to be a very stressful one. However, it is possible that your score on the anxious reactive scale was low because you didn't suffer from the other feedback mechanisms. Therefore, it is important that you carefully consider *each question* that you score 3 or 4 points on to determine how significantly this aspect of stress affects your life.

On the other hand, while these 9 scales are extremely useful tools for you to begin to assess the sources of stress in your life, they are *not* clinically validated psychological tests and should not be treated as such. Such tests are available only from a qualified health professional.

PERSONAL STRESS PROFILE SUMMARY SHEET

Exercise:	1	2	3	4	5	6	7	8	9
	Adaptation	*Frustration*	*Overload*	*Deprivation*	*Nutrition*	*Noise*	*Self Perception*	*Type A Behavior*	*Anxious Reactivity*
	400	40	40	40	40		40	40	40
Scores Indicative of High Vulnerability to Stressors	350	35	35	35	35	105	35	35	35
	300	30	30	30	30	95	30	30	30
Moderate Vulnerability to Stressors	250	25	25	25	25	85	25	25	25

Low
Vulnerability
to Stressors

part III

How to Prevent and Reduce Stress: Intervention and Management Techniques

Introduction: The Holistic Approach to Stress Management

At the risk of redundancy, we have gone to great lengths to try to convince you that stress is holistic. That is, stress is environmental and social; it is mental as well as physical; it involves perceptions, thoughts, and anticipation; it is action and the thwarting of action. Stress is caused by many situations—thus, stress cannot be managed, controlled, or reduced via any one technique. Intervention must be holistic—in this context that means you must formulate a program which attacks the problem on several levels. This is the purpose of Part III.

For the social-environmental component of stress, the next chapter presents social engineering techniques for modifying the personal and social-environmental interaction to reduce their impact. However, even if you are very successful at social engineering, you cannot rid your life of all stressors, so you must personally engineer *yourself* to deal more effectively with stressful situations. This entails altering some aspects of your personality (personality engineering); it also involves decreasing your reactivity to stress—and increasing your immunity to stress—through relaxation training, diet control, and physical exercise. Part III contains more techniques and activities than any one person can master and still have time to live. But different people respond to different activities. In this learning phase, you should learn about all of them, practice all of them, and then adopt the ones which seem to be most effective for you.

9

Social Engineering

The term *social engineering* refers to the willful altering of lifestyle and/or general environment in order to modify exposure to stressors.

Social engineering is the first alleviation technique presented here because it attacks stress at the most logical and often most effective point: at the source, which is the stressor. It is *not* the primary goal of social engineering to change the nature of the stressor. For example, if your job is stressful because your boss is overly demanding, it is probably useless to attempt to change your boss. Therefore, social engineering entails modifying *your* position in relation to the stressor (the boss), not the stressor itself. In this example you could change the amount of time you spend with the boss, change bosses via a transfer, or even consider changing jobs. These are only three social engineering maneuvers that you could make. Only you can ascertain which technique is most desirable.

Many highly stressed people are under the misconception that they *must* live a stressful life. The reality of the situation is usually that they (1) choose to live a stressful life because it is more externally rewarding (that is, offers more money or prestige) than a less stressful lifestyle, (2) don't know of (or haven't searched for) any alternatives to the present lifestyle, or (3) fear an unknown alternative more than they fear the effects of the present lifestyle.

Social engineering allows you to modify stressful behaviors and yet continue to receive suitable rewards for a less stressful life: what reward could be more suitable than health and well-being?

Social engineering strategies are many times not considered, and there are two basic reasons for this. First, the avoidance of stress is too often misperceived as "running away" from stress. In this society running away or avoiding problems has a negative connotation. Many feel that they must stand and fight the problems of life in all cases. While this "John Wayne" mentality is fine for some, it has cost many people their health and well-being. Rarely in the animal kingdom is cowardice seen—when an animal sees that a problem facing it is too great, the animal merely seeks alternatives to that problem. This is the essence of social engineering . . . to seek alternatives or modification of your position in relation to your stressors. Some may use social engineering inappropriately to avoid virtually all stress, and this is not desirable either because the individual might cut himself off from natural, developmental human experiences. Social engineering seeks a balance between the two extremes.

A second reason that social engineering might not be used is that most people suffer from myopic perceptions concerning their own health. Too often we feel, "It can't happen to me." This assumption of immortality can be deadly if it leads to a total neglect of health. Many people are not aware of their unhealthy stress reactions.

To reiterate, then, social engineering strategies are designed to reduce stress by taking the path of least resistance. The specific techniques of social engineering discussed in this chapter parallel the psychosocial and bioecological causes of stress (Chapters 6 and 7). The strategies are summarized in Table 9.1. If you found that you were vulnerable to these stress factors, then consider this section as a starting point for a stress reduction regime.

STRATEGIES FOR ADAPTIVE STRESS

Adaptive stress results from the increased demands for "adaptive energy" that accompany change or novelty. The converse of such change and novelty—*synchrony*—represents the essence of balance and rhythm that is necessary to maintain a healthy body.

Nature is full of examples of balance and rhythm. The establishment of patterns and routines is a basic characteristic of plant and animal life. Even the ant is known for its ability to establish and follow set patterns

Table 9.1

SUMMARY OF SOCIAL ENGINEERING STRATEGIES

Adaptive Stress

    (a) Establish routines when possible.
    (b) Use time-blocking techniques.
    (c) Establish a "mental health" day.
    (d) Remember that a vacation doesn't always mean relaxation.
    (e) If possible, avoid or minimize other changes during periods of massive change.

Stress from Frustration

    (a) Use the Goal Alternative System model to find new alternatives to your frustrated goal.

Overload

    (a) Practice time management and set priorities.
    (b) Avoid overloading situations—avoid overcommitments by learning to say no.
    (c) Delegate responsibility.
    (d) Reduce the task into manageable parts.
    (e) Enlist the aid/support of others.
    (f) Accept fallibility.
    (g) Determine optimal stress level.
    (h) Avoid exposure to stress.

Deprivational Stress

    (a) Plan ahead to avoid potentially stressful situations.
    (b) Realize your vulnerability to deprivational stress.
    (c) Find relaxing activities which are not overly complex or ego-involved.
    (d) Remember that boredom does not equal relaxation.

Bioecological Stress

    (a) Monitor your biorhythms.
    (b) Use nutritional engineering.
    (c) Avoid exposure to noise.

---

of behavior. The physical sciences contain similar examples of synchronous routine. What we think is the basis of the universe, the atom, is also an example of set patterning in subatomic structures. Should the subatomic routine be altered or thrown out of synchrony, the result is the massive release of energy that we witness in nuclear reactions.

To some degree, man needs to conserve energy—to avoid or modify adaptive stress. This can be done through two techniques of social engineering: synchronizing biological rhythms with behavior, and establishing set routines and behavior patterns. If you scored high on the adaptive stress exercise, you should consider these strategies to reduce your stress.

The nature and importance of biological rhythms were discussed in Chapter 7. You should have all the necessary information to chart your biorhythms and then to use them as an effective social engineering technique to alleviate stress.

For most people, establishing set routines reduces stress by conserving adaptive energy and helping maintain homeostasis. The following suggestions will prove helpful in reducing adaptive stress.

1. Whenever possible, set up daily routines or rituals, at work, home, or school. Eventually they will become automatic and greatly reduce the physical and psychic energy you expend.
2. Set aside specific blocks of time for *specific* tasks. This can be done on a daily or weekly basis depending upon the task. This will assure that the task gets done and reduce any anxiety connected with finding time for that specific task.
3. Establish one day of the week as a "mental health" day. This day is to be reserved for true rest and relaxation. Your mental health day should:
   a. Be on the same day of the week, each week, if possible.
   b. Entail behavior that you find truly relaxing.
   c. Be as simple as possible.
   d. Be *strictly* adhered to.
4. Do not use the traditional vacation as a stress-reducing technique. Vacations can be highly stressful if they entail a change of location, scenery, and so on. This clearly requires vast expenditure of adaptive energy.
5. When you notice that there is a great deal of change and adaptation in your life, increase your practice of relaxation and avoid any other changes for awhile.

STRATEGIES FOR FRUSTRATION

Frustration is a stressor because it is by definition inhibitive. Frustration impedes your progress toward some desired goal or it blocks some desired behavior. The best social engineering technique for coping with frustration is to find suitable alternatives.

Frustration explains much of the stress in this country, and much of it is needless. People do not take time to plot alternative courses to their goal or to a similar one. If they did, a setback would prove only a minor concern. Let's examine this social engineering process of alternative exploration as a remedy for frustration.

Before you can find suitable alternatives to some desired behavior, it is helpful to understand just what you are really looking for. Behavioral psychologists suggest that behaviors that are consistently expressed are rewarding. Similarly, desired behaviors are seen as being rewarding or pleasurable. Therefore, when you find yourself somehow frustrated or stifled from doing something you desire, stop and ask yourself *why* you really wanted to do that in the first place, that is, what *specific* outcomes or rewards made that behavior desirable. Then, based on that information, seek alternative pathways to those same rewards, or pathways that result in similar rewards. If you scored high on the frustration assessment, you may want to use the following technique to help reduce the stress of frustrated behavior.

The Goal Alternative System (starting on page 130) is designed to help you cope with frustrational stress by exploring alternatives to goals that have been directly inhibited or stifled.

Step 1 asks you to write down the goal or behavior that has been frustrated. You must deal with concrete goals or behavior. For example, "happiness" is an abstraction; you must consider what concrete things, people, or events make you happy. It is then possible to work through each one of those things separately on the exploration model, if necessary.

Steps 2 through 4 follow a logical progression of thinking on this matter. However, you may discover that one way of obtaining your desired goal is to work directly upon the obstacle, rather than discovering alternatives. So consider some way of removing the obstacle before going on.

Step 5 is the most important step of all in this model, so consider it carefully. Every goal or desired behavior has its rewards, and Step 5 asks you to identify *specifically* what the payoffs or rewards are that you expect to obtain from your goal. You are then asked to assign a point value from 1 to 10 to each of the rewards. This is important, so weigh them carefully.

Step 6 explores the possibility of obtaining the same rewards in Step 5 by any other means. This will help you find the *best alternative* to your frustrated goal by obtaining the maximum rewarding characteristics (as rated by your point system).

Look at the example problem before analyzing your own problem. Playing tennis was the desired behavior here. The malady of tennis elbow made playing tennis impossible. When asked what made tennis really pleasing, this person stated that being outdoors, exercising, the fast action of the game, and the competition were the rewarding characteristics. This person could think of no other sports that were exactly as rewarding. Therefore, the task became that of finding the best alternative to tennis. Of fishing and golf, golf was selected because it was most similar to tennis with respect to the rewards that this person sought. This conclusion was reached by using the point values as the criteria for similarity.

After you have gone through the example problem, try your own problem with the blank form provided.

THE GOAL ALTERNATIVE SYSTEM

Example: Tennis playing

Step 1   What is the desired behavior or goal? *Playing tennis*

Step 2   Is this goal immediately obtainable?

          NO   YES

                     → STOP!   Why are you doing this exercise?

Step 3   What is the obstacle(s) that keep(s) you from obtaining this goal? ←

     Tennis elbow

Step 4   Can this obstacle be removed within a reasonable time period?

          NO   YES

                      If any reasonable methods exist by which you may obtain your goal by removing the obstacle, do so.

Step 5   Consider your desired goal. Take some time and make a list of the specific rewards or desirable characteristics which make that goal desirable to you. Now go back and give each one of those desirable characteristics a score indicative of how important each one is to you. A score of 1 would be the lowest, 10 the highest. Do this very carefully; it is very important.

Rewards	Points
Being outdoors	*8*
Getting exercise	*6*
Fast action	*5*
Competition	*2*

Step 6   Are there any other reasonable ways to obtain those *same* rewards listed in Step 5?

YES	NO
List alternatives, then try them out:	If you have arrived at this point, it seems apparent that *all* of those desirable characteristics listed in Step 5 are currently unobtainable. Therefore, instead of feeling sorry for yourself, make a list of alternatives which *are possible* and which have at least some of the same desirable characteristics as the original goal. Select the behavior that results in the highest point score possible. This alternative is your best one because it is most similar, based on the points assigned in Step 5, to your original behavior.

None

Alternatives   Points

Fishing (outdoors)   8

Golf (outdoors ex-   16*

ercise, competition)

THE GOAL ALTERNATIVE SYSTEM
Blank Form

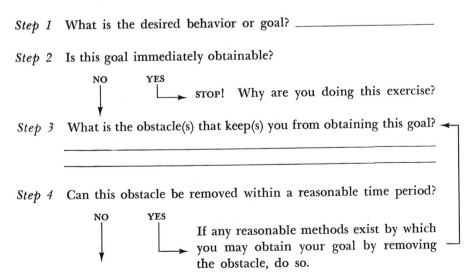

Step 1   What is the desired behavior or goal? _____

Step 2   Is this goal immediately obtainable?

NO   YES

→ STOP!   Why are you doing this exercise?

Step 3   What is the obstacle(s) that keep(s) you from obtaining this goal? ←

_____

_____

Step 4   Can this obstacle be removed within a reasonable time period?

NO   YES

If any reasonable methods exist by which you may obtain your goal by removing the obstacle, do so.

Step 5   Consider your desired goal. Take some time and make a list of the specific rewards or desirable characteristics which make that goal desirable to you. Now go back and give each one of those desirable characteristics a score indicative of how important each one is to you. A score of 1 would be the lowest, 10 the highest. Do this very carefully; it is very important.

Rewards   Points

_____   _____

_____   _____

_____   _____

_____   _____

_____   _____

Step 6   Are there any other reasonable ways to obtain those *same* rewards listed in Step 5?

YES

List alternatives, then try them out:

_____

_____

_____

_____

NO

If you have arrived at this point, it seems apparent that *all* of those desirable characteristics listed in Step 5 are currently unobtainable. Therefore, instead of feeling sorry for yourself, make a list of alternatives which *are possible* and which have at least some of the same desirable characteristics as the original goal. Select the behavior that results in the highest point score possible. This alternative is your best one because it is most similar, based on the points assigned in Step 5, to your original behavior.

Alternatives   Points

_____   _____

_____   _____

STRATEGIES FOR OVERLOAD

You suffer from "overload" when you are faced with excessive demands to the point where your stress response is aroused. You will recall that overload is a function of four major factors: (1) time pressures, (2) excessive responsibility or accountability, (3) lack of support, and (4) excessive expectations. There are several social engineering strategies useful in controlling stress from overload. If you found in Part II that your major stress was from overload, consider these techniques to reduce that stress.

Most of us are forced to face various forms of time pressures, and working under a deadline is the most obvious form of this stressor. Much of this stress can be controlled by effective *time management*. This is the process by which you can set priorities and schedule tasks into the most efficient order possible. When you find yourself faced with numerous tasks to be completed within a given time period, the time management procedures in Table 9.2 may be useful.

Remember, your time management program won't work unless *you use it!*

Many times we create our own overload stress by cramming too much into a short amount of time. The best way to neutralize such a source of overload is to *learn to say no.* Your first obligation is to your health. By committing yourself to do too many things at once you are sacrificing your health for a friendship, or monetary compensation, or other re-

Table 9.2

A MODEL FOR TIME MANAGEMENT

Time management involves matching the best combination of time demands with your supply of available time. The following steps provide a means of achieving that goal.

Time Demands	*Time Supply*
1. List all of the tasks that need to be completed within the given time interval. For example, on Monday consider what things need to be done during the coming week.	4. Look at your calendar for the week. Identify the blocks of time available *each day* for completing the necessary tasks.
2. Estimate how much time will be needed to complete *each* task.	5. Match the tasks with the available time blocks in such a way as to make use of available time most constructively.
3. Go back and increase each of the time estimates in step 2 by 10–15%. This will provide some cushion for error or for unexpected problems.	6. Many times you will find that there is simply not enough time available to complete all of the tasks. Therefore, you must *prioritize* the tasks. List the tasks in order of their importance so that the most important tasks will be completed. If extra time becomes available, you may go on to other, less important tasks.

wards. While there is no doubt that these things are desirable, ask yourself if they are worth your health.

In many cases the stress from excessive responsibility can be reduced by *delegating responsibility* to others. The major obstacle to this strategy is that many people suffer from the need to do everything themselves because they feel that no one else can do it as well. This may be the case, but you should stop and ask if it needs to be done to such a degree of expertise, or if something less will suffice. Another obstacle is the hesitancy to give up control or power. This paranoid-like attitude itself can contribute to excessive stress. Thus, delegation of authority and responsibility can be an effective way to reduce stress and create a more efficient environment.

A common source of overload stress is the responsibility attached to a long and complex project or work assignment. A social engineering technique which will prove extremely effective with this kind of stressor is *reduction* of the task, breaking it down into its smallest workable parts and treating each as a separate task with its own deadlines and requirements. Then all you need to do is to put them together for a completed project. The example of the 50-page report or term paper may prove useful. Most people, particularly undergraduate students would panic at the very thought of having to complete such an assignment. Yet, by reducing the overall topic to numerous sections and subsections, the writer need only write one section at a time. Hence, every separate section may be treated as a separate paper. All that needs to be done then is to put it all together. By using this technique, writing one 50-page paper and writing ten 5-page papers becomes the same task. Yet, which task creates the most stress? When you use this helpful technique of reduction, you have not changed the task, but somewhat altered the approach to make it far less stressful; you have changed the perspective of the excessive responsibility and complexity. The technique of reduction can be helpful in many other areas as well—use your imagination.

Overload that arises from lack of support is difficult to eradicate. The most practical way to intervene would be to enlist the aid of others in the task. When such intervention is impossible, you might consider the many indirect methods of coping, such as the various relaxation procedures which we will discuss later in the book.

Stress from overload may involve expectations that can cause problems. If you have high self-expectation or expectations from others, your performance goals can become unobtainable. In such cases, you must become comfortable with the omnipresent condition of human fallibility and learn to accept the fact that no one is perfect, mistakes will be made. Although you can take steps to minimize the effects of mistakes, you have to realize that they are inevitable.

A more general consideration in dealing with overload is knowing what your *optimal stress level* really is. While there appears to be no empirical test in the strictest sense of the word, the following discussion may give you some clues as to where your optimal stress level lies.

Optimal stress levels (called eustress by Hans Selye) are defined as the maximal point where stress increases and health and performance also increase. Overload (distress) begins where stress continues to increase yet health and performance begin to decrease. Graphically, optimal stress and overload could be shown as a curvilinear relationship shown in Figure 9.1.

Figure 9.1 shows that as stress increases, so do health and performance, until point X is reached. Point X is the point of optimal stress, where stress and health are maximized in a synergistic relationship. However, the shaded area represents overload, where stress continues to increase, yet health and performance suffer.

The best way to find your optimal stress level is to recognize the signs of distress and to continue to reduce your stress to the point where these signs disappear. That, by definition, will be your optimal stress level. While this strategy seems simple, it is not easy to accomplish because most people have become "immune," or have lost their innate sensitivity for excessive stress. The problem, then, is to become sensitive once again to the signs of distress.

Even though stress is unique for each of us to some degree, there are some general clues that usually indicate the existence of excessive stress. We have already said that as a result of frequent exposure to stress, we become insensitive to the presence of the stress. Stress becomes almost the norm and relaxation the unique feeling. This is true in many chronically distressed individuals. Take the example of the hyperkinetic child who is in a constant state of muscular distress. For that child, muscle tension and nervous energy are the status quo. When the child is finally taught that these states are not natural and that relaxation is an alterna-

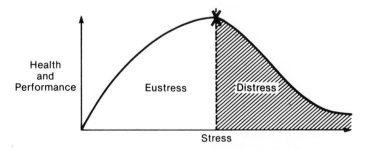

Figure 9.1 Optimal Stress in Relation to Overload

tive, progress can usually be made. Working in a clinical setting it is not uncommon to find patients who, when taught to relax, remark about the "funny" feelings that come over their bodies during relaxation. For these individuals relaxation as a normal bodily state was long ago replaced by distress and tension. Therapy begins with having these people become reacquainted with relaxation as a bodily state.

In order to recognize distress, you should be aware of the three types of stress manifestations, that is, the areas where stress will show itself. The specific cues are called the "signs of distress" and they encompass (1) mood, (2) visceral signs, and (3) musculoskeletal signs.

Stress often becomes recognizable by one's *mood* or *disposition*. Feelings of worry, nervousness, overexcitability, and insecurity are all common mood reactions of distress. Many people, when asked to describe their thoughts during distress, report "racing thoughts," being "rattled," "ill at ease," or being generally "uncomfortable." Insomnia is a common reaction as well.

Another major area within which stress will strike is the *viscera*, controlled by the autonomic nervous system. Signs of visceral reactions during stress are such things as "cold chills," feeling faint or light-headed, a dry mouth, upset or "sinking" stomach, or a ringing in the ears. Some people report a loss of appetite, heart flutterings, or a "flushing" of the face and neck.

Finally, distress becomes most outwardly apparent when it strikes the *musculoskeletal* system. Common signs of this kind of stress reaction are trembling fingers and hands, muscle twitching, muscular tension or tightness, stammering or stuttering, and any other difficulties in fine motor control.

Table 9.3 summarizes these clues to distress. Check the signs that seem to be most frequent for you during periods of distress.

From your check marks in Table 9.3, you can get an idea as to how you respond to stress. If you make note of these signs, you can recognize distress early, and thus perhaps reduce the overload before it causes harm. This identification procedure will also quickly point out your optimal stress point. As soon as these signs materialize, you have passed the optimal stress point and further stress will be harmful.

A final and most effective way to eliminate overload is to *avoid exposure* to your sources of overload. Give this last strategy serious consideration; you may be surprised at how easily stress is avoided.

The social engineering strategies of time management, avoiding overcommitment, delegating responsibility, reduction techniques, enlisting the support of others, accepting fallibility, knowing your optimal stress level, and avoiding exposure are all techniques designed to reduce stress from overload. You may wish to experiment with each of these or use

Table 9.3

WHAT ARE YOUR "SIGNS OF DISTRESS"?

Mood and Disposition Signs	*Visceral Signs*
_____ I become overexcited	_____ My stomach becomes upset
_____ I worry	_____ I feel my heart pounding
_____ I feel insecure	_____ I sweat profusely
_____ I have difficulty sleeping at night	_____ My hands become moist
	_____ I feel light-headed or faint
_____ I become easily confused and forgetful	_____ I experience "cold chills"
	_____ My face becomes "hot"
_____ I become very uncomfortable and ill at ease	
_____ I become nervous	

Musculoskeletal Signs

_____ My fingers and hands shake
_____ I can't sit or stand still
_____ I develop twitches
_____ My head begins to ache
_____ I feel my muscles become tense or stiff
_____ I stutter or stammer when I speak
_____ My neck becomes stiff

various combinations. The most important thing, however, is to find what works for you and then *use* it!

STRATEGIES FOR DEPRIVATIONAL STRESS

As overload is excessive stimulation, boredom (deprivation) is a stressor because it is insufficient stimulation. Like all of the stressors discussed, deprivation is an idiosyncratic and relative phenomenon. Yet, it clearly does result in the stress response because of understimulation.

Boredom is alleviated by increasing the level of stimulation. Such stimulating tactics will be unique to you as an individual, so you must recall the things which *you* feel are capable of alleviating boredom. (During the Korean War, reports told of American POW's using complex mental imagery to alleviate the distress of solitary confinement.) In choosing alleviating techniques, however, be careful not to go overboard and create a situation in which you are now stressed by overload!

There are a couple of things you can do to alleviate deprivational stress if you find yourself vulnerable to such stress.

First, try to plan ahead and recognize situations in which you will be vulnerable to boredom. By foreseeing these situations, you can plan for something stimulating to alleviate your stress.

Also, if you are vulnerable to deprivational stress, a proper relaxation technique is especially important. You may be what Selye calls one of the "racehorses" of life, born to "run" through life. The mistake such people usually make is to overcompensate for their vulnerability to boredom by overloading themselves with arousal. Then when relaxation is genuinely needed, these individuals resort to the conventional wisdom of "doing nothing" to relax. This triggers further distress from boredom. It is important for these "racehorses" to (1) know that they are vulnerable to deprivational stress, and (2) select an appropriate technique of relaxation.

Relaxing activities are things which keep you active but are not mentally complex or laborious, and which also avoid ego involvement. Both overly complex and highly ego-involved activities can create stress of their own. The more active of the formal relaxation procedures, such as neuromuscular relaxation, will be best for this person at first. Remember, do not confuse boredom with relaxation. Many highly stressed individuals, when first learning to relax, become bored and will resort to their old lifestyle for stimulation. If you find yourself in such a situation, reduce your stimulation gradually, but don't resort to your old behaviors. Keep in mind that time spent in introspection is often a prerequisite for successful tension management. The feeling of boredom could become the trigger for saying to yourself, "Now would be a good time to practice some relaxation technique." If you reduce your relaxation activity levels slowly, you will eventually find yourself getting better results from the passive relaxation techniques such as meditation.

Coping with boredom is far easier than effectively dealing with loneliness. Remedying this state of emotional deprivation is beyond the scope of this book. Such remedial processes may involve the enhancement of interpersonal skills and active social involvement. In some cases, counseling may be advisable.

STRATEGIES FOR BIOECOLOGICAL STRESS

This section deals with the biorhythmic, nutritional, and noise aspects of bioecological stress. Many individuals have successfully reduced their stress levels by regular monitoring of biorhythms. By keeping their activity levels in synchrony with their biorhythms, individuals are theoretically maximizing energy expenditures and are gaining confidence in many cases as well. The basis for nutritional stress is that there exist various chemicals or chemical reactions in our daily diets that can lead to distress. These were discussed in Chapter 7 and some specific nutritional engineering strategies were recommended there. In addition, noise, whether psychologically disturbing or physiologically arousing, is also capable of producing the stress reaction. For most of us, some problem foods as well as noise are ever-present, but we can make certain conscious efforts to reduce our exposure to them.

In the case of nutritional stress, the ingestion of caffeine in excess of 250–300 milligrams within a short time span will have a high probability of adversely affecting your behavior. Therefore, you may consider limiting yourself to two cups of coffee in the morning, both of which should be consumed after eating something. As for sodium, reducing or eliminating the salt added to your food at the table could lower your sodium intake by as much as 40 percent. If you are a parent, you may wish to analyze the diet of your children very carefully, as they are more susceptible than adults to the hypoglycemic (low blood sugar) and sympathomimetic reactions caused by chocolate, colas, and "quick-energy" foods. Removing "junk food" from your diet will eliminate much refined sugar and processed flour.

As for tobacco smoke, you may consider staying away from places that contain a high concentration of smoke. Choose nonsmoking areas in restaurants and wherever else possible. If you are a smoker, you are urged to consider cutting down on the amount you smoke, and giving consideration to others around you in close confines by not smoking.

Try to avoid noise by removing yourself from harmfully noisy environments. Turn the stereo or radio down to a lower level and/or buy earplugs at the drugstore and wear them when you are exposed to potentially dangerous levels of noise or any time you are annoyed by sound.

For many people, these things require major life alterations; however, the point that must be underscored here is that alternatives usually exist, if you choose to search for them.

CREATING YOUR PERSONAL SOCIAL ENGINEERING ANALYSIS FORM

To help you employ the techniques of social engineering, we have provided a summary sheet (pages 141–143). Use it to find modifications and alternatives to stressors that may be harming your health. To complete the forms, follow these directions.

1. Select several things that cause you stress. On the summary sheet you will find seven categories of stressors:

Societal Stressors (caused by social activities)

Interpersonal Stressors (personal relationships outside family and work)

Occupational Stressors (related to any aspect of the job)

Familial Stressors (resulting from any aspect of family life)

Academic Stressors (resulting from any aspect of formal education)

Physical Stressors (caused by purely biological mechanisms such as exercise, heat, cold, diet, noise, smoke)

Other (an open category to catch anything not appropriate for any other category)

Place your particular stressors in the first column of the appropriate categories on the Personal Social Engineering Analysis Form.

2. The next column asks you to search beneath the obvious nature of each stressor and conclude what it is about each situation that really results in the stress reaction. Analyze whether stress results from (a) adaptation, (b) frustration, (c) overload, (d) deprivation, i.e., boredom or loneliness, (e) nutritional habits, or (f) noise. If you determine that the stress is caused by one of your *personality* characteristics, this is not the appropriate section in which to analyze that source of distress. Personality engineering will be discussed in the next chapter.

3. The third column is to be used to generate at least two potential strategies for coping with each stressor. These social engineering strategies may be obtained from the text in this chapter or from the summary in Table 9.1. For example, if driving is a form of overload for you, turn to the section on social engineering strategies for overload to see how you might generate specific ideas for alleviation. Don't expect to find *the* answer, but rather look for a starting place from which you can develop a workable plan for your specific problem. List two alternatives and try them.

4. In the next column you analyze what obstacles (if any) arise from your two alternative plans. If none arises, no new plan is needed.

5. If there are obstacles, attempt to formulate a new plan that successfully averts or minimizes the obstacles that you've identified. Don't rush through this! It requires some time to work through obstacles, especially if you've never given them much thought before.

PERSONAL SOCIAL ENGINEERING ANALYSIS FORM

Stressors	Underlying Content (What about this makes it stressful? Why?)	Potential Ways of Alleviating Stress	Obstacles to Alleviation	New Plan
A. Societal				
Example:				
1. Driving in heavy traffic.	1. Too many cars going too fast. Real stressor is *overload*.	1.a. Quit driving. b. Leave earlier to avoid heavy traffic.	1.a. No other transportation. b. Awakening earlier.	1.a. Go to bed early, leave early. b.
	2.	2.a. b.	2.a. b.	2.
	3.	3.a. b.	3.a. b.	3.
B. Interpersonal				
1.	1.	1.a. b.	1.a. b.	1.
2.	2.	2.a. b.	2.a. b.	2.

PERSONAL SOCIAL ENGINEERING FORM (*continued*)

Stressors	Underlying Content (What about this makes it stressful? Why?)	Potential Ways of Alleviating Stress	Obstacles to Alleviation	New Plan
		C. Occupational		
1.	1.	1.a. b.	1.a. b.	1.
2.	2.	2.a. b.	2.a. b.	2.
		D. Familial		
1.	1.	1.a. b.	1.a. b.	1.
2.	2.	2.a. b.	2.a. b.	2.

PERSONAL SOCIAL ENGINEERING FORM (*continued*)

E. Academic

1.
   1.a.
      b.
2.
   2.a.
      b.

1.
   1.a.
      b.
2.
   2.a.
      b.

F. Physical

1.
   1.a.
      b.
2.
   2.a.
      b.

1.
   1.a.
      b.
2.
   2.a.
      b.

G. Other

1.
   1.a.
      b.
2.
   2.a.
      b.

1.
   1.a.
      b.
2.
   2.a.
      b.

10

Personality Engineering

> *Personality* = Values + Attitudes + Behavior

As you may have concluded from reading Part II of this book, regarding the origins of stress, most of the stress you experience is a function of your perception, the meanings and interpretations you give to situations in your life. The manner in which you will define or interpret a life event is determined by the nature of your personality, which is made up of your *values, attitudes,* and *behavior patterns.* We now know that if you can in some way alter your personality, you can significantly reduce your level of stress. The intentional alteration of the stressful aspects of your personality we have called "personality engineering."

Hans Selye said that by adopting the right attitude toward life, one can turn harmful distress into positive stress (called "eustress"). He suggested that this may be the most powerful stress reduction technique in existence. Unfortunately, changing the stressful aspects of your personality is easier said than done.

Perhaps the most ingrained constituent of your personality is your

144

value system. This is a system of evaluative beliefs concerning the relative worth of a person, place, or thing. Values seem to reign as the most rigid and least flexible aspect of personality. Values are learned, usually at an early age, from people whom we love, respect, or highly trust. Many of us might therefore look upon the altering of a value system not only as a rejection of a specific value, but also as an unconscious rejection of the person from whom we learned that value. This explains why most attempts at altering a value through direct confrontation are typically met with resounding failure. Even through intensive psychotherapy, values are the most difficult aspects of personality to alter.

Less rigid than values are our attitudes—our beliefs and motives. Many writers use the terms "values" and "attitudes" interchangeably, but here we are using the term "attitude" to denote a slightly less rigid perceptual process than that inherent in a value. An attitude is more likely to be altered by direct confrontation than is a value, as attitudes are more naturally flexible.

Even less rigid than values or attitudes are behavior patterns, the most expressive forms of personality. Behavior patterns are most vulnerable to alteration, and therefore offer an appealing point for intervention in stress reduction programs.

It would be an incorrect oversimplification to suggest that values, attitudes, and behavior patterns are not intimately interwoven: behavior is the expressive end of the values and attitudes that you hold. But behavior is not as rigid as the other two personality constituents and for this reason behavioral psychologists have chosen this as an intervention point. The practice of behavioral psychology is based upon the intentional alteration of learned behaviors, not merely to gain a short-lived reprieve from problem behavior, but to alter the deepest aspects of personality. Despite all the controversy about behavioral intervention, research has shown that when it is practiced properly, it is a powerful tool in the alteration of personality.

In this chapter you will learn some personality engineering strategies designed to reduce stress by the intentional alteration of personality traits on the behavioral level. These strategies, as seen in Table 10.1, are broken down into three areas, one for each of the three personality causes of stress—self-perception, Type A behavior, and anxious reactivity.

STRATEGIES TO ENHANCE SELF-ESTEEM

Self-esteem is the value that you attribute to yourself. Two common sources of poor self-esteem and depression can be underrating yourself and focusing on the negative aspects of your life. As you grew up, your

Table 10.1

SUMMARY OF PERSONALITY ENGINEERING STRATEGIES

Poor Self-Esteem and Depression

(a) Verbalize your positive qualities.
(b) Accept compliments.
(c) Practice the Assertiveness Ladder.

Type A Behavior

(a) Utilize time management.
(b) Reduce ego involvement.
(c) Use the Goal Path Model for planning.
(d) Practice concentration.
(e) Engage in thought-stopping.

Anxious Reactivity

(a) Engage in thought-stopping.

---

self-devaluation was encouraged by societal edicts of passivity and modesty. How many times were you told to accept compliments with some statement of humility? When complimented on your appearance, societal mores dictated that you respond with some statement such as, "Thank you, you're *too* kind." This humbling mentality may be responsible for many of the self-devaluative assumptions that exist in our society. Many females raised before this generation were particularly vulnerable to this process.

One way to ward off these devaluative processes is to begin appreciating yourself as a valuable and unique individual. Focus on your positive characteristics and minimize the influence of your negative characteristics. All of us have some strong points; unfortunately, the socialization process asked that we repress the urge to discuss our good points, lest we be considered a braggart and a boor. Modesty and humility were emphasized. If you have a poor self-concept, it is time for you to admit to yourself that you really do possess positive qualities and that you do not have to hide them or be afraid of them.

Here are three strategies which have been found successful in increasing self-esteem.

Positive Verbalization

"Positive verbalization" refers to the process whereby you reinforce your self-image by pointing out some positive aspect about yourself. One way to do that is to take seven 3 by 5 index cards, one for each day of the week. On each one write some different aspect of your personality that is positive or that you are proud of. At the beginning of each day place one of the cards in a conspicuous place, somewhere that you are sure to see it and read it several times—on the refrigerator door, in your shirt pocket, in your wallet, or perhaps in your car. At the end of the day place the card at the bottom of the deck and repeat the procedure with the next card on the following day. Eventually you will become comfortable with these positive qualities about yourself. These will also keep you from concentrating on depressive, self-devaluative thoughts.

Accepting Compliments

Learning to accept compliments is another strategy designed to improve your self-esteem. When someone gives you a compliment, simply accept it *without* the traditional statement of humility. In place of the traditional reply, add a statement of agreement. For example, if someone compliments you on a job well done, you might reply, "Thank you, I think so too," or "Thank you, I like it also." These little additions of assertiveness will lay the groundwork for you to really appreciate yourself and to think more positively about yourself.

Assertiveness Training

The entire area of assertiveness training can do wonders for improving self-esteem. Assertiveness training has been found to be an effective strategy for substituting positive, self-assertive behaviors and perceptions in the place of passive, withdrawing, or generally inhibited behaviors and perceptions.

Assertiveness is a positive and productive expression of yourself. On a behavioral continuum between passivity and aggression, assertiveness falls between the poles (see Figure 10.1). Where do you fall on this continuum?

Figure 10.2, the "Assertiveness Ladder," is a hierarchy of assertiveness exercises that you might attempt in your daily contacts with other people. The exercises are listed in order, from least to most difficult. Start slowly at the bottom and progress up through the list. You might spend a week or two practicing each one before moving up to the next. If you begin to experience anxiety, drop back down to the previous exercise for another week; then try to move on again, through the list.

Exercise 1: Greeting Others. Many unassertive people are too shy to greet others or initiate conversations. This exercise consists of initiating at least two exchanges or conversations per day with individuals whom you would not consider close friends. It may be difficult or seem "plastic" at first, but continue trying. You may meet some very interesting people.

Exercise 2: Complimentary Statements. This exercise involves giving others compliments. This is a social behavior that may lead to greater

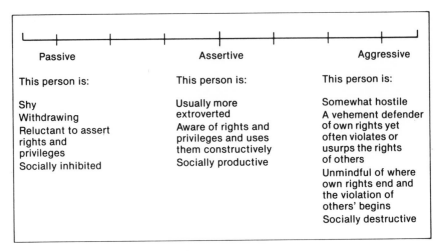

Passive	Assertive	Aggressive
This person is:	This person is:	This person is:
Shy Withdrawing Reluctant to assert rights and privileges Socially inhibited	Usually more extroverted Aware of rights and privileges and uses them constructively Socially productive	Somewhat hostile A vehement defender of own rights yet often violates or usurps the rights of others Unmindful of where own rights end and the violation of others' begins Socially destructive

Figure 10.1 Assertiveness Scale

social horizons. Many unassertive people neglect to give compliments by rationalizing, "Oh, that's dumb," or "Why would they care what I think?" Giving compliments is polite and people probably *do* care what you think, so give it a try.

Exercise 3: The use of "I" statements. Many unassertive people are hesitant or afraid to use the word "I." The reason is that the use of "I" shows ownership, and disagreement with an "I" statement by someone else is often seen by the unassertive person as a rejection of him or her personally. This is not usually the case, though. Don't be afraid to take a

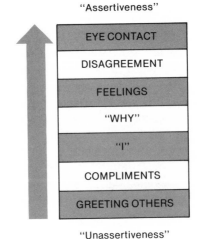

"Assertiveness"

EYE CONTACT

DISAGREEMENT

FEELINGS

"WHY"

"I"

COMPLIMENTS

GREETING OTHERS

"Unassertiveness"

Figure 10.2 Assertiveness Ladder

position. Let your preferences be known; if you don't, they will never be realized.

Exercise 4: "Why?" This exercise involves asking "why?" Many unassertive people feel that to ask why represents a challenge—it does not. "Why?" simply asks for additional information. In this exercise, you should ask "why" at least two times a day from people you consider to be "above" you in status, position, or respect—your boss, for example. If you think the word "why" may be too threatening to that person, substitute "What makes you think that?" or "How is that so?" or finally, "Could you help me to understand that better?"

Exercise 5: Spontaneous Expression of Feelings. Unassertive people often repress feelings. This exercise consists of having you spontaneously react on a *feeling level* to some statement or behavior made by someone else. Repressed feelings are hazardous to your health and well-being; therefore, express them a little at a time. Try to express your emotional reaction at least two times a day. You'll find it gets easier the more you practice. Remember, sometimes it is better to take the risk of hurting someone else's feelings than to keep your feelings bottled up. If that person is your friend, he/she will understand.

Exercise 6: Disagreement. This exercise involves disagreeing with someone when you feel that person is wrong. Many people take such disagreement personally, but that is a problem they must work out for themselves. If the other person is secure, he/she will see that disagreement can be a healthy and positive force for new ideas. Give it a try, but be sure not to be arbitrary—if you disagree with someone, make sure you really believe in what you are saying.

Exercise 7: Eye Contact. Maintaining eye contact is often one of the most difficult things for the unassertive person to do. You may find it awkward at first, but continue trying. The best way to attempt maintaining eye contact is to start with short intervals, 2–3 seconds in length. Eventually extend it to 4–5 seconds, then 9–10 seconds. It is important that you don't *stare* at people: this is too often interpreted as a challenge. Therefore, use this time interval technique. When you break the eye contact, it is important *not* to look down; maintain your basic eye level. Don't look down!

When you can successfully climb up this Assertiveness Ladder, you will be well on your way to becoming an assertive individual and will have done much to improve your self-concept. Remember that not all assertive behaviors will result in rewards; other people may simply be defensive or aggressive. But don't let their problems hinder you. Feel good about yourself and your new assertive personality.

STRATEGIES FOR TYPE A BEHAVIOR

Friedman and Rosenman emphasized that the Type A individual wants to avoid heart disease, not change his/her lifestyle. This fact makes the Type A personality the most difficult personality to work with, because it is the lifestyle and personality that are stressful. When realizing that a lifestyle change is indicated, the Type A who is trying to modify that behavior may quit in frustration. If you are a Type A person, that fact will be the hardest for you to face, but once you realize it, change can successfully occur.

Changing Type A behavior does *not* mean giving up your desire to achieve or excel. It *does* mean changing to achieving and excelling behavior that is more healthfully appropriate.

Time Urgency

The urgency of time is a major problem of concern for the Type A personality. Much of this time urgency stress is self-created. This aspect has been called the "hurry-up" sickness. Type A's rush around, often needlessly. When driving, the Type A will rush through yellow traffic lights only to catch the next red light, and after all of this hurrying the person may save only 5 to 10 minutes at most. But in the rush, the Type A has stressed him/herself needlessly and has missed out on some of the finer pleasures that went unnoticed in the rush.

In an attempt to make the maximum use of time, the Type A will often take on more tasks than are humanly possible within a limited time frame. The result is a stressed individual, both during the rushing process and later when the frustration of not getting all the work done is realized.

Time management is an effective strategy to reduce the stress of time urgency. However, it is important to realize that if you try to take too big a step at once, failure will surely result. You cannot just decide to do away with the time schedule and expect time pressure to disappear. Likewise, you cannot deny the existence of tasks which must be accomplished. The ideal situation for the Type A would be eventually to become time independent, but in the meantime, a more effective intermediate step is time management. Time management involves allocating appropriate blocks of time for tasks and setting priorities for tasks to be completed. This strategy was discussed in the section on social engineering. Table 9.2 is reproduced here as a reminder of the technique.

If you maintain such a schedule, there is no need for rushing or worrying about sufficient time. This system will work in most instances.

150

Table 9.2

A MODEL FOR TIME MANAGEMENT

Time management involves matching the best combination of time demands with your supply of available time. The following steps provide a means of achieving that goal.

Time Demands

1. List all the tasks that need to be completed within the given time interval. For example, on Monday consider what things need to be done during the coming week.
2. Estimate how much time will be needed to complete *each* task.
3. Go back and increase each of the time estimates in Step 2 by 10–15%. This will provide some cushion for error or for unexpected problems.

Time Supply

4. Look at your calendar for the week. Identify the blocks of time available *each day* for completing the necessary tasks.
5. Match the tasks with the available time blocks in such a way as to make use of available time most constructively.
6. Many times you will find that there is simply not enough time available to complete all of the tasks. Therefore, you must *prioritize* the tasks. List the tasks in order of their importance so that the most important tasks will be completed. If extra time becomes available, you may go on to other, less important tasks.

When a major problem arises, don't panic, just sit down and plan the required time and insert it on your priority list for completion.

This same scheduling and prioritizing system can be applied to daily work loads as well. Experiment to find the best combination for you.

Aggression-Hostility

Another aspect of Type A behavior is the aggression/hostility trait which appears to arise from heightened ego involvement. An overactive ego leads to defensive behavior because the Type A puts too much self-esteem on the line in everything he/she does. Type A's defend their work as they would their honor—because for them, the two are synonymous. While it is desirable to have pride in your work, the Type A has carried this principle to an extreme.

The remedy for this problem is to *remove* the ego from its dominating role. The Type A must accept the fact that making a mistake is natural human behavior and does not result in irrevocable condemnation. As

you might expect, this is not as easy as it sounds, and there are no behavior modification techniques which are very helpful. This is one of
those instances when you have to sit down and talk to yourself. One
thing you should consider is your expendability. What would happen
if you took another job, retired, or even died? The company would go
on, someone else would do your work, so why feel so possessive and
defensive about your job? The work is not you, it is just one of the many
things you do. Similarly, it is acceptable to not have the answer to every
question. The Type A employer might regard questions by employees
as direct challenges to authority when they are simply requests for additional information. If a question is seen as an authority threat, the reaction will be defensiveness and the learning process ends; if it is seen
as a request, the question is placed in a proper perspective and the
learning process can continue.

Lack of Planning

The Type A is also noted for rushing into tasks without having adequate planning to achieve the goal. The remedy for this problem is to
learn to plan tasks. To facilitate the skills needed in planning, the
following schema is provided:

THE GOAL PATH MODEL

Step 1   Define the task.
           Can the task be broken down into smaller subtasks?

NO	YES
Continue to analyze	List each subtask and complete the
the task.	rest of this form for each subtask.

Step 2   What personnel or help will be needed? LIST.

Step 3   What are possible sources for personnel?

Step 4   What materials will be needed? LIST.

Step 5   What are possible sources for materials?

Step 6   Estimate costs for steps 2 and 4.

Step 7   Estimate time required.

Step 8   Hypothesize possible obstacles.

Step 9   For each obstacle, go back and develop at least one contingency
           plan, more if possible.

Step 10 BEGIN!

Polyphasic Behavior

The final major area of concern for the Type A is the tendency to do or think about more than one thing at a time. This is called "polyphasic behavior." This behavior is seen as an efficient use of time, but it creates stress because input from several sources stimulates the nervous system simultaneously. In addition, it creates anxiety, causes confusion, and often leads to mistakes.

Several techniques can be utilized to help alleviate this problem. One is to develop the *power of concentration*. Imagine the output, the creativity, the understanding that could result from concentrating all your consciousness on one thing. To train yourself, try to involve yourself in tasks that require concentration. For example, difficult books instead of superficial novels. Or try to use the "Inner" approach (developed first for tennis and subsequently for other activities); with this approach, you avoid overanalysis of performance by substituting non-ego-threatening, purely technological considerations—this necessitates *problem*-centered concentration, leaving little time for spurious ego- or time-related thoughts.

Another technique is that of thought-stopping, which will be discussed in detail in the next section.

STRATEGIES FOR ANXIOUS REACTIVITY

Anxious reactivity was described as a vicious cycle of obsessional thoughts. Everyone experiences some anxiety-producing situations which cause normal anxious arousal. However, in the anxious reactive personality the anxious arousal persists or is rekindled after the stressor is gone. This occurs because the individual obsessively "relives" or "catastrophizes" the stressful situation in his/her mind. This cycle is self-perpetuating, feeding off the obsessional thought processes. The most effective way to attack this problem is to break the anxious cycle. This can be done through a process called "thought-stopping."

Thought-stopping is a technique whereby the stressed person intentionally breaks the anxious cycle by abruptly leaving the obsessional thoughts. This can be done by two different methods:

1. The more traditional technique of thought-stopping involves shouting the word "STOP!" as soon as you become aware of the anxious reliving or catastrophizing. At first the word may be shouted to yourself. If this is not forceful enough, shouting it aloud will successfully destroy the anxious cycle. You may then attend to other less stressful thoughts.

2. Another form of thought-stopping is to switch abruptly to a pleas-

ing, relaxing image or scene in your "mind's eye" as soon as you become aware of the anxious cycle. The scene should be the same one each time and should be a place, real or imagined, that you find aesthetically pleasing and relaxing. After dwelling on this place for 30 to 60 seconds, slowly reoccupy your mind with real world demands. If no such relaxing image exists for you, counting backwards from 5 to 1 will also work. Simply picture the numbers in your mind as large and bright images. By the time 1 is reached, the cycle will be broken and you can begin thinking of other thoughts. If the cycle starts again, break it in the same manner. Continue doing so until the cycle remains broken, no matter how many thought-stopping maneuvers are necessary.

There is a vast amount of research on the thought-stopping procedure as a powerful tool in the elimination of obsessional thoughts. All you need is practice, so keep at it!

CONCLUSION

This chapter has been based upon the premise that by replacing stressful behaviors with consistent patterns of constructive behavior, an ultimate change in personality will occur. This will come about through a slow but reliable process in which the less stressful behaviors become intrinsically rewarding. We have made specific recommendations to effect a change in each of the three major personality causes of stress discussed earlier in the book: self-perception, Type A behavior, and anxious reactivity.

Keep in mind that changing of personality traits requires a long time and a great deal of *practice*. However, once you can make the change, you will find a significant reduction in stress.

11

Altered States of Consciousness

So far we have considered strategies to be used at the intervention points of life events (social engineering) and perception of these events (personality engineering). In order to maintain optimal health, it is also necessary to intervene in the stress-arousal cycle itself. This means you must diminish your overreaction to environmental stimulation, cool the fires of imagination, and above all, reduce the time and energy you spend defending your ego. Considering all of the factors associated with stress arousal, most stress-relaxation problems can eventually be seen as related to ego or ego consciousness. To quiet the mind and achieve relaxation you must experience tranquility, which is nearly impossible while your mind is filled with haunting feelings of failure and is constantly planning, scheming, judging, and wanting. The Greek philosopher Epictetus believed that anxiety was a disorder of the "will to get." He believed that it was "better to die of hunger exempt from grief and fear than to live in affluence with perturbation," and that death was in fact believed to be a "common consequence of chronic perturbation." [1]

[1] *The Works of Epictetus, Volume III*, trans. T. W. Higinson (Boston: Little, Brown and Co., 1890), p. 220.

Not everyone has the philosophical maturity to live a tranquil life, but most people have the ability at least to temporarily alter the normal ego-centered thought process and experience an egoless or altered state of consciousness. An altered state of consciousness is somewhat difficult to understand for many reasons. For one thing, the term "altered" implies being different from the normal state. In this case "normal" generally means that one is in control of the environment and engages in rational, cause-and-effect, goal-directed and reflective thinking. According to Tart (1975) normal consciousness is "consensus reality," a state that is learned within the culture and that shows reality in terms of what is good for society. It is society's prejudice which classifies this state as normal, because it is this state of consciousness that turns the wheels of industry, the state in which we converse, write checks, and make comparisons, a state developed as a specialized tool for coping with society.

To change from the normal ego consciousness, one must alter the normal thought processes away from the planning-doing state to a feeling-experiencing state, sometimes described as an egoless state. In this egoless state of consciousness the environment is perceived as nonthreatening—the proper clothes, cars, colleges, and vacation spots are not important; impressions do not have to be made, images protected, or feelings guarded. It is no wonder that a work-ethic society frowns on a state of consciousness that departs from "normal."

A second reason altered states are difficult to understand is that we are not taught to do so. As we benefit from the part of our cultural development which enables us to make a living, we are diminished by it as well. We have a limited view of reality. We are not taught quiet and tranquility, spiritual search, or in general, how to live. We are not taught to understand and to use the other natural states of consciousness which differ from the "normal" waking, doing state. This is not to diminish the importance of waking consciousness, because it is a naturally developed coping state. But it is also important to explore the other-than-normal states of consciousness, to understand, express, and develop these other natural states as well.

Our culture has not yet developed the words or phrases that can accurately describe the varied states of consciousness. Therefore we will use the language of the normal state and take a scientific approach to describing the workings of the mind. Our scientific understanding of the brain and mind is that we have developed a system of psychological processes which conserve energy for maximum efficiency in achieving their basic goals. These goals are the psychological survival of the personality and the physiological survival of the organism (see Figure 11.1). Under special conditions of dysfunction, such as in cases of acute psychosis, in some drugged states, or in some meditative states, this system of learned

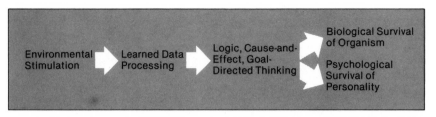

Figure 11.1 The Normal State

thought processing breaks down and permits a less efficient system to take over—one in which everyday activities, feelings, or events are perceived differently or shifted more toward feeling than thinking. When this breakdown of automatic, protective processing occurs, the person shifts from the normal state to an "altered" state.

THE ALTERED STATE

When we are in an altered state of consciousness, we have shifted from the normal, taking-care-of-business state to some other level of consciousness. This other level may be as basic as daydreaming or as spiritual as cosmic consciousness, but the fact is that we all wander in and out of normal consciousness many times throughout the day and night. How often we enter these altered states depends a great deal on our external and internal environments, especially the level of stimulation around us, but the frequency can also be planned or allowed by our own minds.

Environmental levels of stimulation which are either above or below the accustomed range may produce an altered state. For instance, decreasing external stimulation to the point of social deprivation may trigger an altered state. Other low-stimulus activities, in which incoming information is monotonous and nonspecific, may allow you to slip from the normal state. These conditions might develop in solitary confinement, flying at high altitudes in cloudless skies, driving for extended periods on a straight, open highway when you are the only one on the road, or they may be produced by a mother gently and steadily rocking her child. Other conditions, such as religious or spiritual states, passive meditation, floating in water, extreme muscle relaxation, taking depressant drugs, having deep pressure applied as in massage, or a frightened child's being held tightly, all reduce the intensity and rate of stimulation and thus may induce the altered state.

Just as reduced stimulation may bring about an altered state, so may increased stimulation. Such hyperaroused states can be induced, for example, by activities which involve sharp, loud, and ever-changing noise or light, as occurs in some types of revival meetings, in ecstatic trances, and in some brainwashing techniques. Other activities or conditions which have been known to cause altered states of consciousness are the quickening beat of a drum or mounting applause, prolonged vigilance during sentry duty, intense mental absorption (as in many tasks of reading, writing, or problem solving), light tactile touch as in tickling, and taking certain psychedelic or stimulant drugs.

In addition to these predominantly external factors, there are certain "somatopsychological" factors, or alterations in body chemistry, caused by hypoglycemia, dehydration, sleep deprivation, administration of anesthetics, psychedelics, stimulants or sedative drugs, which can induce an altered state of consciousness.

As might be surmised from knowing the various conditions that trigger the altered state, our states of consciousness can range through a vast continuum with extreme *hypo*arousal states on one end, where awareness occurs without thought or action, to extreme *hyper*arousal, manic states and ecstatic mystical rapture on the other end (see Figure 11.2). The normal state is somewhere in the middle.

The two states on either side of normal are behaviorally quite different, yet they do have some common characteristics through which we can distinguish the altered from the normal state.

One of the factors central to most altered states is the change in the level of attention and concentration away from ego-centered consciousness. Memory of an altered state is usually poor, because the usual pattern of thinking and laying down of memory patterns is changed during that state. One does not think in cause-and-effect terms; thus the meaning attached to subjective experiences or ideas is also changed. In many altered states one loses the feeling of being in control of the environment or having a relationship with the environment; thus, self-centered daydreams diminish, a sense of depersonalization occurs, and inhibitions are lessened. There is less attention to time-dictated events, so the sense of time changes. Most often there is a feeling of timelessness or of time coming to a standstill. The perception of body, self, and reality often changes and many times one experiences visual imagery.

Most of us have experienced some or all of these events while daydreaming, or when becoming completely immersed in an enjoyable

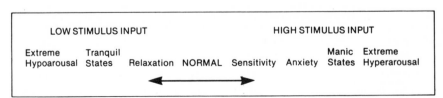

Figure 11.2 States of Consciousness Continuum

activity, or perhaps in meditating. After it is experienced, it is difficult to explain in "I-Coping" consciousness language exactly what was experienced, because the different states do not communicate well. Thus we can, and do, experience dozens of different states of consciousness throughout the day but have little recollection of those changes.

We will not describe here in detail the twenty or more different states of consciousness which have been analyzed by the professionals in the field, but you should be familiar with the five most often recognized and discussed states of consciousness. These are:

Level 1 Deep sleep without dreams
Level 2 Sleep with dreams
Level 3 Waking sleep or identification ("I-Coping")
Level 4 Self-transcendence
Level 5 Objective or cosmic consciousness

Robert DeRopp (1968) discussed these five basic levels in terms of where man is now, and where he must go to obtain ego- or self-transcendence and enlightenment. According to DeRopp, the highest level of consciousness is attainable only by those who can relieve themselves of ego involvement and the search for power over others.

To DeRopp, what is classified as the waking ego consciousness is little better than level 2, sleep with dreams, because modern man does not know where he is going or what he is doing. In fact, he lives a dream, he inhabits a world of delusions, and he is a puppet manipulated by external forces. But, as that is all he has ever known, it is reality. Being surrounded by other sleeping men and never experiencing the freedom of spirit of the fourth level, he becomes complacent to live out his life without ever entering into the struggle to develop his expanded consciousness.

SELF-TRANSCENDENCE

The fourth level in DeRopp's schema has been defined as a state of relative egolessness, free from anxiety and defenses, which allows for expansion of experiences and feelings and for increased knowledge of self. Ego, time, and space are transcended, giving rise to peace and tranquility. It is a state of awareness without thought.

Once this state is experienced, you realize that the feeling is not new; you have been here before, but only for brief glimpses, as it is an experience difficult to sustain. These glimpses were described by the humanistic psychologist Abraham Maslow as "peak experiences" and "the greatest attainment of identity, autonomy, or selfhood." Peak experiences are not to be constantly lived in or planned for; they just happen—

seldom for most people and more often for those whose aim is inner awareness.

COSMIC CONSCIOUSNESS

Many philosophers believe that at the pinnacle of the hierarchy of consciousness states lies a fifth level of consciousness, "cosmic consciousness" or a state of oneness with the universe. Cosmic consciousness, according to the Tao, is impossible to explain or define, as it is a pure feeling state and those who enter it are not in the thinking state which is needed to relate and form memory and explanations. It is a state of universal consciousness where ego boundaries are completely obliterated. It is a oneness with all other living organisms including the highest spirit or divine being. Nature is laid bare and the spirit exists in harmony with the spirit of all things.

Picture every organism as a circle, with an ego consciousness, an inner or subconscious, and cosmic consciousness as layers within the circle. Most of us experience glimpses into the subconscious as premonitions, and unexplained knowledge occurs to us. Some, after intense training and complete attainment of the fourth state, share consciousness with others in the universe and enter the highest circle, cosmic consciousness (Figure 11.3).

ROADS TO TRANSCENDENCE

The road to transcendence may also be thought of as the road back, as transcendence is a natural part of our consciousness which has become

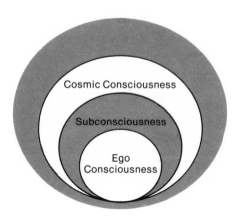

Figure 11.3 Levels of Consciousness

buried beneath our coping, I-normal consciousness. As society has become more complex, so has our pattern of coping behavior. The masks we wear, the roles we play, the plans, the schemes, and the worrying are all "I-centered" activities. We have been taught to fight fire with fire or to fight complexity with complexity, developing a vicious cycle. With the "rebirth" of the ancient Eastern philosophies we are learning that often it is better to fight fire with water or increased complexity with increased simplicity.

The search for self-transcendence is an interesting phenomenon in that those who do not understand the true nature of it continue to use complex and unnatural methods to obtain it. An analogy might be that of digging at an archeological site with a steam shovel. To one group of individuals, the steam shovel represents the easiest, most effortless way of seeing what is buried at the site, when in reality it is destroying the dig. So it is with those people who seek self-transcendence through the use of mind-altering chemicals.

Drugs

A drug-induced altered state of consciousness is often an idyllic experience, but the relationship to the transcendent state is sporadic and tenuous and thus lacks the growth potential of some of the other transcendent techniques. Intensity of the drug-induced experience is dependent upon such factors as timing, the quantity and quality of the drug, the setting, the mood or state of mind of the user, motivation, learned drug skills, general physiology, personality, and expectations. Frustration and disappointment may develop when expectations are not met; and fear, apprehension, and injury can result if the drug is too strong or dangerously adulterated. Either way, the individual is not in control of the experience, and is in a sense imprisoned in an altered state of consciousness until the drug has been metabolized. Often the experience is too intense, too deep, or in a sense, too removed from the learning, remembering, processing, "I-normal" state; thus little is remembered or gained. More important, drugs change but do not stop the flood of sporadic thoughts that bombard the consciousness; thus quieting the mind is almost impossible.

Herein lies the crux of the problem, engendered in a lack of understanding of what constitutes self-transcendence. Psychoactive drugs can induce an altered state of consciousness through either the alteration of incoming stimuli or the deautomatization of thought processes (see Figure 11.1). Psychoactive drugs can change awareness, memory, emotions, moods, and in general, change the ordinary state of consciousness. Such alterations give an air of novelty to everyday occurrences, thus changing their significance and one's interest in them. Motivations become obscure and one may begin pondering the significance of an object, feeling, or idea, forgetting that it was processed before and found to be insignificant. Obligations and goals become obscure and somewhat meaningless, as experiencing the moment becomes extremely pleasurable. The anxiety of passing time is diminished. What is real and important is making sense of the impulses that have the attention of the consciousness. Awareness is heightened, and imagery becomes more stimulating and significant. Touch, taste, and smell are not just stimulators of the senses—their origins can become part of the body or mind. The sense of unrealness and lack of ego involvement are calming, but the learned tendency of the mind to create logic and order often gains awareness, creating alterations in moods that oscillate between pleasure and apprehension. At times, goal-directed activity seems alien and the body is only intermittently disturbed by sporadic arousal. Most often the stress of time, goals, and ego are reduced, as are the pressures of everyday existence.

In order to gain inner awareness—an active process from within—one needs control of thoughts, feelings, and cognitive processes. But all drugs are uncontrollable to a lesser or greater degree, and drugs promote the feeling that the experience is a passive process, externally induced. In the *Master Game*, Robert DeRopp writes that although some transcendence of self is experienced, the drug consciousness is but a glimpse of transcendence.

Mind-Directed States

There are a myriad of currently popular techniques which aim at inducing a self-transcendent, altered state of consciousness through mind direction or control. Yoga, meditation, muscular relaxation, autogenic training, and biofeedback are but a few general examples. Although most of these techniques will be discussed in depth later, with instructions on home practice, a brief description of their relationship to self-transcendent altered states of consciousness seems appropriate here.

As meditation appears to be the simplest, most direct, and the most popular road to the fourth level of consciousness, it is the best example of a mind-directed state. The term "meditation" usually refers to a specific technique, but it should be considered a state of mind. The same state is induced by most of the other techniques mentioned above (yoga, muscular relaxation, autogenic training, biofeedback).

Meditation, as it is known in the modern world, is a complex mixture of philosophies and techniques descended from ancient yoga and Zen Buddhism. As time passed, slight variations in philosophy and/or technique led to the development of numerous forms of meditation until today's marketplace of meditative disciplines is indeed plentiful.

Regardless of their ancestry, all of the meditative techniques have at least two phases: the first is to quiet the body, and the second is to quiet the mind. It has long been recognized that one cannot quiet the mind so long as the cortex and other association centers are being bombarded by stimuli from tense muscles and overactive organs. Thus, elaborate rituals, exercises, and postures have been developed in an attempt to gain the physical quiet so necessary for entrance into the second phase—that of quieting the mind.

Meditation has been explained in a myriad of ways, but the one element common to all explanations is the process of trying to eliminate the surface chatter of the mind, the constant thinking, planning, remembering, and fantasizing which occupies the mind every waking second and keeps the ego firmly implanted in the consciousness. As the ego chatter diminishes, so do the ego defenses. Anxiety is reduced, thus arousal is reduced as both the body and the mind achieve the quiet and the peace natural to the ego- or self-transcendent state of consciousness.

The art of meditation is the ability to maintain a passive concentration state in which alertness and control are maintained, but in such a way as not to be tension producing. The meditator is in complete control of the experience, which is not as intense as the drug high, nor as dangerous or debilitating. The meditator is not trapped in the altered state of consciousness as is often the case with drugs. Because he/she has command over emotions, feelings, and memory, more growth can be obtained from the experience. Physiological processes can be quieted and control can be maintained over the body. Research on meditation has shown that meditation is accompanied by a marked reduction in the activity of most systems governed by the autonomic nervous system.

Meditation is described in terms of awareness of subtle thoughts, energy, and creative intelligence. Although passive, it is an active process that takes thought, preparation, and practice; thus the mediator is left with the feeling of creativity, accomplishment, and a generally positive feeling about the activity. One problem with meditation is the subjectiveness of the process. Most students simply take for granted that if they follow the instructions given them, they are in fact meditating; but many express doubt of obtaining an altered state. When compared with the drug experience the signs are subtle. Occasionally there is visual imagery and a sense of detachment from the body, but most physical sensations are confined to a heaviness or numbness in the limbs and an extreme sense of relaxation and calm. Electroencephalographic studies of experienced students of TM do show that during meditation, brain waves are slowed, thus suggesting that the meditative state and a slow brain wave state are synonymous.

However, some researchers contend that the presence of slowed brain waves do not necessarily indicate a meditative state. It has been generally established that tranquil states are most often related to slowed brain wave states. Thus researchers and clinicians are using electroencephalograph (EEG) biofeedback to train individuals to produce and maintain brain wave states at will to achieve tranquility.

Generally, biofeedback is a system of monitoring bioelectrical signals emitted from the body and transforming that information to visual and/or auditory signals that allow the individual to become aware of internal activity (such as brain states) which are associated with relaxation and calmness. Normally we are not able to experience this feedback from our bodies. With the proper instrumentation one can be taught to induce a state of consciousness characterized by slowed brain wave activity below 13 cycles per second.

The brain is constantly producing electrical activity that can be measured from the surface of the skull. The usual "nonthinking," "blank" or "mind-void" wave of between 8 and 13 cycles per second is called an *alpha wave* (see Figure 11.4). When this pattern desynchronizes in response to stimuli, the *beta* wave pattern emerges and analytical thinking is increased. The beta waves are low-voltage fast waves above 14 cycles per second. Feelings during beta have been described as anticipatory, frustrated, investigative, conceptualizing, and impatient. Alpha has been described as neutral, sluggish, dreamlike, pleasant. *Theta*, a state characterized by waves slower than alpha, has been described as fuzzy, puzzled, unreal, creative, and visionary.

EEG biofeedback has been used for various purposes, from reducing

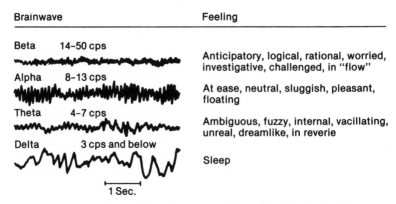

Brainwave		Feeling
Beta	14–50 cps	Anticipatory, logical, rational, worried, investigative, challenged, in "flow"
Alpha	8–13 cps	At ease, neutral, sluggish, pleasant, floating
Theta	4–7 cps	Ambiguous, fuzzy, internal, vacillating, unreal, dreamlike, in reverie
Delta	3 cps and below	Sleep

1 Sec.

Figure 11.4 States of Consciousness as Determined by Brain Waves, and Feelings Often Associated with Each State

stress, to getting high, to increasing creativity. The benefits are similar to those for meditation: a production of an altered state of consciousness, an interaction with the interior self, an increased self-control, self-aware-ness, and self-transcendence. As in meditation, the individual actively produces the state at will and can terminate it instantly, while remaining close to normal thinking consciousness. Unlike meditation, during bio-feedback the individual knows for sure that an altered brain state does exist. However, biofeedback is only a learning tool. The aim of training is to learn to produce the state and sense its presence, and then repro-duce it without the instrument. The sensing is thus transferred to an autosensory system. A drawback to biofeedback is that good instrumenta-tion is expensive. Yet, biofeedback has become so popular that those interested can usually search out a research project, counseling center, or clinic that may offer training.

It is extremely difficult to produce a tranquil, altered state of con-sciousness if the brain is being bombarded with stimuli. For example, if muscles are tense, feedback heightens activity of the reticular activating system (see Chapter 4) and cortex activity is increased, further tensing the muscles and creating a positive feedback system which makes relaxa-tion difficult. This is similar to anxiety reactivity, mentioned earlier. Slowed brain waves may be impossible if such alpha-blocking activity is not reduced. Research has shown that the alpha state is associated with (perhaps responsible for) reduced activity of the autonomic nervous system and results in diminished arousal of most systems including voluntary muscle tension. Biofeedback training of other systems such as muscles, temperature control, and respiration (discussed more fully in Chapter 13) can likewise be techniques of controlling states of conscious-ness.

As in meditation, brain wave biofeedback depends on the art of passive concentration so that alertness may be maintained, but that concentration itself does not induce tension and anxiety. To achieve full relaxation, one cannot be apprehensive; one must void the mind of memories, anticipation, and awareness of pain. Focusing on the internal self in general enhances one's awareness of self and enables one to better recognize the influence of thought and feeling and physical reactions. One begins to see the mind and body as unity.

Just as there are different biofeedback-aided brain wave states, there are also different types of ego-transcendent meditative states of conscious-ness. The alpha state, characterized by the blank or mind-void state (where thoughts are inhibited until a state of awareness without thought is achieved), is analogous to the concentrative or transcendental medita-tive technique. The theta state, although not well researched, is thought to be analogous to the open mind or mind-directed techniques of meditation, in which thoughts are welcomed and followed but the attention is without reaction. There is no identification with the event, feeling or thought. Only when the thought process starts to resemble a daydream or when the meditation starts to control the thoughts are they terminated.

It should be obvious by now that at the core of each mind-directed technique is a thought process directed *away* from the ego and its relationship to the environment. In some techniques that is the primary goal or focus, while in others it is secondary or more of a by-product. The technique of neuromuscular relaxation, also referred to as progressive muscle relaxation, utilizes a series of subtle exercises in which specific muscles are first contracted and then relaxed. It requires intense but passive concentration on the activity itself, but more important, on the feeling of muscle tension. To fully relax the muscles one must be free of apprehension and must void the mind of memories, anticipations, and awareness of pain. The primary end result is the reduction of muscle tension. The reduction of muscle tension reduces stimulation of the reticular activating system and cortex. The secondary end result is a focus of attention away from ego consciousness.

Likewise, Hatha Yoga teaches posture and subtle exercises to redirect blood flow, to realign organs with gravitational pull, and as a discipline of the body and mind. However, one cannot assume the postures only with the body: the mind must be intimately involved and as a result the consciousness tends to shift away from the ego.

CONCLUSION

One might view the roads to altered states of consciousness as a hierarchy. On the low end are the drug-induced states. Except for potential physical dangers, side effects, and a lack of internal control, they may be better than no experience at all because drugs may afford glimpses of self-transcendence and moments of egolessness.

Next on the hierarchy are what one might consider the techniques. These are a more positive approach than drugs, not only because they are less dangerous, more socially acceptable, and more controllable, but also because they are active and creative, requiring and promoting self-control and self-discipline. These are learning exercises which result in temporary feelings of self-transcendence, thus providing the foundation and motivation needed to reeducate one's thoughts and coping processes. If mastered, they lead from ego consciousness toward cosmic consciousness—an egolessness, or ego-extended state in which ego boundaries are infinitely extended.

Many philosophers believe that at the pinnacle of the hierarchy lies the fifth major state of consciousness, cosmic consciousness or a state of oneness with the universe. Drugs, meditation, or alpha-theta states may provide either glimpses of or temporary presence in such a state, but if it is obtainable at all, it is so only after years of training and complete attainment of the fourth state.

12

Meditation

According to the teachings of Buddha, the source of man's problems is his extreme attachment to his senses, his thoughts, and his imagination. Peace can be attained only when he frees himself from these attachments, directing his awareness inward, transcending the incessant bombardment of the consciousness so as to experience a quiet body, a subtle mind, and a unified spirit.

Buddha's thoughts generally state the simple goals of meditation, which have motivated millions of seekers for hundreds of years. Although the goals are simple, the fundamentals of meditation are often misunderstood, as meditation itself is difficult to define. Meditation is not a physiological state, nor is it any specific psychological feeling or state. It is not a philosophy, it is not a religion, it is not a technique and it is not a state of mind—but it is a combination of all of these. Meditation is so basic that it has transcended time, culture, races, religions, and ideologies. It is so simple that millions have used it, yet so advanced that it represents the highest order of human activity—the living condition which most closely approximates the divine state or universal oneness.

Meditation can be best understood as a state of mind, of consciousness, or of spirit. But it is most often defined in terms of an act or a technique. There are numerous techniques of meditation embodied in different philosophies and religions; although it is intended to be a central component in one complete style of living, a few have been successfully extrapolated by Western culture to be techniques of relaxation and tension reduction.

The philosophical goals of meditation cannot be achieved without training. The great number of meditation groups or "sects" which have arisen throughout the world are the result of differences in techniques and ways of mastering techniques rather than different philosophies. The most popular meditative techniques in Western society are based on specific concentration and contemplation practices of ancient yoga and Zen Buddhism.

Yoga, a Sanskrit word meaning "reunion," is an elaboration of philosophies and teaching that Lord Krishna gave to his disciples and that have been transmitted from generation to generation by enlightened masters. There are several yoga paths which have developed into spiritual schools, and in many instances these paths have become separate disciplines in themselves. Bhakti Yoga, the path of devotion to God, uses devotional chanting and worship. Jnana Yoga, the path of knowledge, teaches wisdom and understanding. Some others are Karma Yoga, the path of action and selfless services; Hatha Yoga, the path of health using exercise as a means to physical and mental harmony; and Raja Yoga, or Royal Yoga, the path of self-realization and enlightenment. According to Palanjali's Sutras, the most authoritative source of yoga philosophy, all other forms of yoga are just preparation for meditation and realization of the Raja Pathway, through which the divine potential of the soul can be revealed. Although yoga practices are used by various religious groups, yoga is not a religion, thus it is free of dogmatism and orthodoxism. Yoga teaches methods of concentration and contemplation to control the mind, subdue the (primitive) consciousness, and bring the physical body under control of the will. It releases the innermost consciousness to release the true forms of the self.

Zen, as originally conceived, was not a philosophy; it had no doctrine and was anti-intellectual. Having no doctrine, it was not a religion and did not deny or affirm the existence of God, a soul, or a spirit. Specific doctrines, rituals, and intellectual inquiries associated with it were merely attempts by various sects to discipline and guide the seeker. Zen seeks to open the mind itself, to make it its own master to be free of unnatural encumbrances. In this sense, Zen is chaotic, undisciplined, and unteachable. So, to accomplish the goals of Zen, various disciplines have grown with each teacher who thought of a better method to teach the undisciplined mind to reach this freedom. Meditation is at the core of all the techniques.

CONCENTRATION

Common to all meditation are concentration and the closely related techniques of contemplation and mental repetition.

Concentration here implies attention to one subject, thus controlling of the mind's usual habit of flipping from one subject to another. Control of the mind through selected attention reduces ego consciousness, and nondirected attention heightens awareness and in some disciplines is thought to release energy. Concentrating on physiological processes or internal sensations as the mystical "third eye" or getting into the rhythm of breathing are used in several different disciplines. One type of yoga, Kundalini Yoga, theorizes potential energy coiled up in the nervous system which can be awakened by relaxing and thinking that you are able to magnetize the entire body until you feel that light and heat are flowing from your body and that a great ocean of consciousness is flowing around you. Visual imagery is used by Hindu and Buddhist practices; the mind's eye concentrates on the thousand-petal lotus. Another more popular Zen Buddhist practice is to concentrate on breathing by counting breaths while working to eliminate all other thoughts and feelings. When ten breaths are counted without one's losing the count, the mind is more ready to contemplate mu. (Mu is an example of a mantra—see below.)

Another vehicle for concentrative meditation is the verbal or mental repetition of a word or sound called a *mantra*, meaning "hymn" or "calming sound." A mantra can be a single word such as "mu," or "om," or a phrase from holy scripture, a name for God, Hare Rama, Hare Krishna, or specially selected words thought to be calming because of resonance qualities, as is the practice in the popular Transcendental Meditation (TM). TM is a classical Hindu mantra technique based on the teaching of the Hinda teacher, Sankaracharya, and made popular by Maharishi Mahesh Yogi through the ambitious worldwide organization called the Students International Meditation Society.

Maharishi Mahesh Yogi, born Mahest Prasod Varma in 1918, received a degree in physics at Allahabad University in 1942, but before he began the normal prearranged (destined) lifestyle, he met and became a disciple of a religious leader, Swami Brahmanada Saraswati, and spent the next thirteen years studying with him. After this period of intense study and meditation, he was given the task of finding a form of effective meditation simple enough that everyone in the world could learn it.

After spending two years in a Himalayan cave, he began traveling throughout India addressing small gatherings of people on the technique of meditation he had founded. Realizing it would take twenty years of this type of practice to reach the rest of the world, and not being averse to the use of mass communication and advertising, he launched a worldwide campaign to bring TM to everyone. Realizing that things happen faster in the West and that Americans were open to new ideas, he concentrated his efforts there.

TM is not a religion or a philosophy and does not demand any particular lifestyle of its practitioners. This fact is particularly responsible for its wide acceptance in the West. TM is described as a technique of expanding conscious awareness and producing a state of restful alertness, indicative of the fourth state of consciousness, self-transcendence. Unlike the contemplative techniques, TM is not an intellectual analysis, but a direct experience of going beyond surface thought to reach the quiet, subtle awareness which is the desired outcome of most meditative techniques. The technique of TM is a simple mantra which is said to be somehow matched to each meditator. The mantras themselves are not unique to TM, but come from Sanskrit texts still in use today. Examples of Sanskrit mantras are "Shyam" which is the name of Lord Krishna, and "Aing" a sacred sound of the Divine Mother.

The secrecy of the mantra, a much criticized practice of TM, is an attempt to discourage those other than regular TM instructors from teaching the technique. However, TM readily advertises that it is a simple, natural technique which takes only twenty minutes to learn as it is the most fundamental aspect of the self.

The Maharishi claims that TM is neither a contemplative or concentrative technique because the mantra is passively allowed to repeat itself in the mind. However, especially in the initial phases, the mantra is actively concentrated on; but as with other concentrative techniques, the vehicle may soon disappear, leaving attention without focus, awareness of nothing, also referred to as "pure consciousness." The Maharishi theorizes that thinking the mantra has a vibratory effect on the nervous system that dissolves stress and frees the mind to pursue its natural subtle state of consciousness.

CONTEMPLATION

Contemplation, *zazen* or *dhyana* in Sanskrit, is one of the three basic branches of Buddhism. It is closely related to concentration, the primary difference being that the object of contemplation (usually an external object, *mandala*) has symbolism and it is the significance rather than the object that becomes the focus. The Zen Buddhist *koan*, which is a question puzzle or riddle such as "What is the sound of one hand clapping?", has no answer, but is an artificial instrument to force an open mind and develop in students the Zen consciousness. In most meditative techniques, *dhyana* (sitting quietly, cross-legged in contemplation) is an end in itself. However, in pure Zen, *Dhyana* or *zazen* is practiced as a means of solving the *koan* and is not an end in itself.

The same is true for Christian meditations which use objects such as the crucifix, a picture or statue of a religious figure, or spiritual passages and prayers as a focus for contemplation which is a means to Christ consciousness. One of the more complete systems of Christian or religious meditation has been outlined by the Association for Research and Enlightenment, made up of the followers of the "Sleeping Prophet," Edgar Cayce. Cayce was adamant in his belief that contemplation should be only a means and not an end, and he quoted Jesus's warning in the Parable of the Displaced Demon in which the evil spirits that were cast out of an empty mind quickly returned bringing other devils, leaving the man worse off than before. To Cayce, meditation was attuning the mental and physical body to its spiritual source, seeking to know the relationships to the Maker. There is no emptying in the mind-void sense, only emptying of that which hinders the creative forces from rising along the natural channels or centers. The seven spiritual centers or *chakras* are recognized as the endocrine glands, which provide energy for psychic and religious experiences. Cayce additionally defined meditation as a prayer from within the inner self and distinguished between prayer and meditation by stating that prayer was external attunement, a pleading, a petition to the Holy Spirit; while meditation was an internal attunement, a seeking to know our relationship with God, an inpouring from the Holy Spirit. The Cayce-based form of meditation uses the Lord's Prayer as a focus for contemplation.

Christian meditation contemplation techniques are similar to other types in that they seek transcendence of ego consciousness. The primary difference is in the end focus of the contemplation. Whatever the technique, though, the sought-for outcome is control of consciousness and direction of the mind.

MEDITATION AND THE REDUCTION OF STRESS AROUSAL

The primary purpose of meditation—peace, enlightenment, and spiritual growth—cannot be obtained as long as the mind is in turmoil and the body is aroused. Thus, most meditative techniques have seemingly elaborate preparatory procedures designed to induce physical relaxation, and meditation itself quiets the mind. Relaxation, an indirect product of meditation, can be therapeutic in the treatment or prevention of psychosomatic disorders.

Even though meditation is thousands of years old and the physiological feats of yoga masters is legend, the "scientific" study of the psychophysiological processes of meditation is still in its infancy. Meditation only recently became scientific when Wallace (1970) published the results of a study showing that during meditation the oxygen consumption of the body was significantly decreased, thus producing a hypometabolic state, that is, a slowing down of the body processes. Wallace also found that during meditation the skin had increased resistance to the passage of an electrical current; this indicated decreased arousal of the autonomic nervous system. He also found a decrease in the lactate ion concentration, another measure of decreased metabolism; a decrease in heart rate and cardiac output (quantity of blood pumped by the heart per minute), indicating a reduction in the workload of the heart; a decrease in respiration rate; an increase in the percentage of time the brain is emitting slowed brain waves, indicating a more restful state. This restful state physiologically resembled sleep in many ways, but in totality it was significantly different from sleep. The meditator was found to be in a restful state, but was awake and alert, and exhibited an increased reaction time, improved coordination, and improved efficiency of perception and auditory ability.

Later research both supported and refuted, at least in degree, Wallace's early findings. This only points out the difficulty of such research due mainly to subject variability and differences in technique of meditation. For example, the variance in the length of each meditative session and the experience of the meditator are extremely important. Obviously, the more one meditates the greater should be the ability to change psychophysiological states. EEG records of Zen masters show a predominance of alpha and theta brain waves during meditation, which become more marked with years of practice; beginning meditators, on the other hand, show only slight changes in brain wave patterns.

Another difficulty in research is the difference in the meditative state itself. As previously mentioned, meditation is not a unitary phenomenon, but a series of stages which include a sitting quiet stage, a passive concentration stage, a mental deautomatization or desynchronization stage, a neutral or mind-void stage, and, especially in accomplished meditators, a brain-directed stage. Measurements taken during each of these phases could yield different results. More recent research has found a decreased oxygen utilization in meditators, but a decrease not nearly as dramatic as Wallace's, whose subjects' metabolism seem to have been somewhat above normal when they started (Pagano, 1977). This indicates that the significance of the results may be related to the starting point of the subjects and illustrates the fact that immediate benefits are related to the initial arousal of the individual. Even though hundreds of studies have been conducted and thousands of words written, we are just now starting to understand the physiological state of meditation.

Stress arousal is a psychophysiological response to a particular psychosocial or environmental situation. Each situation produces an immediate stress response, but may also leave a residual amount of tension in the body. Response to subsequent stressors is augmented by the residual left over from previous responses. As the day wears on, response overactivity results from the inability to dissipate residual tension. The physiological relaxation experienced by the meditator is a short-term phenomenon, but the more the relaxation state is induced, the more the carryover to the nonmeditative state. Meditation helps dissolve tension by quieting the mind's tendency toward "after thoughts" which prolong the stress response and at least temporarily reduce the physical arousal of the organs. Thus each new stressful situation will produce a reaction sufficient to deal with that particular situation without the add-on effect of previous stress arousal. The longer one meditates, the more his/her general state of arousal resembles the meditative state, and the ongoing tensions most detrimental to the body are greatly reduced. Gradually, this psychophysiological state becomes a stable part of the personality structure of the meditator. The overactive, rushed individual can become a slowed, cooler reacting individual, who has the ability to respond with the intensity demanded of each situation as an isolated incident.

Chronically stressed and anxious people often do not perceive internal states of arousal and do not associate physical states with emotional arousal, but the unattended physical arousal causes anxious feelings which further augment physical arousal. In a similar manner, relaxation not only diminishes physical arousal, but promotes stress desensitization by allowing the individual to experience previously stressful situations in a relaxed state, gradually diminishing the stressful experience in their lives and reducing anxiety.

As often mentioned throughout this book, one essential for mental health is the ability to live each current situation in reality without the effect of adding imaginary consequences which could or should happen. Perhaps the primary therapeutic benefit of meditation is the development of the ability to concentrate attention on the present, to quiet the imagination, and to distinguish reality from fantasy. The accomplished meditator develops the ability to direct thoughts away from the ego self, the primary source of stress. The meditator experiences temporary transcendence, but just as the physiological state gradually becomes a stable trait, so can an individual learn to live a life of increased ego transcendence.

HOW TO MEDITATE

There are many types of meditation, each representing a variation in purpose and technique. The type presented in this section is thought to be the best suited for stress reduction, the easiest to learn, and the one most devoid of cultic, religious, and spiritual overtones. The technique is complete for the purpose of meditation; however, it can also serve as an introduction to more specific types as they all have at least this technique as their core experience.

What follows is both explicit instruction and clarifying explanation. The instructions will be in italics; the explanations will not. You may want to read the instructions into a tape recorder and play them back during the first few meditation sessions, so that you will have a chance to practice it while hearing the instructions.

The first essential is a quiet environment—both external and internal. A quiet room away from others who are not also meditating is essential, especially while you are learning. Put out the dog, cat, or whatever. Take the phone off the hook or find a room without one. Generally, do whatever can be done to reduce external noise. If you cannot completely eliminate the noise, as is often the case in busy households or in college dorms, use ear plugs, play a record or tape of soft instrumental sounds, or use any of the numerous environmental sounds which have been commercially recorded. Many enterprising people take their tape recorders to the woods to record the sound of the wind whistling through the trees, a mountain stream, or just the birds at dawn. The sounds of the waves at the seashore also make an excellent background for meditation. Beside blocking out noise, such sounds help promote a sense of relaxation, as they usually bring back memories of pleasant feelings.

Next, work on quieting your internal environment. One way is to reduce muscle tension. Remember, it is practically impossible to induce a meditative state while the reticular activating system is bombarding the cortex with sensory signals being emitted from the muscles. Muscle tension represents one of the largest obstacles to successful meditation. Spend some time, no more than 5 minutes, relaxing your muscles. You may want to choose one or several of the neuromuscular relaxation exercises from Chapter 14 and work on your particular tensed area.

One way to reduce excess muscle tension is to *sit comfortably*. You may not feel like a real meditator unless you use the Asian, cross-legged, lotus position; if you desire this position, sit on the floor with a pillow under your buttocks. In this position the legs are crossed so that the left foot rests on the right thigh and the right foot rests on the left thigh. Unless you have practiced this position or are naturally flexible, you will find this uncomfortable, however. A simple tailor's position will suffice, if you really want to sit on the floor. If you don't mind being too Western, *sit in a straight-backed, comfortable chair, feet on the floor, legs not crossed, hands resting on the thighs, fingers slightly open, not interlocked.* You should sit still, but remember, meditation is not a trance; if you are uncomfortable or feel too much pressure on any one spot, move. If you itch, scratch. *Do not assume a tight, inflexible position or attitude. Relax.* Do not lie down or support your head or you will tend to fall asleep. Keep your head, neck, and spine in a straight vertical line. A small but significant amount of muscular effort is needed to maintain this posture, and this effort helps prevent sleep from occurring. If shoes, belt, bra, tie, or collar are too tight, loosen them. The goal is to diminish sensory input to the central nervous system.

Most people like to have a clock where it can be seen at a glance to reduce the anxiety that arises from the feeling that more time is being spent than was anticipated. Twenty to thirty minutes is the standard amount of time spent per session, although five minutes is better than none. Although not recommended for the first few sessions, occasionally interspersing a one-hour session has been reported to be most profound and relaxing.

Before you start, relax and stretch your neck muscles. Move your chin toward your chest, then back in place. Repeat this three times. Move your head toward your back. Do this three times. Rotate your head clockwise three complete rotations. Repeat this counterclockwise three times. Now relax your neck. Allow your head to drop slightly forward. This is more comfortable than slightly backward. *Sit quietly. Close your eyes.* Notice immediately how that simple movement acts to quiet the environment. Most of our sensory input enters through the eyes; the simple act of closing the eyes does much to quiet the mind. The ambient noise is reduced, the eyes are closed, muscle tension is reduced, and tactile sensory stimulation is at a minimum. The external and physical environment of the body should now be quiet. Now *concentrate on quieting the mind.* Foremost in this effort is developing a tranquil or passive attitude. Even if meditation is done for a specific reason, such as to reduce hypertension, cut down on smoking, or increase self-assuredness, you must not dwell on the outcome of meditation or even on how well that particular meditation is proceeding. Such thoughts represent an ongoing ego-involving type of thought process which the meditation is trying to suppress.

Direct your thoughts away from your self, away from the parts you play in the stories of your mind. If you have music or environmental sounds playing, *direct your attention to the sound. Float with the sound like a cloud, white and fluffy against the blue sky . . . like a leaf floating down a stream, floating, twirling around the rocks, over a waterfall.* You may notice some warmth or heaviness in your arms or legs. This is an indication of muscles in those areas beginning to relax. You might also notice your head drooping with relaxation of your neck muscles. *Your breathing is probably slower and a bit deeper. For a moment, concentrate on your breathing. As you breathe in, think "in," let the air out, and think "out." You should breathe in through your nose, think "in," and breathe out through your mouth, think "out," but do not force the expiration . . . just open your mouth and let the air out. Think . . . in . . . out . . . in . . . out. . . . Now each time you breathe out, count the breath. Count ten consecutive breaths without missing a count. If you happen to miss one, start over. When you get to ten, start at one again. Concentrate, anticipate the breath, block all other thoughts from your mind.*

Concentrating on breathing is a means of focusing attention inward away from the self in relation to the external world. It is an example of a mental device. Most meditative techniques utilize some form of mental device to direct consciousness away from logical, cause-and-effect, goal-directed thought processes. The device may be a spiritual contemplation, the contemplation of geometric designs, concentration on a body process such as breathing, an internal light, or an external light, as in a biofeedback display, but most often the device is a word or chant called a mantra.

The mantra (calming word) is used to quiet the mind. One can think of the mind as a lake, choppy on the top but calm below. Just as the choppy waters of the lake are caused by the external environment, so too are reflective thoughts churning around the cortex (top layer of the brain) in response to external stimulation of your senses, your memory, your habits of thought. Concentrating on the mantra, in most cases a meaningless (in Western culture) word, directs your attention toward it. But because the word has no meaning, stories are not formed, memory is not stimulated, imagination is quieted, arousal does not occur. Automatization of brain function breaks down and you drift into an altered state of consciousness. As in the quiet depths of the lake, the quiet, more subtle state of mind emerges into consciousness. Gradually, the concentration on the mantra will also disappear and you will remain in a neutral state until a new thought pops into your consciousness, as sporadic thoughts often do. At that point, you can consciously void the thought just by telling yourself, "No, I do not want to think about it," or you may want to go back to the mantra, or you can direct the thought to a pattern of nonstressful thinking consistent with the particular type of meditation being practiced.

In all cases, you are teaching the mind not to think about or form stories around sporadic thoughts. You are just eliminating a bad habit acquired throughout your life. It is a form of reeducation of the mind and the central nervous system. An analogy can be made to dieting. Dieting can help you lose weight and, you hope, the practice of dieting may help you to develop new eating habits to lessen the chance of becoming overweight again. Similarly, meditation will help make you calm, and the practice of meditation can help develop new thought habits which should diminish stress arousal in the future.

An example of a mantra suggested by Herbert Benson in *The Relaxation Response* is simply the word "one." This is a soft, noncultic word which has little meaning as a number but can be considered as "unity" and takes on greater significance. If you prefer a word in a foreign language, try the Sanskrit "om," which is considered the universal mantra. It also means "one."

At this stage of learning, your primary goal is to achieve a neutral or mind-void state. Thus the meaning of the word is not important. If you go on to mind-directed contemplative types of meditation such as Zen Buddhism, it will take on greater significance.

Breathe softly, but now do not concentrate on your breathing. Repeat one of the mantras aloud. Say it over and over. Each time say it softer until it becomes just a mental thought with no muscular action involved. Pace yourself, gradually lengthening the interval between thoughts of the mantra. Allow the mantra to repeat itself in your mind. Do not force it, just let it flow. Gradually the mantra will fade, your mind will remain quiet. The quiet will occasionally be broken by sporadic thoughts. Let them come, experience them, go with them until you feel like you are controlling them to some preconceived outcome. At that point they become daydreams and usually involve ego arousal. At that point, stop the thought process and go back to the mantra.

Remember, meditation is a feeling, a state of mind. It is not a technique, it is not saying the mantra. *Sit quietly for 10 to 15 minutes and meditate.* Keep your movements to a minimum, but if you are uncomfortable, move; if you are worried about time, look at a clock or the discomfort and anxiety will prevent the full attainment of the meditative state.

When you finish meditating, do not be in too much of a hurry to get up. Open your eyes, stretch a little. Contract your muscles and reactivate yourself slowly. Having at least temporarily altered your emotional reactivity, continue your day with renewed inner capacity for meeting the day's challenges.

One of the greatest obstacles preventing the full attainment of the meditative state is usually the lack of physical and/or mental quietness. Physical quietness is the easier of the two to surmount. A quiet room, dim lights, closing the eyes, working to relax the muscles, sitting comfortably, and loosening clothes all tend to diminish sensory stimulation. You should also eliminate the stimulation which can come from a full stomach and psychoactive drugs by abstaining from either before meditating. Meditation is a discipline which necessitates having faculties at full command, and psychoactive drugs have no place in the practice.

Mental quietness is more difficult to attain, especially at first. But do not be discouraged. It took many years to develop your current thought processes and they do not change overnight. Many people are uncomfortable with quietness. They have been so bombarded with stimulation every waking minute since the cradle that they have not learned how to sit still by themselves and simply think of nothing. When one finally does sit down and seek quiet, the mind is flooded with, "The car needs a tune-up," "What time will Dick be home? . . . I hope he remembers our anniversary," "Should we buy the new TV?" . . . But as you learn to disregard these thoughts, they will gradually diminish and finally disappear.

Meditation is not difficult to learn, but many people are hindered by lack of confidence in their ability. They make the mistake of comparing themselves to masters who have spent their lives in meditation. That is just as foolish as saying you cannot drive a car because you cannot race at Indianapolis, or you can't hike in the woods because you cannot climb Mt. Everest. Meditation is not so simple, however, that the mere ritual will by itself overcome the hyperactivity of the mind busied by planning, scheming, thinking about and reacting to the myriad distractions to which we are all subjected. One cannot be full steam one minute and tranquil the next. Preparation for quietness is an essential step.

The biggest hindrance is attitude. Meditation is work, but one cannot labor at it. You cannot force yourself into transcendence. Often one hears, "I just must lower my blood pressure . . . I must obtain tranquility . . . I just have to straighten myself out." Don't constantly analyze and rate your meditation, and above all, don't continually search for evidence of change or enlightenment. Such an attitude is not only a hindrance to meditation, but an abuse of it.

Another abuse of meditation is withdrawal through meditation. The purpose of meditation is to enhance the experience of life, not to be a vehicle for withdrawal from life. The meditative period of tranquility trains the mind to allow active participation in an active life without unnecessary stress. Meditation is not a substitute for living.

13

Biofeedback

When you become frightened, anxious, angry, or generally stressed, numerous changes occur in your body—most of them negative. If the stress is moderate to severe, you will have no trouble in recognizing the outward signs. For example, the heart rate speeds up and often you can feel the palpitations in your chest. The palms of the hands become moist with increased sweating, skin may flush or become excessively pale, the pupils of the eyes may change size, your mouth may become very dry, or in some instances salivation may become excessive, muscles may tense to the point of pain or feel so limp your legs threaten to give way, the stomach "turns over" and you may feel nauseated, breathing rate may increase, and you may have a difficult time swallowing.

Often the stressor is overt—you know what it is or you know you are in a tough situation. More often, what produces stress is more subtle, not readily apparent. In these situations it is the bodily reactions mentioned above which signal a state of stress and are the triggers for initiation of coping behavior. If you have ever felt any of these symptoms, you have experienced biofeedback—that is, feeding back of biological signals to the source of that activity.

Try a little experiment. Find your pulse and record a resting pulse rate. Take it for several minutes to be sure you have a good sample. Jot down the rate in beats per minute. Now, as you sit quietly, try to imagine a scene or story you find particularly exciting. Really get into it until you can vividly see yourself involved in the situation. After a couple of minutes, stop, take your pulse, and record the beats per minute. Chances are that if you really got yourself into the imagined situation, and if the situation was one you found stressful, you found the second heart rate to be higher than the first.

Try another one! Stand in front of a mirror. Closely observe the pupils of your eyes. Occasionally they will change size. When they do, try to recall what you were thinking of at that time. Your emotions and what you are thinking will influence the size of your pupils—a biological signal of the stress response. If you happened to hear a noise or if someone startled you while you were standing in front of the mirror, you probably noticed an increased dilation. To particularly note the effect, have someone clap suddenly and unexpectedly as you look at your pupils in the mirror.

Both the heart rate and pupil size exercises are examples of getting feedback from the body. If you could monitor your heart rate continuously and if the stimulus were steady, just having the information would provide you with the primary ingredient in the biofeedback system—self-knowledge. The fact is that you would get tired of the process, your attention would wax and wane, and you would miss some information. However, through the miracle of technology, an electrical instrument can monitor the heart rate for you. In addition, this handy device can modify the signal to make it more useful. Most important, it can transform the heartbeat into a light or sound, so that our senses can interpret it easily. Diagrammed in Figure 13.1 is an example of a modern biofeedback system. Such an instrument senses, processes, and gives or feeds back to the individual immediate and continuous electrical signals which represent biological activity, activity that the individual would not usually be aware of. Having such information better enables the person to adjust his/her action and augments the learning process.

Monitoring biological activity with sophisticated electrical instruments might be thought of by some as a medical device. However, although biofeedback is used in the practice of medicine, it is best described as an *educational tool* which simply provides information about performance—much the same as an examination is used to test a student's progress in the classroom or the bathroom scale is used to give information about body weight.

The body is constantly telling us about its activities. We have learned to key into some feelings, sounds, and outward signs of mind-body func-

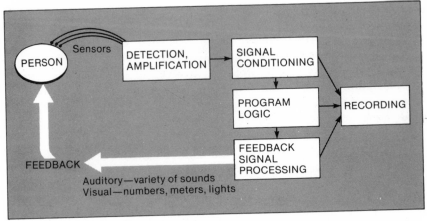

Figure 13.1 Typical Biofeedback System

tion. Stomach contractions are interpreted as hunger; diarrhea and constipation are indicators of gastrointestinal problems; redness and swelling are possible indicators of infection. We have also learned to use physiological parameters like heart rate and blood pressure to assess the body's functioning. When an increase in blood pressure is detected, the individual has some information about the cardiovascular system, and during treatment subsequent blood pressure readings are a constant measure of the success of treatment.

Biofeedback is to some extent a refinement of that feedback system. Instead of diarrhea, which is a rather gross measure of intestinal action, one could measure the minute muscle contraction of various intestinal segments. Thermal measurement of skin can indicate blood flow to a particular region of the body. Measuring contraction of skeletal muscle can detect muscle action before it reaches the stage of producing pain and discomfort.

INTERACTION WITH THE INTERIOR SELF

Biofeedback is more than just a means of self-monitoring physiological states. It can be used to promote self-exploration, self-awareness, and self-control. Barbara Brown in *New Mind, New Body* appropriately described biofeedback as an "interaction with the interior self."[1] Through such interaction one learns, by actually feeling (visceral learning), that what he/she is thinking influences body processes and that body processes or states influence thought processes. Feelings and emotions can be seen as more a part of the cognitive experience. The

[1] Barbara B. Brown, *New Mind, New Body* (New York: Harper & Row, 1974), p. 1.

knowledge of the "inner space" becomes more a part of the total thought and action process. Behavior becomes more internally directed and less habitually conditioned to external forces.

Biofeedback training is itself a conditioning, or perhaps better stated, a reconditioning process. Tranquility neurophysiologically conditions the tonus of the nervous system to be less reactive, desensitizes reactive behavior, and one begins to change behavior by "becoming" a more tranquil person. Research has reported decreases in trait anxiety and Type A behavior, and as a person feels and behaves, he/she eventually becomes (Girdano & Girdano, 1977). The reconditioning or relearning process disciplines the mind to reduce the constant mundane chatter. One experiences (perhaps for the first time) thought which is clear of imagination and anticipation, allowing greater concentration and often revealing insights and creativity heretofore subdued by self-doubt. What results is often an increased sense of self: self-concept, self-esteem, and self-realization. Equally important is the enhanced discipline (self-discipline) and increased control (self-control).

Thus, what started out as an exercise in relaxation quickly turns into a development of self-awareness and self-control. These qualities are an integral part of a holistic health program, as they are central not only in stress reduction programs, but also in weight control programs, programs for the aged, fitness programs, cardiovascular rehabilitation, and general health counseling, to mention a few applications.

HOW BIOFEEDBACK WORKS

The complex electronic instruments and the almost science-fiction-like accounts of results obtained using biofeedback give it an aura of mystery and magic. But there is no magic, and the mystery surrounding it pertains only to some as yet unexplained phenomena regarding the limits of human regulatory capacities. In order to understand the mechanisms of action, we can divide the processes into three phases:

1. *Physical or physiological phase*: The release of energy (physical, chemical, thermal, electrical—usually all of these) which can be measured with the appropriate device.

2. *Psychophysiological phase*: Mind and body controlling the energy-releasing process; coordination of voluntary, involuntary, and endocrine systems.

3. *Psychological or learning phase*: Voluntary control or conditioning process in which biofeedback becomes an essential link.

The body's response to stress is a physical release of energy which produces action and constitutes the function of the organ system. The interaction between cells is one of constant exchange of chemicals (hormones, electrolytes, metabolites, etc.) through the membrane of the cell. These chemicals often carry an electrical charge and sometimes produce physical movement of the cell structure (as in muscles) or movement of cellular secretions (such as in the hormonal, gastrointestinal, and cardiovascular systems). Finally, such movement releases excess energy in the form of heat. Any one of these processes can be measured with an appropriate device, and this constitutes the first phase listed above. The muscles offer a good example. Stimulation of the muscles results in movement of cellular electrolytes which carry an electrical charge. This shift results in a change in the equilibrium of the structural components of the muscle, attracting them toward one another, causing the cells to shorten and the muscle to move. A by-product of that movement, friction, causes the release of heat. Again, any of these processes can be measured and used as biofeedback. Most biofeedback systems measure the shift of electrolytes and thus measure muscle contraction as an electrical phenomenon.

At the beginning of this section you monitored your heart rate by physical means. The contraction of the muscles in the heart reduces the size of the heart chambers, thrusting blood through the arteries. When the surge of blood passed through the section of artery beneath your finger, that section swelled to such an extent that it could be felt on the surface of the skin. You counted the pulsations and thus became your own biofeedback device. A more efficient system which would accomplish the same purpose would be to monitor the shift of electrically charged chemicals which precede each heart muscle contraction and to allow the instrument to count them for you. (This is one of a variety of functions of an electrocardiogram.)

A more sophisticated system changes the swelling of the artery into electrical energy and measures that. Or, as the blood transfers heat, one could measure the heat shift into an extremity, and use that as a measure of cardiovascular function. There are numerous possibilities, but in each case, the instrument becomes your tireless monitor and can transform that energy into a more easily recognizable form. This, then, is your biofeedback instrument.

The second or intermediate phase is represented by the psychophysiological control systems, the endocrine and central nervous systems. The central nervous system is divided into two main components, the voluntary and involuntary. You may wish to refer back to Chapter 4 to refresh your memory. You will recall that the involuntary part of the nervous system is referred to as the autonomic nervous system. This system is a fantastic array of interconnecting nerve cells with which Mother Nature has cleverly endowed us. When a room becomes too warm, peripheral blood vessels located under the skin will dilate to release body heat. It is automatic; we do not have to direct our attention to it and nothing need be done on a conscious level. However, if this action is not sufficient and body temperature continues to rise, conscious centers of the brain will be alerted. Association will be made to the environment, memory of past solutions will be triggered, and voluntary action (getting up and turning down the heat) will be instituted.

The autonomic control centers are primarily in the "lower centers" of the brain, which include the brain stem and interbrain structures of the limbic system, the reticular activating system, the thalamus, and especially the hypothalamus, which monitors body heat very precisely. The hypothalamus also measures blood sugar level, regulates the gastrointestinal tract, and aids in the control of blood pressure, heart rate, sweat glands, and size of pupils, just to mention a few of its constant tasks. And most important to this discussion, the homeostatic action (restoring balance) it takes need not be pondered by the consciousness centers of the brain.

Theories of psychosomatic illness slowly began to emerge as scientists were confronted with diseases caused or at least exacerbated by over-stimulation of the autonomic nervous system, seemingly elicited by conscious perception of environmental and social events. In other words, consciousness was interacting with and influencing the autonomic nervous system. It was then reasoned that if the central processor could influence the autonomic nervous system with fears, worries, and plans, then why couldn't the same process be turned around and have a more tranquil consciousness *reduce* the activity of the autonomic nervous system? Such a feedback system is pictured in Figure 13.2.

The third phase considers the learning mechanisms that operate in biofeedback. In the final analysis there is no one explanation which can fully account for the learning and which can develop through the use of biofeedback. Actually, there are several events linked like a chain forming a circle, each adding a measure of control, each influencing the others.

As you can see in Figure 13.1, biofeedback represents a closed loop system. The control system (the instrument) senses the physiological output from the person (through the sensors, in the illustration) and the person senses the electrical output of the control system (represented by Feedback in Figure 13.1). However, it is more than just a stimulus-response situation. The biofeedback instrument is capable of making some decisions about the incoming information and can change the output (feedback) to fit some predetermined criteria. Likewise, an intelligent organism has the ability to recall memory of events related to previous responses and problem-solving attempts and instantly alter the response in relation to the feedback signal. In other words, the individual acts,

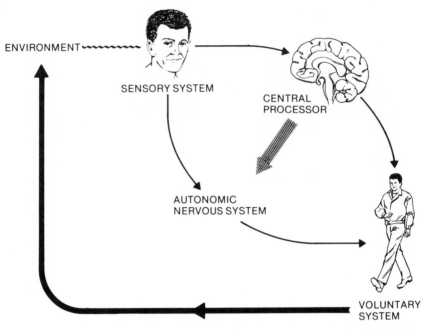

ENVIRONMENT

SENSORY SYSTEM

CENTRAL
PROCESSOR

AUTONOMIC
NERVOUS SYSTEM

VOLUNTARY
SYSTEM

Figure 13.2 Interaction between Central Processor and Autonomic Nervous System

gets feedback, and acts again, but the subsequent action may be changed from the first if the individual was not satisfied with the results of the previous action.

The output of the biofeedback instrument is electrical activity in the body and represents automatic responses of the brain. The closed loop or circle can be influenced by neural activity occurring in smooth muscle, skin, blood vessels, or any of the levels of the brain previously mentioned.

Let's take a trip around that closed loop and focus in on a few examples of possible mechanisms. One explanation for the action of biofeedback is that it deploys attention away from ego-centered, stress-producing consciousness and, in the manner of meditation, induces an altered state of consciousness. Instead of a mantra, the feedback and/or the organ "language" it represents become the focus of attention. In one sense, there is a reduction in the impact of potential environmental stressors, not because the event is altered in any way, but because the focus of attention is changed inward, away from the event. Even without biofeedback the body is a closed loop system. For example, as in anxious reactivity, cognitive or autonomic arousal can increase muscle tension, which feeds back impulses to the central nervous system, further increasing general arousal, which further stimulates the muscles. Often awareness of muscle tension causes further muscle tension. Deployment of attention away from the stressor temporarily reduces the arousal output to the viscera, reducing muscle tension, which in turn decreases stimulation back to the central nervous system. While this is a temporary situation, two things happen. First, the central nervous system, specifically the limbic and hypothalamic areas, are being conditioned. You will recall from Part I that this general area of the brain exhibits a tone which to a large extent determines stress reactivity. This tone can be conditioned to be relatively volatile and overreactive, or, by the mechanism just outlined, can be conditioned to be more tranquil, increasing one's tolerance to outside stressors.

Second, the cognitive centers now have memory patterns set up for relaxation, or at least reduced arousal, and these patterns can be recalled. The biofeedback learning laboratory should create an optimal situation for relaxation. The instrument provides instant feedback, which allows the cognitive mechanisms to associate the feedback with the visceral feeling, and perhaps a mechanism for reproducing that state will develop. The mechanism may be the development of memory patterns for the response, or a development of more efficient neural patterns for production of the response. It is by this same process that control over any visceral activity can be learned. Again, the cognitive can influence or be influenced by the emotional set, and these can in turn affect the autonomic arousal, and so on around the loop. In addition, motor output from the brain can issue specific instructions which are constantly being altered in relation to feedback until the desired outcome is accomplished, be it general relaxation, fine control of one muscle, or the change in blood flow to any one section of the body.

THE MANY USES OF BIOFEEDBACK

Illness, especially that thought to have psychosomatic roots, is the malfunction of organ systems. "Treatment" may be generally thought of as removing the exacerbating condition and allowing the body to heal itself, or as a process which aids the body in healing itself. Some forms of treatment are: surgery, to remove a foreign object or harmful growth; drugs, to destroy bacteria or to augment defense mechanisms; the discontinuance of stressful behavior, or a strengthening of the psychophysiological coping mechanisms.

Considering the previous discussion of mechanisms, it is not difficult to see how biofeedback can aid in the treatment of illness. Even though biofeedback is an educational instrument, its primary use to date has been as a tool to aid in the treatment of conditions as dissimilar as anxiety neuroses and musculoskeletal disorders. Barbara Brown has indicated that "Biofeedback still appears to be the closest thing to a panacea ever discovered," and that "there are more than fifty major medical and psychological problems in which biofeedback has been used with either greater success than conventional treatments or at least with equal benefits." [2] The exciting aspect of biofeedback as treatment is that it is noninvasive and has almost no adverse side effects. It works by allowing the body to heal itself—more specifically, by aiding the body to correct imbalances simply by giving information about imbalance and about the success of the rebalancing action.

We will not attempt to give a complete list of the conditions for which biofeedback has been used; the list would be outdated by the time it appeared in print. Rather, we will briefly discuss the major types of biofeedback; together with knowledge of a particular condition, this discussion should give you the ability to evaluate the potential of using biofeedback in that particular situation.

Any system in the body that emits energy can be used in the biofeed-back process. Because of anatomical and physiological considerations, some systems are more difficult to use than others, but by and large, bio-feedback technology has advanced to the point where almost anything is possible. The systems which have become most popular for biofeedback are the ones with the most practical application. These include the mus-cular system, brain waves, and the cardiovascular system. Other forms of feedback that are becoming increasingly more useful are the skin and gastrointestinal systems.

Muscles and Biofeedback

There are two distinctly different applications of biofeedback to the muscular system:

1. Muscle tension and relaxation
2. Neuromuscular rehabilitation

Both utilize the electromyograph (EMG), which is an instrument that measures the activity of a muscle. More specifically, the EMG measures the electrical energy emitted by the flow of electrically charged particles in and out of a muscle cell just before contraction. The strength of the muscle contraction depends on the quantity of these particles; thus the EMG can give an instantaneous and continuous evaluation of muscle contraction.

Before we go into the application of biofeedback to the muscular system, we should review what we know about the muscle's reaction to

[2] Brown, *New Mind, New Body*, pp. 2–3.

stress (Chapter 5). A muscle is a mass of millions of cells which have the ability to contract, or to shorten, thus producing movement. As we learn how to perform activities, patterns of muscle movements are ingrained in our memory and become automatic functions. You do not have to think about how to pick up a pencil, but rather just think of the act and the muscles respond. Other muscle action patterns are learned as well, such as striking out, running away, bracing for anticipated harm, to mention a few. When a threatening situation occurs, each muscle does not have to be commanded to act; one just thinks of the action "run," and the legs move.

This concept is simple enough when the threatening situation is obvious. The muscles contract and the job gets done. However, in our modern, socially controlled world there are few physically threatening situations one must face in the average day. Most threats encountered are symbolic and do not necessitate all-out action of fighting or running. But social forces do cause anger and threaten ego, so subconsciously one prepares for action. This process is referred to as "alerting" or "bracing." Muscles contract, but not to the extent that movement occurs; thus, one does not get feedback as to the extent of the muscle activity. What results is an incomplete or partial contraction referred to as "muscle tension." Muscle tension, then, is muscle contraction that is inappropriate or in excess: no work is done and it serves no purpose. If the tension is prolonged, the muscles set up a learned pattern of response and chronically assume this state. Chronic, long-term tension has been related to numerous disorders, and because the origin of the muscle tension is in the defensive or alerting attitude, these disorders are considered psychosomatic.

Sit back in your chair, close your eyes, and try to focus your thoughts on your muscles. Bend your arm up so that your hand touches your shoulder. The muscle tension is obvious as movement occurs. Next, just think of that same movement. You almost have to hold the arm back as it seems to want to move. Feel the muscles contract ever so slightly. Try the same activity with your forehead. Frown; feel the muscles contract. Then just think of frowning and feel the tension develop. Next, try thinking of an activity which is unpleasant to you, and try to feel the tension which may develop in that area. You are, of course, getting feedback of subtle muscle activity which does not produce movement only because you have not willed the movement.

But just as the gross movement can be controlled, so can the more subtle muscle tension if its existence is known. Unfortunately, most humans possess limited ability to sense muscle tension. It is here where the EMG biofeedback instrument can be helpful. If sensing electrodes are placed on the skin over the muscle, the subtle contractions can be measured. The signal is specially processed and converted to a light or sound and is fed back to the individual, who can use that information to direct the muscle to relax. In most tension reduction or general relaxation programs, muscles of the face and/or neck are used. Tension in these areas generally reflects moods and emotions.

Edmund Jacobson, one of the eminent experts on muscle tension and relaxation popularized the concept of mind-muscle interrelationship. He indicated that anxiety and muscle relaxation are incompatible and formulated the idea that one effective way of reducing anxiety was to reduce muscle tension. This concept formed the basis for the most-often used biofeedback program, which uses EMG biofeedback as a technique to develop self-awareness and an awareness of the relationship between emotion and tension. EMG biofeedback has also been used to promote general relaxation, to reduce anxiety, to treat phobias, and to relieve a myriad of other conditions commonly associated with muscle tension, such as tension headache, migraine headache, premenstrual distress, and insomnia.

The second major application of EMG biofeedback is in neuromuscular reeducation. This process uses the same principle of mind-muscle communication, but here the goal is to make the muscle (which has for any reason lost its function) contract in a coordinated movement pattern. An action command is given, and even if the limb does not move, the EMG will sense even the most minute stimulation of the muscles. Thus, one can keep correcting the thought process until eventually a coordinated movement is possible. One tends to see the restoration of lost function as a modern medical miracle—and indeed it is—but the miracle is the human potential to relearn activities and behaviors and to regenerate damaged tissue. Technology has provided a technique of giving information concerning the appropriateness of the action which facilitates the learning process.

Brain Waves and Biofeedback

The most popular biofeedback system (as gauged by the current media blitz) is the alpha/theta brain wave instrument, which roughly resembles the EEG. The EEG measures the electrical activity of the brain in a manner similar to the way the EMG measures muscle activity. There are some important differences in that nerve cells, unlike muscle cells, are always acting and do not stop generating electrical activity until death. The nerve cell membrane potentials (the electric differential between the inside and outside of the cell) are not fixed, but oscillate continuously near threshold level. Electrical potentials in any part of the nerve cell create an open field of current flow which can be detected at the surface of the scalp. This continuous variation and accompanying impulse discharge produces a spontaneous and often rhythmical flow of current.

The analysis of brain waves is an extremely complex activity, and biofeedback represents but one of the more general applications. The brain wave, like all the other energy waves emitted from the body, has two primary characteristics of interest to biofeedback. These are the frequency with which the wave occurs and the strength of the signal. The frequency, as we mentioned in an earlier chapter, can range from less than one cycle per second to 50 cycles per second. As one might expect, with millions of cells simultaneously performing thousands of functions, it is impossible for the entire brain to be producing activity at any one frequency at any given time. Thus, the EEG shows a complex pattern of mixed wave forms occurring at varying frequencies. However, at any given point there does appear to be a dominant frequency emitted from a specific section of the brain, and the analysis of this dominant frequency has become an important area of study as researchers have begun to associate brain wave patterns with cognitive functioning, emotion, and states of consciousness, as shown in Figure 13.3.

The slowest wave pattern, the delta wave, is present while you are awake, but is dominant only during sleep, and its presence is often used as an indication of sleep. Delta signifies a state of consciousness which is not interacting with the external environment. Yet, a few researchers have reported that they have observed delta-dominant brain wave states accompanied by apparent sleep, but with a measure of consciousness heretofore thought to be impossible. One such report was made by Elmer and Alyce Green, who worked with an Indian yoga, Swami Rama. In experiments where the Swami was demonstrating various levels of control

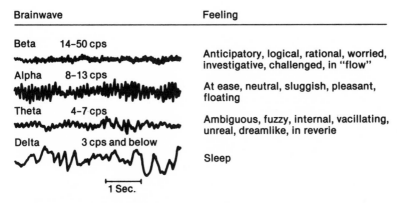

Figure 13.3 States of Consciousness as Determined by Brain Waves, and Feelings Often Associated with Each State

over his consciousness, he produced a state which gave the appearance of sleep, that is, he was lying down, eyes closed, snoring lightly, with delta-dominant brain wave patterns. Yet, after a twenty-minute period he remembered 90 percent of what was said in his laboratory room. The Swami referred to this state as yogic sleep, in which he instructed his mind to rest but to be attentive, not to wander, and not to busy itself warring. Thus, as will be shown with the other brain wave states as well, what is considered the normal characteristic of a state is not necessarily the exclusive function of that state.

The next wave pattern on the frequency continuum is theta, if theta waves can be called patterns—as these usually occur in sporadic spikes. They consume less than 10 percent of the daily awake EEG and are most often associated with the hypnogogic state. Try to remember how you feel when you are just starting to fall asleep. While not quite asleep and not quite awake you may have experienced dreamlike hypnogogic imagery which can be visual, auditory, olfactory, tactile, or of taste. In this state the brain is active but is not actively involved with outside situations, nor are the thoughts directed by the will as in daydreams. The theta state is not necessarily a quiet and relaxed state, as the mind is active. This activity is often associated with creativity. Like the delta state, the theta state is thought to be an internally directed, but not controlled, state of consciousness in which "thinking" in the usual sense does not occur. Rather, "thoughts" are bursts of images which are not temporally related to external events and are not "controlled" by learned inhibitions. Thus, thoughts are often original and, when they are remembered, represent something new and creative.

It might well follow that the conscious inhibitions or "blocks" that often interfere with creative thoughts also interfere with learning. Thomas Budzynski and colleagues at the University of Colorado Medical Center conducted some interesting research with individuals who were taught to maintain the half-awake-half-asleep theta state. During this time a taped message was played, and the tape would stay on only when the theta wave was dominant in the EEG. Varying types of information were presented and, in general, it was found that individuals who had previously been blocked from assimilating the information or idea seemed to learn it or accept it during the theta state. The hypersuggestibility is probably a result of the fact that in the theta state there are no learned inhibitions which may prevent acceptance. There seems to be an uncritical acceptance of the information which circumvents learned and conditioned blocks.

This type of learning seems to work better with holistic ideas than with factual pieces of information—for example, it is effective in reducing prejudice, guilt, or test anxiety, or in changing certain types of eating behavior or stressful patterns of thinking, rather than in learning specific historical dates. The information must be presented in the drowsy, dreamlike, theta state. As this state does not readily communicate with the awake-rational state, most subjects report little learning, but when retested, they just seem to know the information or behave differently. Budzynski (1977) points out that as this information is being directed to the side of the brain which processes ideas rather than factual knowledge (the "nondominant" hemisphere of the brain), what is learned through this method should be tested using nonverbal recognition techniques. To facilitate learning, the Colorado research team first taught relaxation, then increased the voluntary production of slowed brain waves and coded the information within the rhythm of background music.

Although more research needs to be conducted, it appears that the factual information usually processed by the dominant hemisphere is better learned through traditional methods with the learner in the alert rational mode of consciousness. Westerners have been taught primarily through analytical processes, and as a result our dominant hemisphere learning is highly developed. It is only recently that interest in nondominant learning has increased. The theta or twilight learning appears to be one method of facilitating this neglected mode of learning.

It is the famous alpha state which is responsible for the rapid growth and popularity of EEG biofeedback. The resurgence in popularity of yoga and meditation, coupled with our reverence for time- and energy-saving machines, has given rise to an alpha fad. Many people are convinced that the mere presence of those magical little 8–13 cycles per second brain waves is instant mind control. Intuition, accelerated healing, control over pain, higher I.Q., improved sleep, even weight loss is attributed to gain in control over alpha.

There is nothing mystical or magical about alpha. It is a slow, synchronized wave, which means that it occurs in rhythmical stepwise fashion indicative of a predictable, nonfluctuating, nonprocessing state. Everyone has alpha waves. When you close your eyes, alpha bursts begin to appear. Sit with your eyes closed in a quiet environment and alpha will appear with greater frequency. It is more difficult to remain willfully in alpha for any length of time than to produce it in spurts, but one can be trained to do so.

Subjective reports of the feelings which accompany the alpha state indicate that it is an awake, alert, but calm, restful, and peaceful state, often described as idyllic. It is often difficult to validate such subjective accounts as most people hold preconceived opinions as to what alpha is supposed to be like. However, most (but certainly not all) authorities in the field agree that alpha waves characterize a state of consciousness free from ongoing ego-involved thought processes. It is this relative absence of sustained thought pattern which is responsible for the more relaxed feeling. We have said that a large part of stress is triggered or augmented by ego-involved arousal thoughts, and these are not present during the typical alpha state. Feeding information back to an individual about the general activity of the brain promotes the ability to decrease the potentially stress-producing thought patterns.

The fourth and fastest of the major brain wave patterns is beta. Most of the beta activity occurs below 25 cycles per second. Faster beta is also present but has not been sufficiently studied; however, technological advances in biofeedback instrumentation have increased the likelihood that 40 cycle per second beta will be a rich source of study in the near future. Beta is a fast wave of relatively low voltage when compared to alpha. It is not synchronous, which may indicate that it is a diversity of unpredictable thought patterns responding to the outside environment. During beta the brain is usually considered to be working faster than in other states and to be involved in more analytical thought. That does not say anything about the quality of thinking or about right or wrong analysis; it just indicates that the brain is more active. Certainly, not all thinking activity is stressful. One may be in a beta state, thinking, problem solving, feeling challenged, but not threatened, and not at all stressed. However, while beta does not necessarily mean arousal, arousal almost always occurs during beta. One seldom encounters physiological arousal during alpha.

While it is difficult to describe brain wave biofeedback without the typical four-state classification of delta, theta, alpha, and beta, it is misleading to think of them as clearly demarcated states. Brain waves represent a continuum of frequency activity which seems to parallel a continuum of mental alertness and activity. Years ago behavioral states were roughly associated with frequency, and generalizations about that behavior have been responsible for the sharp lines which appears to divide the states. More recent research clearly shows that such sharp behavioral lines do not exist. For example, the 6–7–8–9 frequency range is a blend of characteristics of both theta and alpha, and the 12–13–14–15 range blends aspects of alpha and beta.

Cardiovascular System and Biofeedback

It has long been known that the cardiovascular system is very responsive to stress arousal. Ancient scientists observed this relationship, but postulated a purely autonomic reflex action. It is now clear that our thoughts and anticipations can increase the action of the heart in preparation for activity which may or may not ever occur. At the beginning of this chapter, when you monitored your heart rate, you observed how what you were thinking influenced the rate of cardiac contraction. Because it is so easy to measure, heart rate activity represented one of the earliest biofeedback systems. By itself, a faster or slower heartbeat has little significance until one understands that cardiac activity is a balance between the two major divisions of the nervous system, the sympathetic (which stimulates the stress response in the body) and the parasympathetic (which counteracted the effects of the sympathetic and is responsible for the day-to-day functioning of the organs). (See Chapter 4.) Thus, in this instance the mechanism that slows the heart is more important than the actual change, as a decrease in heart rate signifies a shift to parasympathetic dominance.

There is some evidence to suggest that a shift in this system represents a total shift in dominance which would act to reduce stress arousal. But even if the shift is only in the cardiovascular system, it feeds back to the central nervous system and further influences arousal via a positive feedback loop. Individuals who suffer anxiety reactions often report palpitations and this awareness of cardiac activity further heightens general stress and anxiety. Again, learned control would help reduce this vicious cycle. Finally, heart rate is a good window into the self and is often used to promote self-awareness and self-control over emotional states.

Another cardiovascular biofeedback system which has proven to be beneficial in clinical situations involves blood pressure, which generally reflects the vasoconstrictive and vasodilation properties of the arteries. This is explained more fully in Chapter 5. Essential hypertension, or high blood pressure of unknown origin, is one of the most prevalent diseases in our society. Even though the exact cause is unknown, we do know that the mechanisms for increased pressure can be influenced by stress arousal. The hypertensive is characterized as an aggressive, sometimes hostile individual who internalizes the anger. The cardiovascular mechanisms serve to prepare the body for the anticipated venting of this anger, which usually does not occur.

Early studies show that feeding back information about pressure resulted in the learned reduction of blood pressure which, of course, had tremendous clinical significance. The problem at the present time is the biofeedback instrumentation itself. The standard blood pressure cuff or *sphygmomanometer* has been slightly modified to become a feedback device. However, constant inflation of the cuff produces erroneous readings and the feedback derived from stethoscope sounds leaves much to be desired. A newer method, which has impressive experimental credentials but is still clinically unproven, is the pulse wave velocity technique. In this technique, with each pulse the movement of the artery is transformed into electrical signals which can be taken without a pressure cuff. The time it takes the pulse to reach the extremities is correlated with blood pressure and can provide instant (pulse by pulse) feedback on change in pressure.

The most popular cardiovascular-related biofeedback system relates to control over vasoconstriction (constriction of the blood vessels) and vasodilation (dilation of the blood vessels). It was found that information about the activity of the arteries could be gained by simply measuring the temperature on the surface of the skin. The skin is profusely supplied with blood vessels which aid in the conservation and release of body heat. Generalized vasoconstriction is a function of sympathetic tone (remember most of the blood vessels constrict during stress) and vasodilation is thought to be a change in the tone or an increased dominance by the parasympathetic system. Stressed individuals often exhibit strong sympathetic tone, vasoconstriction, and thus cooler skin temperature, especially in the extremities.

Based on the pioneering efforts of Drs. Elmer and Alyce Green at their Menningers Clinic laboratory, skin temperature biofeedback has developed into one of the most versatile and valuable clinical tools. Conditions such as migraine headache, hypertension, and Raynaud's syndrome (a disease in which the blood vessels of the extremities constrict) have been helped with this technique. Skin temperature feedback involves the most simple of all biofeedback systems: a simple thermistor or diode which changes resistance in response to temperature is attached to a meter or sounding device and the feedback loop is complete. Usually the fingers are used, but other common sites include the forehead, feet, face, back, and abdomen. Multiple site selection is also employed and averaged to obtain mean temperature, or differential techniques are used to obtain finer control, that is, hand warming, forehead cooling, as was done in the original migraine headache research. Control over skin temperature can be very specific. Several demonstrations have been made where various individuals have exhibited the ability to increase the temperature of one part of the hand while simultaneously decreasing the temperature elsewhere on that same hand. Control can also be general in that an increase in temperature is thought to reflect a generalized state of relaxation. More importantly, temperature feedback represents a learning exercise for the development of self-awareness and self-control.

The usual protocol for a skin temperature exercise incorporates not only biofeedback, but some auto-suggestion or visual imagery techniques as well. The individual must learn to attend passively to the biofeedback while very subtly reflecting upon specific thoughts. The mind has memory engrams set up for feeling states, and recalling those states can help the body return physically to a condition which dilates the peripheral arteries. An example of such statements are, "I am relaxed, I am quiet.

. . . My arms feel heavy. . . . My hands feel heavy. . . . Warmth is flowing through my body. . . . My hands feel warm. . . . My hands feel heavy and warm. . . . I feel relaxed. . . . My hands are warm."

As previously mentioned, measuring skin does not entail the sophisticated instrumentation necessary in the EEG and EMG systems. In fact, several programs have reported satisfactory results simply by taping a baby thermometer to the finger and using that as the feedback device. Granted, the more sophisticated instrument will aid learning tremendously, but this is one system that does not cost great sums of money.

THE MECHANICAL GURUS

This chapter has presented the basic information on the most-used biofeedback systems. There are other systems, such as those involving the galvanic skin response, the gastrointestinal system, respiration, and sex organs, but these are not as popular or as well-developed. The Bibliography at the end of the book lists some sources which discuss those systems. We have endeavored to report only the findings which are generally recognized as factual, spiced with some avant-garde projects by noted researchers. This approach was an attempt to reduce the sensationalism which surrounds biofeedback. The fact is, however, that many of the results reported from both clinical and research programs are sensational. To those who do not understand the interaction of the mind and body or the mechanisms of nervous system control, biofeedback does seem magical.

To those hunting for a passive shortcut to Nirvana, biofeedback has become the latest "in" fad. But these novitiates have become prey for the small unethical element of our society which seems to be ever-present, offering something for nothing. If you look at the advertisement section in most of the popular scientific journals, you will find a myriad of psychophysiological instruments and techniques for sale: EMG, EEG, temperature gauges, alpha/theta monitors, plethysmometers, and dream recall machines, to mention a few. To add to the confusion, one finds advertisements for instruments ranging in price from $29.95 to $10,000 on the same page! It is difficult for the reader to know whether the more expensive models offer sophistication or fancy wood-grain cabinets. You can make better use of your money if you know a little bit about electronics and some basics about the psychophysiological parameter to be measured or trained.

Biofeedback equipment can be classified as (1) home trainers, which are relatively inexpensive and virtually worthless ($29.95 to $200), (2) clinical trainers, which are useful and fairly accurate, but limited in versatility ($250 to $1,000), and (3) research units, which are amazing, but expensive ($1,000 to $10,000).

The home trainers are fraught with drawbacks. One generally does not need an instrument to distinguish between a relaxed and contracted muscle. What is needed is an instrument that can distinguish a resting muscle from a relaxed muscle. Most home trainers are not sensitive enough to sense such low-voltage charges nor are they sophisticated enough to filter out environmental or instrument noise. Furthermore, the delay between energy output and feedback is so long with these instruments that it is difficult to determine what feeling or movement was responsible for the change in feedback.

A good example is the most popular feedback system in the home trainer class—the alpha/theta brain wave instrument. The popularity of yoga and meditation has increased the interest in these instruments as an adjunct to meditation or as an alternative method of obtaining "instant Zen." But the lack of sensitivity and filtering capacity allows false signals to trigger the feedback. There are numerous reports of individuals who, simply by moving or focusing the eyes, trigger the feedback and think they are meditating because their alpha trainers are sounding off. False feedback can be produced by improper placement of electrodes, improper technique of preparing the placement site, and inability of the instrument to filter out muscle twitches, eye movements, swallowing movements, heartbeats, or electrical noise from the environment.

Safety

In testimony given in Congressional hearings which investigated the safety of medical devices, it was emphasized that, to date, there is no documentation of harm resulting from the use of a biofeedback instrument. Nevertheless, it is fortunate that most inexpensive home trainers are battery operated, as electrostatic (or Faraday) shields which protect the user from electric shock are not mandatory in the United States.

Policing safety and effectiveness of manufactured products is a difficult task, as is evidenced by the attempt to control over-the-counter drugs. It seems more feasible to focus on the promotion and advertising of such instruments, as few of them can live up to promotional claims. And while the systems are not harmful, they are a diversion of time and money and constitute a consumer health problem.

Another concern related to safety is contraindications. Biofeedback is a powerful tool which can help change psychophysiological functioning, but there are some instances where such changes can exacerbate an existing medical problem. In these instances training should be carried out under special conditions, with the cooperation of a physician, especially if medications are involved. Normally, biofeedback is contraindicated in the following conditions: when there are physical conditions such as colitis and digestive hyperacidity, diabetes mellitus, high or low blood pressure, or a variety of musculoskeletal difficulties, especially skeletal joint and spinal cord problems; when medications are being taken; when there are psychological conditions centering around depression, hysterical neuroses, and in obsessive-compulsive or schizoid personalities.

SUMMARY

Biofeedback can be considered one of the most significant biomedical and educational advancements of our times. Although used in the practice of medicine, biofeedback must be considered as an educational tool giving information which can aid in the learning of self-control. Often such control can eliminate the cause of or exacerbation of a physical condition which may lead to disease. Biofeedback is not as economically practical as meditation or autosensory neuromuscular relaxation, but it is more efficient and is exact enough for research. As always, the faddist, the instant seekers, and fast-buck promoters are finding ways to misuse and to bilk, but this abuse is far overshadowed by the immense potential which biofeedback, yet in its infancy, promises.

14

Relaxation Training

Take a moment and move your attention from this book to your body. First note your general overall position. Are you sitting comfortably? Is your body supported by the chair, or are your back muscles being strained? Are your arms supported, or are you holding the book in the air? Are your fists clenched? Think back to times when you were writing something. Did you ever notice that you were holding the pencil or pen so tight that it was leaving an indentation in your fingers? Think of another activity, such as driving a car. Have you ever found yourself with a death grip on the steering wheel, producing tension up your arms, to your shoulders, neck, back, and even to your head and face muscles?

These are examples of tension being exhibited through the muscles. More specifically, it is excess and needless muscle tension, as it is far more than what is needed to accomplish the task. This excess muscle tension is both a response to stress and a cause of stress. Think of stress as an expression of the internal state, and of muscle action as representing the outward expression of that state. The often-mentioned fight or flight syndrome is muscular expression, as are speech, facial expression, and eye movements.

Most movements are readily observable—that is, you can see your fingers move a pencil as you write, but it takes a second look to notice if there is excess pressure. Excess exertion has nothing to do with the writing movement. It is an outward expression of the anxiety or resentment over what you are writing and/or it represents the general state of tension constantly with you. It is no mystery that people experienced at observing stress can quickly pick out stressed people by analyzing certain characteristics of their penmanship.

Much of the harmful, stress-producing muscle tension is extremely subtle and almost impossible to detect. If you are thinking defensive thoughts, you start to assume a defensive posture. It is practically impossible to think of an action and not have your muscles prepare for the potential action. To illustrate this phenomenon, take a pendant that is on a chain, or tie a key to a string, and hold it out in front of you. Close your eyes and without moving your hand, imagine the object swinging toward and away from you. After a minute open your eyes and chances are it will be moving. Move it side to side, or imagine it circling. Even though your hand did not actually move, the thought was translated to your fingers and tension developed in a rhythmical pattern with enough force to cause the object to move. This shows that we have the ability to anticipate, and this ability is necessary for preparation. Unfortunately, we often spend so much time in unproductive imagined preparation that our bodies adapt by increasing *general* muscle tension. At several points in this book we mentioned Selye's concept of the disease of adaptation. Muscle tension represents a good example. The anxious individual who is defensive and is constantly imagining actions creates a situation where the body becomes very efficient and adapts by maintaining a chronic state of muscle tension.

If such a condition is permitted to exist for an extended period of time, a wide variety of physical disorders may be produced or exaggerated. A few of the more common disorders are tension headaches, muscle cramps and spasms (such as writers cramp), limitation of range of movement and flexibility, susceptibility to muscle injuries such as tears and sprains, insomnia, a wide variety of gastrointestinal maladies—constipation, diarrhea, colitis—urinary problems, dysmenorrhea. The list seems endless, but remember that the muscular system is involved in every body process and every human expression of emotion.

The connection between inordinate muscle tension and disease was made hundreds of years ago, but it was not until the end of the last century that systematic relaxation programs were formulated. The names of Schultz, Sweigard, Maja Schade, and Jacobson became synonymous with relaxation training, as their pioneering work formed the basis of most of the relaxation programs in existence today. There are literally hundreds of techniques now, but all have the same basic objective of teaching the individual to relax the muscles at will by first developing a cognitive awareness of what it feels like to be tense and then what it feels like to be relaxed. If one is able to distinguish between tension and relaxation, control over tension follows almost effortlessly.

NEUROMUSCULAR EXERCISES [1]

Neuromuscular relaxation trains not only the muscles, but the nervous system components which control muscle activity. The benefits are, of course, the reduction of tension in the muscles; as the muscles make up such a large portion of the body's mass, this represents a significant reduction in total body tension. In addition, this training develops a sense of tension awareness. Using the muscles as a biofeedback device, one can develop an inherent autosensory awareness to the point that a little internal alarm goes off when tension starts to rise.

Another benefit is mind control, which has been mentioned often throughout this book. To accomplish any of these techniques one must learn to center on the task or problem and control the mind's tendency to wander aimlessly in daydreams. Neuromuscular relaxation requires concentration but passive concentration which was previously discussed. As you perfect your ability, you can practice relaxation anywhere, even in short spurts—for example, while stopped for a red light, while waiting for an appointment or while watching television. Just think of how much time you spend each day just sitting around waiting for things to happen; you might view this "wasted time" as an opportunity to practice relaxation. Two things will happen. First, you will easily get in 30 to 60 minutes of practice a day, and second, you will lose the concept of wasted time—a very important philosophical development necessary for enlightenment.

The Learning Phase

What follows is a detailed set of instruction on how to practice muscular relaxation. The learning phase of course necessitates more structured time involvement, more concentration, and more commitment than will be necessary once you master the technique. Once you have perfected it, you will be able to choose the particular exercise sequence that is most beneficial to you and that meets your immediate needs. It is very im-

[1] We are indebted to Vinod K. Bhalla, who is primarily responsible for the development of these exercises. We have included only those which have been shown to be most beneficial to his physical therapy patients and to his university students in his past years of practice.

portant, however, that in the learning phase you follow the instructions
to the letter.

The exercises which are being presented in this chapter have been used
for ten years in our clinical practice and have been proven to be quite
effective and easily learned. While they are theoretically based on the
concepts of the many similar relaxation techniques which have preceded
them, significant differences exist. We follow a natural patterning to
provide a constellation of exercises which we have found more effective
and more easily learned than other current relaxation techniques. First
you practice the gross muscle actions which you initially developed during
the prenatal as well as the neonatal stage. These movements are innate to
human locomotion and can be easily identified and controlled. Since these
movements provide an excellent basis for cortical learning, you can gain
awareness and conscious control over these motor actions. Then you can
progress to higher levels of skilled muscle activity. Another important consideration which was taken into account when these exercises were developed was that they include group action rather than single muscle
activity. The brain knows nothing about muscles, only about movements
which involve many muscles working together. Trying to relax one
muscle is difficult and retards learning. Finally, the exercises start from
distal muscle groups (feet and legs) and proceed to proximal groups or
muscles closer to the head and trunk.

Preparation for Exercise

In order for the learning experience to be as effective as possible, you
should do whatever you can to create an environment that enhances
concentration. A few minutes spent preparing the environment and the
body will be a good investment.

First, concentrate on the environment. Generally do whatever you
can to reduce external noise. Find a room away from traffic, with no
telephone and with indirect or dim lighting. As was suggested in the
section on meditation, you may want to use ear plugs or earphones, or
play soft instrumental music or environmental sounds. As you become
more proficient at these exercises, you will not have to take such elaborate
precautions, but anything which may enhance initial learning will reduce
learning time.

Next, work on preparing your body. A reclined or semi-reclined position with proper support under the legs is best (see Figure 14.1). Lie
down; place your arms at your sides, elbows flexed at about 60 degrees
so that the hands and wrists rest on the abdomen. Your hips will naturally flex to about 25 degrees, so don't attempt to hold your legs together. Your legs will naturally rotate outward; don't force them straight.

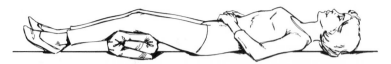

Figure 14.1 Preparatory Position for Relaxation Exercises

In other words, allow the body to assume a position that does not require muscle action to maintain a position. If you wish, you may support your neck with a small, soft pillow. If it is difficult for you to maintain a lying position without pain in the lower back, due to unusual pull on the lumbar spine, place a pillow under your knees. This helps flatten the back against its support and relieves strain on the lower back. Also, if you have a history of low back pain, lumbar disc disease, or any other musculoskeletal disorders or postural conditions such as round shoulders, overdeveloped muscle mass, or cervical lordosis, you should take individual cautions and adopt the most restful and comfortable position to promote maximum concentration and learning. Any tight clothing, jewelry, belts, and the like should be loosened or removed. In preparing for relaxation, if you experience tingling or numbness in a body area, change your posture to relieve the pressure on that area. Above all, if pain or cramps develop during relaxation, rest the muscle until they diminish, and then proceed with less intensity.

Breathing Patterns

Ancient yoga philosophy states that mind is the master of the senses and breath is the master of the mind. Yoga knowledge has long advocated breathing as an elixir of life. These breathing techniques and patterns have numerous benefits: the pulmonary system is strengthened and conditioned, the cardiovascular system function is enhanced, greater oxygenation is promoted, the nerves are calmed, and restfulness occurs. The breathing centers in the brain have a close relationship with the reticular activative system; therefore, constant, steady, restful breathing promotes relaxation.

The practice of breathing techniques not only facilitates neuromuscular relaxation, but plays a vital role in the prevention of respiratory ailments. Individuals with respiratory disorders like asthma and emphysema can benefit not only from increased oxygenation, but also from learning correct, efficient, and less stressful breathing patterns. Emphysema sufferers who are unable to exhale fully due to a loss of recoil properties of the air sacs of the lungs can be taught breathing patterns with emphasis on forced expiration. Similarly, an asthmatic can learn to reduce tension and maintain open air pathways. But even in those of us without respiratory problems, breathing is often labored and inefficient. At rest we normally use only one-third of our lung capacity, and at seven breaths per minute we utilize only one-eighth of the average lung capacity. By using breathing exercises, you can vitalize these functions and regulate your breathing patterns, building up respiratory reserve as well as increasing the capacity to get oxygen into the blood to be carried throughout the body.

Breathing Exercises

The first step in learning more efficient breathing patterns is to learn to differentiate among the three types of breathing patterns. This can be done by performing the following exercises.

Upper Costal Breathing. Use your hands to sense the action of the respiratory movements. Place your hands on the upper one-third of the chest wall, preferably crossing the hands, at the wrists, with the fingertips resting comfortably over the collarbone. Keeping your abdominal wall relaxed, inhale through your nose, expanding the upper ends of your lungs as fully as possible. With your fingertips in the open space between the collarbone and the trapezius muscle, which runs behind that bone, you can easily sense the expansion of the upper lobes of the lungs. Hold your breath for a period of three to five seconds and then let go, exhaling

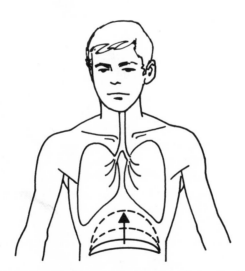

Figure 14.2 Action of the Diaphragm. When we breath in, the diaphragm expands downward and the ribs move out so that the chest cavity increases and the lungs fill with air. When we breath out, the diaphragm rises and the ribs close in, reducing the chest cavity; the lungs become compressed and they expel air.

slowly, letting the air gently flow from the mouth. Repeat this exercise five to six times, resting for a moment between each breath. The pause in between is important, because you want to avoid hyperventilation and allow yourself time to center your thoughts on the activity and reflect on what was sensed and felt. This type of breathing is very stimulating, as it clears lung congestion and improves oxygenation, facilitates lung tone, and builds up pulmonary reserve.

Middle Costal Breathing. Again let your fingers be your sensors. Place your fingers on the middle one-third of the chest wall below the nipples (sixth rib). Keeping your abdominal and upper costal area relaxed, inhale through your nose, expanding the mid-chest region as fully as possible. Hold for three to five seconds and gently exhale through the mouth. Repeat this five or six times and then relax quietly.

Diaphragmatic Breathing. Breathing with the diaphragm is performed by taking in a deep breath and letting the belly be pushed out by the movement of the diaphragm, thus allowing lower lobes of the lungs to inflate fully. The hands are placed on the lower ribs and should easily sense the breathing motion. With the upper chest relaxed, inhale deeply. The abdominal wall is pushed up and out. Hold for three to five seconds and exhale, feeling the abdominal wall descend toward the spine. Repeat this exercise five or six times. Diaphragmatic breathing stretches the lower lobes of the lungs, thus allowing for more fresh air to enter. It also corrects shallow breathing habits.

Levels of Breathing

Once the three types of breathing patterns have been learned and practiced, develop your respiratory ability further by adding the following different levels of breathing.

Very Deep Breathing. Start by inhaling very deeply, taking as deep a breath as you possibly can, taking in every last bit of air you can hold. Hold your breath for three to five seconds and then exhale slowly through the mouth; let the air flow completely out of the lungs, making a heaving sound as long as you can. Repeat this exercise four to six times, pausing to rest between breaths. The emphasis in this exercise is placed on expiration, which is very slow and very even. Concentrate on the breathing process, become part of it. Visualize the air moving slowly out of your lungs.

Deep Breathing. The very deep breathing exercise is utilized initially just to focus your attention on the process; it need not be a part of each practice session. However, deep breathing is an integral part of every training session. Inhale deeply and fully, but do not use the extra force as in the deep breathing exercise. Although deep breathing is not the usual normal form of breathing, it is nevertheless a natural process and you should be able to perform it effortlessly. Try five or six deep breaths. Breathe from your diaphragm, naturally and effortlessly. Concentrate on the air traveling through the air passageways. With each expiration feel a sense of increased relaxation. Feel a sense of letting go; begin to feel the looseness in your body, an uncoiling feeling as you settle down and pull your mind and body together. Gradually begin to breathe normally. Breathe in through your nose and out through your mouth or nose with long, slow expirations. Concentrate on the breathing process, become part of it. Do not allow your mind to wander; center in on the quiet breathing process. Sit quietly for a minute or two and concentrate on this normal breathing exercise.

The entire breathing sequence (very deep, deep, and normal) should eventually take no more than five minutes. It is a good way to center yourself and mentally prepare for the other exercises to follow. Be careful not to overbreathe or hyperventilate. If at any time you feel light-headed, dizzy, or nauseated, simply lie down or relax, resuming normal breathing. This will not happen if you do the exercises slowly, allowing sufficient time between breaths. Table 14.1 gives a summary of the breathing exercises. Try each one again.

Now here is a detailed plan of exercises for muscular relaxation. Note that the exercises are subdivided into simple joint activities for convenience and simplicity of learning. Follow the order of exercises given here, at least until the practice is mastered. The plan involves groups of muscles in gross movement patterns, starting with lower extremities and progressing to the trunk and abdominal muscles, then bringing in shoulder, elbow,

Table 14.1

SUMMARY OF BREATHING EXERCISES

Very Deep Breathing	Breathe in and out as deeply as possible. . . . In . . . hold 5 seconds . . . and out . . . Force the breathing! Deeply in . . . and deeply out . . .
Deep Breathing	Now slacken off the breathing, and breathe in and out more easily. In . . . and out . . . and in . . . and out . . .
Normal Breathing	Breathe quite normally now, and follow your breathing movements with your thoughts. . . . Concentrate on the breathing and put everything else out of your mind.

wrist, and hand muscles in a stepwise progression. Last are the neck and facial muscles. By the time you get to them, you should have gained the finer control necessary to manipulate these muscles. Breathing exercises should not only precede the other exercises, but should be an integral part of each exercise. Get into the habit of breathing *in* during muscular contraction and *out* during relaxation.

Lower Extremities

The Ankle. The first exercise involves the ankle joints (Figure 14.3). No other joints should be involved here. You should be lying in the preparatory position shown in Figure 14.1 and should have proceeded through the breathing exercises. Now pull your feet toward the front of your legs (the movement involved in taking your foot off the gas pedal). The contraction should be felt only in the muscles on the front and outside of the lower leg, not in the calf muscles, which will feel stretched. Your toes should be pulled forward toward your legs as hard as possible until you feel uncomfortable (short of pain—if pain develops, rest for a moment and proceed less vigorously). Center your thoughts in the muscles experiencing the tension. Try to visualize the tension. Form an image in your mind about this tightness. Hold for a few seconds and let go. Repeat the exercise, this time being sure to synchronize your breathing. Breathe in, pulling the feet up, hold your breath, hold the contraction—then let the air out, relaxing the muscles. Lie quietly for one minute and then repeat.

After you have done this several times and feel comfortable with the activity and the breathing pattern, turn your awareness more toward the relaxation than the contraction. As you breathe out and relax, allow the muscles to go limp. As you pass over the peak of the contraction, begin to unwind. Try to form a visual image of this relaxed state and hold it in your mind. Repeat this exercise until you have gained confidence in your ability to relax those muscles.

Next move on to another group of muscles called the plantar flexor group or calf muscles. They are the exact opposite of the first group. Thus tightness will be felt in the calf area and the stretching sensation will be felt in the muscle group in the front of the lower leg. Start by taking a deep breath, while pushing your toes down (as in pushing down

Figure 14.3 Ankle Exercises

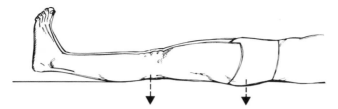

Figure 14.4 Hip and Knee Exercise

on the gas pedal) and away from the body as far as possible. Keep the heels down. When you reach the peak of your breath, hold the breath for five seconds, holding your toes in the pointed position. Now, slowly exhale while allowing the feet to come back to a resting position.

Repeat this exercise three to five times, attempting to synchronize your breathing with the contraction and relaxation phases. As you exhale and let go of the contraction, form a visual image of the tension in the calf muscle flowing out with the air from your lungs. Imagine an unwinding or letting go. Concentrate on the feelings of tension, the feelings of relaxation, and the difference between the two states.

The Hip and Knees. The best exercise in this group is the extension of the knee and hip, the knees being pushed down into the bed while the legs are kept straight (Figure 14.4). For this exercise, remove the pillow from under your knees if you were using one. The tightness will be felt in the front of the thigh and in the buttocks area. You will not be aware of any appreciable stretching force, because these muscles are long and serve more than one joint. As always, begin with a deep breath, pushing your hips and knees down into the mat as hard as possible, heels off the mat. Hold at the peak of your breath, then exhale and allow the muscles to rest. Again, form an image of the tension; feel the letting go.

Table 14.2 gives a summary of lower extremity exercises. Put these together in three successive movements. Allow about thirty seconds between each exercise.

Table 14.2

SUMMARY OF LOWER EXTREMITY EXERCISES

Dorsiflexion of Ankle Joints	Bend up the feet . . . Pull hard . . . Harder! And let go . . .
Plantar Flexion of Ankle Joints	Push the feet down as far as you can . . . Push harder! And slacken off the muscles completely . . .
Extension of Knee and Hip	Straighten the knees as much as possible . . . Now press the legs down into the mattress . . . Hard . . . Harder! Now relax . . .

Figure 14.5 Trunk Extension

The Trunk

The first of these two exercises utilizes the extensor muscles of the lower back. This exercise is particularly good for you if you have lower back discomfort not related to deformity or injury. As a large proportion of our population suffers from tension-related low back pain, remember the earlier warning: If this or any of these exercises produces pain or spasms, stop the exercise and rest. Then continue with only a moderate amount of contraction, gradually increasing the strength of contraction over several weeks. If pain persists, discontinue this type of relaxation training. In this exercise you hollow or arch your back, as shown in Figure 14.5. Move your chest slightly toward your chin. The pelvis is fixed on the mat. You will feel the tension in the lower back area. Synchronize the exercise with your breathing, concentrating on the feelings of tension and relaxation. Repeat five times.

The second exercise is pulling in the abdominal muscles. Keep the legs, pelvis, and shoulders in contact with the mat. Breathe in, contract the stomach muscles, and flatten the lower back against the mat. Hold for five seconds, exhale, and relax.

The trunk exercises are summarized in Table 14.3. Try them both, one after the other with three-second rest intervals between them. At this point, go back and repeat once each the exercises you have learned thus far. Concentrate on the feelings of tension and relaxation. The visual imagery is just as important as is the performance of the muscular exercise.

Table 14.3

SUMMARY OF TRUNK EXERCISES

Extensor Muscles of the Spine	Push the chest forward until you have hollowed the back strongly . . . Lift a little more! And let go . . .
Abdominal Muscles	Pull in the abdominal muscles until they are quite flat . . . Pull a bit more . . . And rest . . .

Figure 14.6 Wrist and Finger Extension

The Upper Extremities

This group of exercises is for the muscles in the upper limbs around the shoulder, elbow, wrist, and fingers. Remember to start each exercise with deep breathing and follow all the progressive steps as discussed on page 207.

The first exercise in this group is the extension of the wrist and fingers (Figure 14.6). Exercise both your left and right extremities at the same time. Pull your hands and fingers simultaneously back toward your forearms, keeping your fingers straight. You should feel the tension on the backs of your hands and the backs of your forearms below the elbows. A little pain might be felt near the wrist—this is ligament stretch, don't strain. Hold the tension for 5 seconds; then relax. Make sure you give yourself a proper rest period so you can focus on the relaxation. Repeat this exercise 5 times.

The next exercise (Figure 14.7) reverses the previous one. Turn your

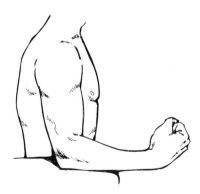

Figure 14.7 Wrist and Finger Contraction

Figure 14.8 Arms Straight Against Sides

wrists in (stretching the back of your hand) and clench your fists very tightly. Hold the tension 5 seconds; then relax. Repeat 5 times.

Next, straighten your arms against your sides, keeping your fingers straight (Figure 14.8). Press both arms tightly against your sides. Hold the tension for 5 seconds; then relax. Repeat this exercise 5 times.

Finally, do this exercise for your shoulders. Shrug your shoulders up as high as you can—try to touch your shoulders to your ear lobes (Figure 14.9). Hold the tension 5 seconds; then relax. Repeat 5 times. This exercise is excellent for stiff necks and shoulders from excessive desk work.

Head, Neck, and Face

The primary exercise in this group is rotation of the head. The muscles in this region are overworked, because we tend to hold a steady partial tension for hours at a time, especially while doing desk work or driving. If you have chronic neck problems, *use extreme care.* To do this exercise, shown in Figure 14.10, first close your eyes. Touch your chin to your breastbone. Return, rest for a breath, and move the head backward toward the spine. Return, rest, and then rotate the head so as to look over the right shoulder. Return, rest for a breath, and then look

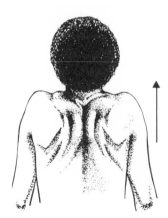

Figure 14.9 Shoulder Shrug

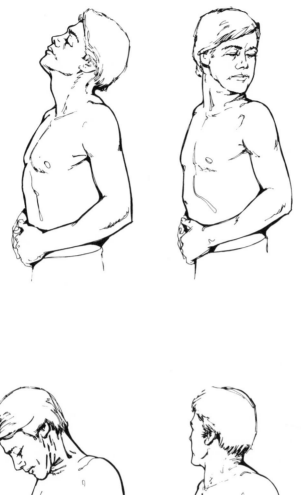

Figure 14.10 Head Rotation

Table 14.4

SUMMARY OF UPPER EXTREMITY EXERCISES

Finger and Wrist Extension	Straighten the fingers and pull back the wrists . . . Pull hard.
Flexion of the Fingers and Wrists	Clench your fists and curl your wrists inward.
Adduction of Shoulder Joints	Straighten the arms against your sides . . . Press tightly.
Shoulder Shrug	Shrug your shoulders high . . . Higher . . . Touch your ears.

over the left shoulder. Consider these four moves as one exercise and complete them in succession, but do not hurry. Synchronize each move with your breathing: contract, relax for a few breaths, and continue with the next movement.

Another group of overworked muscles is the facial muscles, especially those involved in talking and chewing. To exercise these, clench your teeth together, drawing your facial muscles up tightly (Figure 14.11). Always remember the correct emphasis on breathing. Repeat five times and then relax.

Conclusion

The learning phase will take time and concentrated effort, but as learning progresses, it will take less time to complete the exercises. In the beginning, you may tend to fall asleep during practice or feel

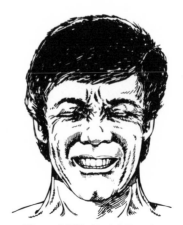

Figure 14.11 Facial Exercise

Table 14.5

SUMMARY OF HEAD, NECK, AND FACE EXERCISES

Rotation	Shut the eyes . . . Now roll the head slowly forward, then slowly back . . . Roll the head to the right, then slowly to the left . . . It's heavy . . . and it's rolling easily . . . front to back, side to side . . . Now stop, with the face turned forward, and rest . . .
Facial Exercise	Clench the teeth together. Now draw up the facial muscles very tightly . . . Tighter! And relax . . .

lethargic afterward. This reaction is due to your mind set, if the only time you relax is when you are too tired to do anything else. However, these are precision exercises which require concentration (albeit passive), and as you become more proficient you will feel rested, relaxed but alert, and full of vigor, strength, and enthusiasm for your daily activities. These exercises are more than relaxation promoting, they are a learning process which provides awareness of states of mind and body in relation to everyday life. Slowly you will begin to notice your posture, how your hand grips objects, your sitting position, and your neck and facial expression. Being aware of such neuromuscular states is the first step in the change process and finally you will be well on your way to not only combating tension, but preventing it.

AUTOGENIC RELAXATION TRAINING

Almost every form of relaxation training presented in this book could be considered *autogenic*, which means self-generating. Yet, over the years the term has been most often used to describe a form of relaxation associated with self-directed mental images of relaxed states. The psycho–physiological mechanism underlying this technique has been presented a number of times throughout this book: it is simply a conditioned pattern of responses which become associated with particular thoughts. Recall how thinking of yourself or your loved ones dying or being involved in a serious accident gives you chills or raises the hair on the back of your neck. This represents a conditioned physiological response to that particular association. The opposite is just as true and produces an equally dramatic physiological response. Imagine sitting on a quiet beach with the sun warming your body, and a relaxation response is triggered. Unfortunately, many of us have become more conditioned to negative thoughts than to positive ones. Thus the technique of autogenic relaxation was developed to help condition relaxation.

215

Autogenics is actually a very advanced form of relaxation training in that you can learn it more rapidly if you already possess some other relaxation skills. For example, relaxation is somewhat of a suggestible state, and self-suggestions are also used in autogenics. Autogenic training is also helped by your ability to vividly imagine a scene or feeling state and by your ability to concentrate without arousal. This, of course, is passive concentration which we have spoken of many times.

Let's look at a common technique used in autogenic training. It is known that one of the physical responses which accompanies relaxation is vasodilation or widening of arteries in the skin of the extremities. This produces a warm, heavy sensation as blood flow increases in that area. If you can imagine warmth, or on a feeling level can reproduce the heavy sensation, your body has the tendency to "relive" or "reproduce" that state. A shift in blood flow is impossible without a change in nervous system tone, and you'll recall that the parasympathetic system takes over to dilate blood vessels during relaxation.

If you have read this book through from the beginning and have practiced the exercises as they were presented, you have already begun this conditioning process. Now is the time to refine it, practice it, and put it in a form you can readily use. The following exercise is an example of how you might use the autogenic technique. Read through it, trying to get the feelings suggested here; then close your eyes and relax, and try to reproduce that feeling.

Tell yourself that you are relaxed, relaxed and calm. By this time the thoughts "relax" and "calm" should start to produce a relaxed and calm feeling and physically promote a relaxation response. Help it along by *feeling* the heaviness move into your arms and hands. Let your arms feel heavy and warm. Tell yourself that your right arm is heavy. Tell yourself you are relaxed and calm, very quiet, calm and relaxed. Your right arm is heavy, warm, and very relaxed. Your left arm is also warm, heavy, and relaxed.

Typical phrases which are often used during this exercise are:

I am relaxed.
I am calm.
I am quiet.
My right arm is heavy (if right-handed; left, if left-handed).
My right arm is heavy and warm.

My right arm is warm and relaxed.
I am calm and quite relaxed.
My left arm is heavy.
My left arm is warm.
My left arm is heavy and warm.
My left arm is warm and relaxed.

Other body parts can be added here, for example, the solar plexus (located above navel, behind stomach—imagine the center of the body).

My solar plexus is warm.
My body is warm and relaxed.
I am quiet and at peace.
I am relaxed.

After you obtain a degree of proficiency, you can add a more complex imagination process by visualizing a time and place which was particularly relaxing to you. Before going on, fill out the following Relaxation Recall questions; they should help you remember that special place which will be used in the next relaxation exercise.

RELAXATION RECALL

Recall a time in your life when you felt very relaxed, peaceful, and tranquil. It may help to close your eyes, relax, and let the images come to you.

Describe the place in the following terms:

a. When was it? _____

b. Who were you with? _____
   Note: Even though you might have traveled with another person, do not list anyone else unless that person's image is vividly associated with the relaxation feeling.

c. Where was it? Look around, describe what you see, describe your feelings and sensations:

_____

_____

_____

_____

_____

_____

_____

_____

Note: Feelings and sensations are more important than exact topographical descriptions. Below is an example of c, somewhat overdone to drive home the point that the location *must* have feeling:

See a lonely stretch of beach with the waves forcefully pounding the rocks and teasing the sand. With each wave the sand feels cool, solid and resisting, then warm and accepting, caressing my feet. The gentle breeze massages my skin and my hair resembles the grass, bending in response to the wind's gentle persuasion. The sun seductively bathes my skin with warmth, which is then cooled by the breeze. The gulls, precocious and curious, clamor for attention as they proclaim the ecstasy and freedom of flight. My spirit soars with their flight, and as I ride the wind I feel free, open, part of the wind, the sun, the sea, the universe.

The place you have described here is your relaxation place. Use it in the following exercise:

Putting It All Together:
The 8-Minute Relaxation Plan

Minute 1   In a quiet room and in a comfortable chair assume a restful position and a quiet, passive attitude. Take four deep breaths. Make each one deeper than the one before: Hold the first inhalation for 4 seconds, the second one for 5 seconds, the third one for 6 seconds, and the fourth one for 7 seconds. Pull the tension from all parts of your body into your lungs and exhale it with each expiration. Feel more relaxed with each breath.

Minute 2   Count backward from 10 to 0. Breath naturally, and with each exhalation count one number and feel more and more relaxed as you approach 0. With each count you descend a relaxation stairway and become more deeply relaxed until you are totally relaxed at 0.

Minutes 3–7   Now go to that relaxation place outlined in the previous exercise. Stay there for four minutes. Try to vividly, but passively, recall the feelings of that place and time that were very relaxing.

Minute 8   Bring your attention back to yourself. Count from 0 to 10. Energize your body. Feel the energy, vitality, and health flow through your system. Feel alert and eager to resume your activities. Open your eyes.

SUMMARY

If it was not evident before, it should be evident after practicing the techniques presented in this section that relaxation is not an exercise in passivity. On the contrary, relaxation is an active, mind-directed state where excess stress and tension are replaced. However, it is difficult to replace what one cannot see, so most of the exercises were dedicated to developing the ability to recognize tension and to become aware of the feelings of relaxation.

Set aside some time and practice what has been presented. Measure your success by your ability to control your thoughts and your ability to truly feel the presence and then the absence of tension. Without directly pursuing it, you will naturally condition a relaxed state.

15

Stress Reduction Through Physical Activity

Contributed by Dorothy Dusek-Girdano, Ph.D.

There have been a number of relaxation techniques presented so far in this book, and in final analysis these techniques share the denominator of ego loss and body awareness. This chapter presents a natural body-emphasis technique which is absolute knowledge to all who love to lose themselves in physical activity—to revert to an original mind-body unity, to rediscover play. Physical activity is a natural way of putting mind-body back together. The movements of dancing, running, skiing, and walking through the woods are natural and necessary for normal growth and development.

In Chapter 1 you learned that when the mind-body split, the mind became of great importance to mankind and the body was left with relative unimportance, except when in ill health. The pendulum started to swing toward the mind when man found that the mind could accomplish more than the body through its use of written and stored information, the basis of technology. The body had been quite perfected by this time and, with no great need for bionics, it lived in harmony with mind and nature. This human body was delicately balanced, with an innate drive to conserve energy—energy gained equaled that expended. (If the movement involved in gaining food expended more energy than the food gave, then the person quickly perished.) Thus, all species survived by becoming efficient, by reading the current and swimming only when necessary. We began to let the mind work while the body conserved its energy, and the mind began to think of ways of extending the body without expending human energy—enter the machine. Through use, the mind grew into the fantastic organ that we still don't fully understand.

To that innate drive of energy conservation man added a learned one of time efficiency. Reducing the time involved in one activity allows for completion of more activities. The mind is responsible for technological advances, so it is no wonder that development of the mind has taken precedence over development of the body. But as we move away from a mere survival epoch to one of life quality, we have begun to ask the questions: "Save energy for what?" "Save time to do what?" We have also begun to realize that physical inactivity results in degenerative disease and have found it increasingly difficult to cope with the mental overstimulation that accompanies rapid technological growth. Perhaps this is an epoch in which we allow the body to "catch up" with the giant strides of the mind.

The physical nature of man has gone through a resurgence, but instead of casting off technology, we have learned to live with it by replacing physical work with "artificial work" in the form of recreational activity. The difficulty in finding an open tennis court, the packed ski area parking lots, and the colorful world of runners' warm-up suits all attest to the fact that physical activity is making a strong comeback. In conjunction with its recreational nature, physical activity is regaining recognition for its potential as a relaxation technique, which is in some ways similar to those already discussed, but with several unique characteristics as well.

Relaxation techniques such as meditation, neuromuscular relaxation, or autogenic training are highly preventive in nature; they contribute little to alleviation of tension once the stress response has occurred. A primary contribution of physical activity, on the other hand, is the alleviation of stress product buildup, with prevention being a secondary aspect. This being the case, we will focus here on three aspects of physical activity: (1) using activity to dissipate or use up the stress products which are produced by fear, threat to the ego, or whatever has evoked the hormonal and nervous systems into defensive posture, (2) using exercise preventively to decrease one's reactivity to future stress, and (3) using physical activity on a high-level motivation plane involving a feeling of well-being, tranquility, and transcendence.

PHYSICAL ACTIVITY AS TREATMENT

Let us look at the treatment role of physical activity in stress management by focusing on a particular problem. Imagine yourself in your work situation being asked to give more time than you can give to do more work than you can possibly accomplish. Then imagine that your personal relations at home begin to be strained because of the overload, the high work expectations on you. Your family wants more of your time. An underlying state of tension is becoming a part of your life and you begin to doubt your personal effectiveness. Then the crowning blow comes—you are berated in front of your co-workers by your boss and you undergo a massive stress response. Anger, fear, indignation, and rage boil through your body. This is the response we have described many times before—the hormonal and nervous systems ready the body for fight or flight. Now is the time to do one of these, and do it *physically*.

It is important to understand that the stress response endowed in us was intended to end in physical activity. The outpouring of sugar and fats into the blood are meant to feed the muscles and the brain so that they might contend actively with the stressor which has provoked the system. The dilation of pupils occurs to give better visual acuity, to take in apparent threats visually. The increased heart and respiration rates are to pump blood and oxygen to active muscles and stimulated control centers in the brain. This is not a time to sit and feel all of these sensations tearing away at the body's systems and eroding good health. This is the time to *move*, to use up the products, to relieve the body of the destructive forces of stress on a sedentary system. Appropriate activity in this case would be total body exercise such as swimming, running, dancing, biking, or an active individual, dual, or team sport that lasts at least an hour. (This is assuming you are in adequate physical condition to perform the task.) Such activities will use up the stress products that might otherwise be harmful and that are likely to play a part in a degenerative disease process such as cardiovascular disease or ulcers.

We have mentioned that during the stress response the two adrenal medullar hormones, epinephrine and norepinephrine, are pumped into the system to ready the body for fight or flight. In laboratory experiments, when norepinephrine is injected into the body, it makes one feel an underlying anxiety until a social situation triggers a known emotion. For example, if one is injected with norepinephrine and is then annoyed by someone, the reported feeling is one of anger; if intimidated by someone or a situation, the feeling reported is one of fear. As norepinephrine is a product of the stress response, it makes one highly volatile and vulnerable to adverse emotions if it is not used for its intended purpose

—physical activity. The mental and emotional implications here should be apparent. How many times under stress do you "fly off the handle" at very little provocation?

A crystal clear picture that should be forming is that Mother Nature intended that the stress response be nothing more than preparation for physical activity. Thus, a natural release, which is also increasingly socially acceptable for everyone, is no less than bodily movement. It is a treatment form that everyone can afford.

This treatment is notably used by two professional coaches. A former Redskin coach would go out and run after football games to wear off the stress products and bring himself down after the game. The other, a basketball coach, has four piles of dirt in his backyard and moves dirt pile A to spot B and so on until his stress level subsides. In American life, we are all coaches of sort—we watch the game being played, we get emotionally involved, and then we sit back and suffer the consequences of not interacting physically. The key factor for each of us is to *recognize* when we're stressed and *act physically* on that response soon after.

PHYSICAL ACTIVITY IN THE PREVENTION OF DISEASE

The second nature of physical activity is that of prophylaxis—preventive treatment. The values of physical activity in preventing the untoward effects of stress are such that if they could be bottled and sold for people to take a dose a day, the bottling and sales agents would be rich beyond compare, so effective is the product.

Deep within most of us we fear abnormality of the heart; if it beats too fast or too loudly or "skips a beat" we become anxious, because we *are* this muscular organ, when it expires, we are expired! The heart, just like other muscles, is the epitome of *syntropy*—it becomes stronger as we use it appropriately. Even though exercise is a stressor in itself, the system is set up to make itself stronger through activity. The heart gains in muscular strength during exercise and that carries into the resting state: When it is strong, fewer beats are required to supply the body with blood so the heart gets more rest and relaxation time.

The respiratory system reacts to exercise in the same syntropic manner, increasing its capacity to take in air and exchange oxygen for carbon dioxide at the capillary level. This respiratory efficiency also carries over into the resting state.

The working muscles, the hormonal system, metabolic reactions, the responsiveness of the central nervous system, all the systems of the body react in a like manner to physical activity, strengthening one's ability to cope.

The unifying feature here is (1) that during activity the body reacts in an *ergotropic* manner, that is, all systems are stimulated for action, and (2) that after physical activity, the systems are slowed down, dominated by the parasympathetic nervous system which occurs synonymously with tranquility. About 90 minutes after a good physical bout of exercise there occurs a feeling of deep relaxation. If you are a consistent exerciser, you know that feeling and perhaps are aware of its lasting effects throughout the day. The relaxation that comes after exercise brings with it a certain imperturbability, a lowered resting reactivity to the environment that helps the regular exerciser to react more appropriately to stimuli. Your step is a little lighter, your attitude more positive, and it takes more to get you upset.

In using activity as a preventive agent, you should use up stress products daily rather than wait for a psychosocial stressor to trigger the system. This calls for a regular exercise regime. In a preventive exercise program your motivation is of a higher level than the urge to run or hit a ball against a wall when angry or upset. Because of this difference in intensity of purpose, a regular pattern of exercise to prevent over-reactivity must somehow be rewarded in its initial stages until it becomes a reward in itself. Exercising with a partner, joining a club, or making certain to engage in an enjoyable activity is helpful for this purpose.

EXERCISE FOR WELL-BEING, TRANQUILITY, TRANSCENDENCE

The highest purpose status of physical exercise is that of well-being: participating because it feels right (and conversely, feels wrong when you don't), because it enhances positive feelings toward yourself which bounce off others as positive energy, because it helps make life complete. The tranquility state, the oneness, the internal calm that has been experienced by those who really become involved in their activity make the prospect of a regular exercise program intriguing.

Exercise is a natural form of expression. We were made to move. And when we do, if social sanctions against it are not too harsh on our psychological acceptance of the activity, we rediscover the original unifying thread of mind-body. It makes us feel naturally healthy, just as we feel when we know that we're eating the right foods and dealing with social problems in a self-enhancing manner. But we cannot achieve this feeling unless we enter into activity in a *noncompetitive* way.

Ego-Void Exercise

In all three aspects of physical activity—treatment, prevention, and especially enhanced well-being—there is an important commonality: in order to get all the benefits of the exercise, you must choose an activity that is *not ego-involved*. Playing a highly competitive game of golf and wrapping a putter around a tree is not a relaxing activity. Nor is a game of tennis when your ego is on the line. This is one reason why singular activities such as running or biking or skiing often have greater relaxation rewards than competitive sports in which winning is more important than playing your best.

We are competitive people with a competitive heritage. We compete for money, jobs, space, and glorification of the ego. It may seem odd that our leisure and recreation activities, intended as diversions from competition, are themselves competitive. We become conditioned to seek ego enhancement from beating others, and there is no reason to believe we can stop competing just because we are not on the job—the drive to win carries over into all aspects of life. Most of us measure ourselves by comparison to others. As was mentioned, exercises will burn off much of the stress arousal products, but competitive exercise often creates *more* stress in the form of lingering self-doubt, anger, and embarrassment. Think about your recreational activities. How transcendental are they? Do you lose your sense of time, do the hours seem like minutes? Or do you lose your temper and/or patience with yourself and others? Do you lose your sense of self? Or are you constantly "seeing yourself" and admonishing yourself for bad performance?

Competitive sports are not the only leisure activities which are the culprits here. Performance of singular activities (such as running or skiing) are no guarantee of ego transcendence. "Can I run three miles? Am I running as fast today as yesterday? What if I can't make it the entire distance? I really don't have it any more. Why can't I make a simple parallel turn? Mary can do it, why can't I? I don't think I am skiing any better this year than last year." Some activities are not directly competitive, with a winner and loser in each event, but we can make them competitive by constantly rating our performance against our past performances or against the performance of others (we even take it upon ourselves to compare our performance with that of a professional athlete!). More important, we allow the performance to influence our feelings about ourselves. "It seems as though any reasonably intelligent and halfway coordinated person should be able to learn to ski in a year, why can't I? What kind of a man can't even run one mile without stopping?" This is the "terrible athlete, therefore terrible person" syndrome.

In two important books on play, Tim Gallwey (1976, 1977) explained the ego-void state, called "Self II," as the noncritical, inherent athlete in all of us who can perform without constant self-instruction. It is the part of us which hits that "lucky shot" and is responsible for the better performance which often paradoxically accompanies not really trying. Unfortunately, most of us have enslaved our Self II by our critical, ego-protecting, self-directing Self I. Again, we might look at conditioned response in our society. We have spent so many years of our education in learning and analyzing with our minds in total control that we have lost faith and ability to let Self II take over, to get lost in the joy of the movement, to flow with the feeling of the activity, and to correct movements through somatic and visual feedback, not through highly critical cognitive analysis in which we paralyze ourselves by overanalysis.

High-risk Activity

Each year more people than ever before take to what is called high-risk recreation. They try to exist in the wilderness for days with no food, tents, or weapons; they climb high mountains, navigate wild rivers, and do other crazy things. Educators have even organized such activities into Outward Bound programs for rehabilitative purposes. The reasons for the upsurge in the popularity of high-risk activities are numerous, but one which stands out is the pleasure and exhilaration one receives from success. Many of these situations are "dare not lose" (in the sense that to lose would mean death), so survival is winning. More important, survival is possible only if one totally concentrates on the activity. The innate survival instinct takes over and "demands" total attention. There is no one to clap when you make a good shot or boo when you don't. You don't worry about the appropriateness of your dress, and you cannot allow yourself the luxury of self-indulgence. There are no "what if's."

This was vividly experienced not long ago while we were doing some "light" mountain climbing. (The term "light" is used to avoid giving the false impression that we were climbing Mt. Everest. In "heavy" climbing, you can kill yourself by falling a mile to your death, whereas in light climbing, you fall only half a mile!) Without really intending to do so, we found ourselves in a situation clearly beyond our expectation of danger. Too far up a cliff (of what appeared to be pleasantly climbable boulders) to turn back—climbing down a cliff is more difficult than climbing up it—we went on, vowing to help each other and carefully analyzing each rock, each foothold, each move before making it. The hours passed like minutes; fear was present only in brief fleeting moments when we stopped to rest or thought about the other person falling. While in motion, it was difficult to feel fear, for we didn't really exist, we were "climbing machines" concentrating on the terrain; and while we analyzed our moves, it was in a calculating and businesslike way, with little or no thought to how we looked, what our form was like, nor to the consequences of failure. "Up" was assumed, "down" was not an alternative. The view from the top was more exhilarating than the view from any mountain ten times its majesty that we have easily hiked. We were fatigued, but not tired. We felt alert, alive, and a part of that mountain. We had succeeded.

SUMMARY

One does not have to be a stock market analyst to realize that one of the fastest growing industries in the world is recreation. True, we have more leisure time and we need to fill a void, but beyond that, people are beginning to recognize that it is very difficult to remain healthy performing only sedentary tasks. So while some are driven to physical activity to counter boredom, others are trying to prevent degenerative diseases, and still others are driven to activity because the activity itself is "right" and reinforcing. To many, physical activity is the only transcending experience they have ever had, so they seek to reproduce the feeling and search for more active leisure-time pursuits.

Unfortunately, modern men and women (at least in the industrialized world) are obsessed with recreation and pursue it with the same diligence and competition with which they pursue work. In fact, for many the only difference between work and recreation is that one may be done behind a desk and the other is done on a golf course. Everything else is the same. Critical analysis is present, as is competition and ego defense, so the participant is often left with self-doubt and extended worry over performance and its reflection on personality and character.

In order for you to use a physical activity as a relaxation technique, it must be void of competition and ego involvement. Otherwise it is a mere diversion of your time.

STOP!!

Activity Self-Assessment

The following self-assessment of your activity level lists activities which are daily routine for many people. In addition, a sample of other activities are given. If you engage in activity other than that listed, try to approximate that activity with one given here and use the points accorded to it. After completing the exercise, you will have 24 hours of activity listed. For each hour or partial hour, multiply the weighted score given for the activity and then total the points. This is your physical activity score.

After filling out the activity assessment, answer the four questions dealing with your motivational state and physical activity.

How many hours per day do you spend:

Sleeping	__10__ hours @ .85 points/hr.	_____

Sitting   @ 1.5 points/hr.
   Riding/driving _____ hours
   Study/deskwork _4_ hours
   Meals _1_ hours
   Watching TV _____ hours
   Reading _____ hours
   Other _____ hours
   _____ hours
   _____ hours   (total sitting × 1.5) _____

Standing   @ 2 points/hr.
   Standing _____ hours
   Dressing _____ hours
   Showering _lo_ hours
   Other _____ hours
   _____ hours   (total standing × 2) _____

Walking
   Slow walk _____ hours @ 3 points/hr.   _____
   Moderate speed _____ hours @ 4 points/hr.   _____
   Very fast walk _____ hours @ 5 points/hr.   _____

Occupational
  Housework,
  light physical
  work _____ hours @ 3 points/hr.   _____

Heavy total body physical exertion
   Rapid calis-
    thenics _____ hours @ 4 points/hr.   _____

Slow run
   (jog) _____ hours @ 6 points/hr.   _____
Fast run _____ hours @ 7 points/hr.   _____
Recreational
  racket
  sports _____ hours @ 8 points/hr.   _____
Competitive
  sports _____ hours @ 9–10 points/hr.   _____
Stair climbing _____ hours @ 8 points/hr.   _____

   Total Hours: 24   *Total Points:* _____

Do you have an exercise outlet for stress buildup? Yes _____ No _____

Do you use it? Yes _____ No _____

Do you exercise regularly for its
preventive rewards? Yes _____ No _____

Have you discovered the transcendental
nature of exercise? Yes _____ No _____

If you score below 40 points, you are a very sedentary person and should consider engaging in an activity which is higher in the point system than the activities you usually engage in. If you score above 55, you are probably enjoying the benefits of physical activity. Everyone who is physically able should have some regular activity which is worth more than 5 points per hour. To be a "regular exerciser" you should perform that activity five times a week for at least a half hour per session.

Concerning the last four questions on the exercise, if you do not use physical activity to burn off stress products, try it. Choose an activity compatible to you and your lifestyle (Table 15.1 on pages 230–31 may be of help) and try it out the next time you can't seem to calm down after a confrontation. Do it long enough for it to be physically effective—you'll need to walk longer than you would run to use up similar energy products. If you find you can tolerate this activity, try doing it regularly so you can keep a low stress profile. And if you really learn to love the activity, you will recognize the rewards and want to pass them on to others.

Table 15.1

ACTIVITY CHART

Activity	Energy Use *	Advantages	Possible Disadvantages **
Walking	++	No cost, no equipment, no special facilities. Everyone can participate. Year-round activity.	Time committment, must walk fast for conditioning effect.
Jogging (less than 5 miles per hour)	+++	Promotes weight loss, leg strength, cardiovascular endurance. No special facilities.	May be hard on knees and other joints. Must have physical checkup, proper shoes.
Running (more than 5 miles per hour)	++++	Promotes weight loss, cardiovascular conditioning, and well-being.	Must have physical checkup, good shoes. Can be hard on joints.
Dancing (Disco, other fast dances)	+++	Promotes weight control, total-body conditioning, esp. aerobic dancing (doing cardiovascular exercises to music). Year-round activity.	Must be brisk for conditioning. Requires coordination, rhythm for set dance patterns. May be hard on joints.
Biking	+++	Good cardiovascular conditioning, promotes weight control, easier on joints than walking, jogging, running. Energy-saving transportation.	Danger from autos, cost of bike, requires a learned skill.
Alpine skiing	+++	Promotes total body conditioning, esp. legs. Enjoyable, apt to promote well-being.	Requires learned skill, expensive equipment. Can be dangerous, esp. if not in condition, from falls, cold weather, and altitude. Seasonal.
Cross-country skiing	++++	Excellent for cardiovascular conditioning, total body fitness. Little jar to body joints. Apt to promote well-being.	Requires some learned skill, special equipment. Cold and altitude may be a negative factor. Seasonal.
Swimming		Excellent for cardiovascular conditioning and muscle toning. No jar to joints.	Requires some skill, pool, minimum cost of swimsuit.

ACTIVITY CHART

(continued)

Activity	Energy Use *	Advantages	Possible Disadvantages **
Racket sports (tennis, squash, racketball)	+++(+)	Excellent total-body conditioner if fast game is played. Promotes weight loss.	Requires learned skill, special equipment and facilities. Must play at high level for conditioning effect.
Golf (walk, carry own clubs)	++	Enjoyable and relaxing if not self-critical. Some same benefits of walking.	Requires learned skill, special equipment. Walking briskly without intermittent stops is a better conditioner.
Bowling	+	Relaxing and enjoyable if not self-critical. Better than just sitting.	Almost no conditioning effect. Requires learned skill and special equipment. Not recommended as treatment or preventive relaxation technique.
Calisthenics	++	Brisk, total-body exercises have conditioning value, esp. muscle toning. No cost, little or no equipment. Year-round activity.	May exacerbate existing muscle problems. Tendency to overdo initially.
Weight lifting	++	Increases strength, improves physique and may improve self-image. Can improve cardiovascular efficiency by lifting lighter weights for greater repetitions or by circuit training.	Requires special equipment. Some risk of muscular injury unless properly trained and prudently utilized.

* All energy use, of course, depends on the intensity at which one pursues the activity, so only a relative rating system is used here. One "+" denotes least strenuous activity and minimal energy use, while four "+" signs denotes highest energy use.

** A possible disadvantage in most of these activities is high-level, ego-involved competition.

Epilogue

The Inner Nature of the Holistic Approach

Your original reason for being interested in this book was probably that you were under pressure, living a hurried or anxious life, and as a result, felt stressed. You were determined to get that aspect of your life under control. As you read the material and practiced the techniques, you began to realize that stress was not just an isolated part of your life, but was a constant factor in your life situation, and was keeping you from being truly happy and from living up to your full potential. This is not at all unusual, for most people who carry out this type of a program eventually realize that stress is just the tip of the iceberg, a symptom of fear, inhibition, frustration, unfulfilled potential, and blocked energy.

Stress and tension responses, anxiety, and psychosomatic illnesses are a few behaviors which offer a convenient window into the inner working of the mind and body; thus they become the focal point upon which to concentrate intervention efforts. One theory states that when you change a particular behavior, you also elicit a change in the mechanism that is causing it. Handwriting analysts have long felt that if you change an aspect of your handwriting, the process can result in a change in that aspect of your personality reflected in the writing. Similarly, biofeedback therapists have found that the process of reducing tension in one muscle often reduces general tension and acts to change some aspect of personality or behavior which caused the tension. So, too, can the process of controlling stress and tension change many aspects of your life which caused the stress. Thus, the *holistic approach* logically offers more chances of ultimate success because it promotes a little change from many aspects of your life without causing a major upheaval in any one area.

Consider the techniques of social and personality engineering. If you were successful in reducing stress arousal, you, to some degree, had to change your relationship to the stressor. In most instances that required only minor adjustments in daily living habits; but as you eventually saw the improvement, there were subtle but significant changes in your relationships with family, friends, and society in general. Even the small changes are quite difficult, as we are constantly reinforced for behaviors which mirror the values of the collective mass rather than live up to our own values. Unfortunately, what is often felt to be good for society is not always good for the individuals who make up that society.

To some degree you had to throw off some of the bonds of enculturation, become somewhat selfish, and regain the naturalness of the body, mind, and spirit. In their book, *The Adjusted American*, Snell and Gail Putney related: [1]

> The adjusted individual is one who is able to fit readily into the normal patterns of his society, but it cannot be taken for granted that one who is adjusted is psychologically healthy. . . . Normal human behavior, then, is not natural, but rather habitual behavior that over a period of time has become typical in a particular society.

The complex nature of your life is to remain natural and free and to be true to yourself while working, living, and communicating with those who demand conformity and "normalness" and who seek, even unintentionally, to lock up your energy. In the process of freeing yourself from stress and tension, you free yourself from inhibitions, you exert the will power to say no. You naturally and subtly have made changes in your life script as you reduced your ego involvement. You care less about winning and losing and, in general, competition means less to you, in that winning, power, and control diminish both the victor and the vanquished. In general you have had to withdraw somewhat from other people's expectations and thus you have become less critical and judging of them and paid less attention to their judgments of you.

Stress is a blocker; it blocks and consumes your energy. When you free

[1] Snell Putney and Gail J. Putney, *The Adjusted American* (New York: Harper & Row, 1964), p. 9.

yourself from stress, you create a void which can be filled with a sense of energy and power needed to risk, take a different path, throw off your fixed belief system, or, if need be, to turn your world upside down to find peace, tranquility, happiness—enlightenment. Stress is the bottled-up energy which becomes blocked when you stuff yourself into a restricted life in which you trick yourself into giving up what you need for nourishment and growth (Daniels and Horowitz, 1976). Now you have taken the first and most vital step: you have begun to know yourself and to be directed by your inner feelings. You can free your energy to power you into the natural flow of life.

We all slip backward from time to time and we sometimes *choose* depression, dependency, powerlessness, stress, even illness. The measure of success is how much time we spend there and our ability to break out, to recognize these states as stimuli for growth.

In the quiet of one of your relaxation practice sessions, perhaps for the first time in your life, you began to know yourself. Beneath the constant surface chatter of the mind, you were able to look at yourself objectively with a sense of ego detachment and find a sense of security and well-being. Although alone, you might have felt closer and more a part of the world around you. Perhaps you have learned to like yourself more, to feel more secure. If you know yourself better and accept yourself, you are less likely to be influenced by what others think you should be, you can forget the past and worry less about the future (and thereby live a rich today), thus reducing anxiety and becoming more spontaneous. You can cling less and love more and feel aloneness without being lonely. Finally, you can begin to slow down and hurry less, for your destination is within you and in constant easy reach.

Bibliography

PART I

CANNON, W. B. *The Wisdom of the Body* (2nd ed.). New York: Worton, 1939.

CAPRA, FRITJOF. *The Tao of Physics.* New York: Bantam Books, 1975.

DUBOS, RENEE. *Man Adapting.* New Haven: Yale University Press, 1965.

DUNBAR, H. *Emotions and Bodily Changes.* New York: Columbia University Press, 1935.

GELLHORN, E. *Autonomic Imbalance and the Hypothalamus.* Minneapolis: University of Minnesota Press, 1957.

HESS, W. R. *Diencephalon, Autonomic and Extrapyramidal Functions.* New York: Grune and Stratton, 1954.

HINKLE, L. E., "The Concept of 'Stress' in the Biological and Social Sciences," *Science, Medicine, and Man,* 1:43, 1973.

SELYE, HANS. *The Stress of Life.* New York: McGraw-Hill, 1956.

SILVERMAN, S. *Psychological Aspects of Physical Symptoms.* New York: Appleton-Century-Crofts, 1968.

SOLOMON, G. F., A. A. AMKRANT, and P. KASPER. "Immunity, Emotions, and Stress," *Annals of Clinical Research,* 6:313–322, 1974.

235

TOFFLER, ALVIN. *Future Shock.* New York: Random House, 1970.

WEIL, J. L. *A Neurophysiological Model of Emotional and Intentional Behavior.* Springfield, Ill.: Charles C. Thomas, 1974.

WOLF, S., and H. G. WOLFF. *Human Gastric Function* (2nd ed.). New York: Oxford University Press, 1947.

PART II

CODDINGTON, R. D. "The Significance of Life Events as Etiologic Factors in the Diseases of Children," *Journal of Psychosomatic Research*, 16:205–214, 1972.

DUBOS, R. Environmental Determinants of Human Life. In D. C. Glass, Ed., *Biology and Behavior: Environmental Influences.* New York: The Rockefeller University Press and Russell Sage Foundation, 1968.

ENGLE, G. "Emotional Stress and Sudden Death," *Psychology Today*, (11)6:114–118, 153–154, 1977.

FREEDMAN, J. L. *Crowding and Behavior.* San Francisco: W. H. Freeman and Co., 1975.

FRIEDMAN, M., and R. ROSENMAN. *Type A Behavior and Your Heart.* New York: A. A. Knopf, 1974.

FRIEDMAN, M., R. ROSENMAN, and V. CARROLL. "Changes in the Serum Cholesterol and Blood Clotting Time in Men Subjected to Cyclic Variation of Occupational Stress," *Circulation*, 18:852–861, 1958.

GALDSTON, I. *Beyond the Germ Theory.* New York: Health Educational Council, 1954.

GEER, J. H., G. DAVISON, and R. GATCHEL. "Reduction of Stress in Humans through Nonveridical Perceived Control of Aversive Stimulation." *Journal of Personality and Social Psychology*, 1970, 16:731–738.

GLASS, D. C., and J. SINGER. *Urban Stress.* New York: Academic Press, 1972.

GRAYSON, R. "Air Controllers Syndrome: Peptic Ulcer in the Air Traffic Controller," *Illinois Medical Journal*, 142:111–115, 1972.

HOLMES, T. H., and R. H. RAHE. "The Social Readjustment Rating Scale," *Journal of Psychosomatic Research*, 11:213–218, 1967.

KRYTER, K. *The Effects of Noise on Man.* New York: Academic Press, 1970.

LAZARUS, R. S. *Psychological Stress and Coping Processes.* New York: McGraw-Hill, 1966.

LESHAN, L. *You Can Fight for Your Life.* New York: M. Evans and Co., 1977.

LYNCH, J. J. *The Broken Heart: The Medical Consequences of Loneliness.* New York: Basic Books, 1977.

McLEAN, A. *Occupational Stress.* Springfield, Ill.: Charles C Thomas, 1974.

MARX, M. B. *et al.* "The Influence of Recent Life Experiences on the Health of College Freshmen," *Journal of Psychosomatic Research*, 19:87–98, 1975.

MEISSNER, W. W. "Family Process and Psychosomatic Disease." In Z. J. Lipowski,

D. Lippsitt, and P. Whybrow, Eds., *Psychosomatic Medicine*. New York: Oxford University Press, 1977.

MILGRAM, S. "The Experience of Living in Cities." *Science*, 1970, 1461–1468.

National Institute of Mental Health. *The Mental Health of Urban America*. Washington, D. C.: U.S. Government Printing Office, 1969.

RAHE, R. H. *Life Crisis and Health Change*. Report Number 67–4, U.S. Navy Bureau of Medicine and Surgery, February 1967.

ROSENBERG, H. *The Book of Vitamin Therapy*. New York: Berkley Windhover Books, 1975.

ROSENMAN, R. H., *et al.* "Coronary Heart Disease in the Western Collaborative Group Study: a Follow-Up Experience of 2 Years," *Journal of the American Medical Association*, 195:86–92, 1966.

SELYE, HANS. *The Stress of Life*. New York: McGraw-Hill, 1976.

SIMONTON, O. C., and S. SIMONTON. "Belief Systems and Management of the Emotional Aspects of Malignancy," *Journal of Transpersonal Psychology*, 7:29–48, 1975.

SINGER, J. "Commuter Stress." *Science Digest*, August 1975, 18–19.

TANNER, O. *Stress*. New York: Time-Life Books, 1976.

TOFFLER, ALVIN. *Future Shock*. New York: Random House, 1970.

ZUCKERMAN, M. "The Sensation Seeking Motive." In B. Maher, Ed., *Progress in Experimental Personality Research*, Volume 7. New York: Academic Press, 1974.

PART III

BENSON, HERBERT. *The Relaxation Response*. New York: Avon Books, 1975.

BROWN, BARBARA B. *New Mind, New Body*. New York: Harper & Row, 1974.

———. *Stress and the Art of Biofeedback*. New York: Harper & Row, 1977.

BUDZYNSKI, THOMAS H. "Biofeedback and the Twilight States of Consciousness." *Psychology Today*, 11(3), August 1977, p. 38.

DANIELS, VICTOR, and LAURENCE J. HOROWITZ. *Being and Caring*. Palo Alto, Calif.: Mayfield Publishing Co., 1976.

DEIKMAN, A. J. "Deautomatization and the Mystic Experience," *Psychiatry*, 29:324–338, 1966.

DEROPP, ROBERT S. *The Master Game*. New York: Dell Publishing Co., 1968.

EPICTETUS. *The Works of Epictetus, Volume II*, trans. T. W. Higinson. Boston: Little, Brown and Co., 1890.

GALLWEY, TIMOTHY. *Inner Tennis*. New York: Random House, 1976.

GALLWEY, TIMOTHY, and BOB KRIEGEL. *Inner Skiing*. New York: Random House, 1977.

GIRDANO, DANIEL A., and D. D. GIRDANO. "Performance-Based Evaluation," *Health Education*, 8(2):13–16, 1977.

MENNINGER, KARL A., and W. C. MENNINGER. "Psychoanalytic Observations in Cardiac Disorders," *American Heart Journal*, 11:10, 1936.

PAGANO, R., *et al.* "Oxygen Consumption, H, EMG and EEG during Progressive Muscle Relaxation (PMR) and Transcendental Meditation (TM)." Report to 8th Annual Meeting of the Biofeedback Society of America, Orlando, Florida, 1977.

PUTNEY, SNELL, and GAIL J. PUTNEY. *The Adjusted American.* New York: Harper & Row, 1964.

TART, C. T. *State of Consciousness.* New York: E. P. Dutton and Co., 1975.

WALLACE, R. K. "Physiological Effects of Transcendental Meditation," *Science*, 167:1751–1754, 1970.

Index